ordinary people
extraordinary lives

inspiring stories from rural Australia

Margaret Carroll

To the best of storytellers, my dear Dad, Paul Hamilton,
and to my brother Robbie, who has shown me how precious life is.

Published in Australia in 2001 by
New Holland Publishers (Australia) Pty Ltd
Sydney • Auckland • London • Cape Town
14 Aquatic Drive Frenchs Forest NSW 2086 Australia
218 Lake Road Northcote Auckland New Zealand
86 Edgware Road London W2 2EA United Kingdom
80 McKenzie Street Cape Town 8001 South Africa

National Library of Australia Cataloguing-in-Publication Data:

Carroll, Margaret.
Ordinary people, extraordinary lives : inspiring stories from rural Australia.

1. Rural women - Australia - Biography. 2. Rural men -
Australia - Biography. 3. Australia - Rural conditions. I.
Title.

307.720994

ISBN 1 86436 685 0.

10 9 8 7 6 5 4 3 2 1

Publishing Manager: Anouska Good
Project Editors: Jennifer Lane and Sean Doyle
Copy Editor: Jacqueline Kent
Designer: Nanette Backhouse
Cover design concept: Linda Dickson
Production: Wendy Hunt
Reproduction: Pica Digital, Singapore
Printer: Griffin Press

This project has been supported
by the National Council for the
Centenary of Federation.

Foreword

By the Rt Revd Dr Peter Hollingworth ~
Governor-General of Australia
(former Chairman of the National Council for the Centenary of Federation)

The Centenary of Federation is much more than the anniversary of a system of government.

It is about the way people have shaped Australia over a century of nationhood.

When Margaret Carroll approached the National Council to support her idea to interview and photograph 'ordinary' rural Australians, we had no hesitation in backing it as a centenary project.

Alongside the more scholarly and historic ventures we had funded, this publication highlights a group of people tackling some of the big issues our nation faces today: our natural environment; reconciliation; depression and suicide; the city/country divide.

While those involved in politics or academic life discuss and debate these issues from afar, here are real people getting on with life and, in the process, making an enormous contribution to the community around them.

Margaret has skilfully allowed her subjects to speak with their own voices, to the extent that readers will imagine they can hear the different accents and turns of phrase. More than that, they'll smell the Australian landscape, feel the red dust on their skin.

There's great tragedy exposed in these stories and images, as well as great courage and great warmth.

As individuals, each one of Margaret's subjects has an inspiring story to tell.

Together in this moving publication, their stories offer a special, panoramic view of a remarkable and fortunate nation.

3 July 2001

Preface

It is very fitting that this book was written for our Centenary of Federation, for it highlights the strength, resolve and tenacity of some of the extraordinary people of this great nation. Trial and tribulation have worked together over past centuries to form our nation and, along the way, many truly great Australians. You will meet some on these pages.

This is a book you can pick up at any time and draw upon for courage and inspiration when the going gets tough. The people in these stories are real, everyday Australians who have excelled because the need was there, a tragedy had to be averted or a dream needed to become a reality. Journey through pages of courage, determination and just plain guts—live the dreams, visions and overall enthusiasm for life. By walking these different life roads you gain, spiritually, the tools needed to face life in general. It is a very therapeutic book for dealing with everyday problems. For me, reading this book was a trip down memory lane—so many places and people that were known and familiar, and so many other extraordinary people I would like to meet.

Almost all of us seem to have a fascination or connection with the land, so I am sure these stories will strike a chord in your heart and cause a stirring in your soul. This book is about what truly makes us achievers, champions and mates. Read it and gather the strength, wisdom, enthusiasm and determination to follow your dream. It proves that the problem is never too big, the tragedy never too great, and that dreams achieved not only change the dreamer's life, but the lives of the people they inspire. Finally, it proves the most important fact of all—that one person really can make a tremendous difference.

The heart of Australia beats between these pages. I always knew there were stories out there that made my life seem like a stroll in the park, and I was right. People are the threads of the great tapestry that is our society, our Australia. There are truly golden threads woven through these pages and, like the author, they are not ordinary people.

Sara Henderson

Acknowledgements

First and foremost I would like to express my heartfelt gratitude to my family—Robbie, Beck and Duncan, my sister Sahni Hamilton, my mother Helen Hamilton and especially my husband Bill, who shared much of the journey of these stories and never doubted I could turn my hand to photographic stories.

My project reviewer, Mike Beckingham, former Executive Director of the Australian Rural Leadership Program (ARLP), set me off on this joyous but risky path in the Kimberley in 1997. I thank my generous sponsors for the leadership scholarship: the New South Wales Country Women's Association and the Rural Industries Research and Development Corporation, and the Australian Rural Leadership Network for its support. This collection of stories is my small contribution to the shared vision for a strong, self-reliant and caring rural Australia, developed with my ARLP Course 4 friends and colleagues in 1997–98. My special thanks to my friend, writer Sue Butler, who edited endless drafts, supported and continually walked with me. And to Rick and Mim Butler, who put up with the 'ghost' in their guest room for two months.

The book would not exist without the enthusiastic and patient involvement of all my storytellers—you are my inspiration, and it has been my great privilege to hear and record your lives. I am indebted to those who recommended various storytellers: Sara Henderson, Ian and Delsia Mitchell, Sara Potter, Marg Cooper, George Gardiner, Robyn Tredwell, Jenny Towers-Hammond, Peter Taylor and Sally Tonkin. And the book would have been impossible to produce without the generous support of the National Council for the Centenary of Federation. Heartfelt thanks to the Rt Revd Dr Peter Hollingworth, Governor-General of Australia and former chairman of the National Council for the Centenery of Federation, for writing the foreword and launching the book, and to Sara Henderson, well-known writer about the triumphs and tribulations of outback life on Bullo River station in the Northern Territory, for the preface.

Thanks to Deborah Nixon at Lansdowne, my initial publisher, and all those at New Holland: publishing manager Anouska Good, project editors Jennifer Lane and Sean Doyle, copy editor Jacqueline Kent, designer

Nanette Backhouse and publicity co-ordinator, Melissa Wilson, all of whose quest for excellence, attention to detail and sensitive advice have made a great deal of difference. It was a fortunate day for me when our paths crossed.

I am grateful to: ABC journalist Kieren McLeonard for interviewing tips; to my advisory group, Sue Butler, Irina Dunn, Executive Director of the New South Wales Writers' Centre, and Bruce McKenzie from the University of Western Sydney, Hawkesbury; my keen team of interview transcribers: Alex Dowling, Patricia Harrap, Elizabeth Roberts and Josie Ringuet; Liz and Robbie Scott, for constant encouragement and installing a special program so I could 'talk' to their computer; Peter Andren, my stalwart local Member of Parliament for supporting my funding application; Kerry Cochrane of Sydney University, Orange, for teaching my students while I wrote the stories; my brother-in-law, former New South Wales Supreme Court Judge, 'Dusty' Ireland for legal advice; and the many friends around Australia who supplied shelter, sustenance and support as I travelled.

Thank you to the people who read various stories and gave great feedback and encouragement—particularly Penny Marr, Jan Howe, and Central West Writers' Centre members Liz Edwards and Diana Brooks.

Lastly, my sincere gratitude to all those helping to market the book in the nooks and crannies of this vast country.

Contents

Challenging Stereotypes

Triumph of the Spirit

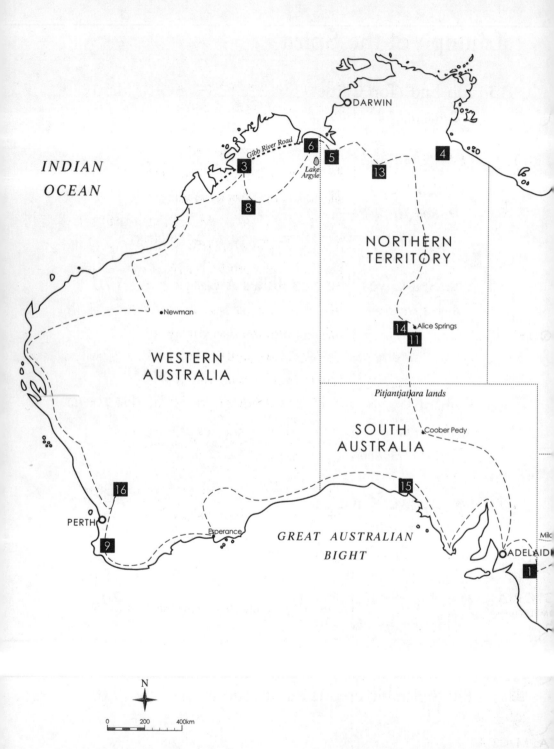

INDIAN
OCEAN

DARWIN

Gibb River Road

3

6

5

13

4

Lake
Argyle

8

NORTHERN
TERRITORY

•Newman

WESTERN
AUSTRALIA

14 •Alice Springs

11

Pitjantjatjara lands

•Coober Pedy

SOUTH
AUSTRALIA

16

15

PERTH

9

Esperance

GREAT AUSTRALIAN
BIGHT

Milc

ADELAID

1

N

0   200   400km

‑‑‑‑‑‑‑‑‑ Author's journey 1999–2000

Introduction

You won't find the rich and famous between these covers. You will find Australians like yourselves, each an ordinary person leading an extraordinary life, each asking, 'Why me?' when asked for an interview. The answer is because who they are and what they have done is inspiring, and because they have immeasurably enriched my own life. Lest you think these people are a rare breed in the bush, I could have written hundreds of stories, given enough time and energy.

Why do such a collection of stories?

The popular picture painted of life beyond the black stump is often bleak, depressing and hopeless as rural Australia fights drought, debt and dying towns. Through my work in many fields and travel to remote corners of this country I have met people whose spirit lights the seemingly dark interior. I hope their stories will resonate with you, the reader, as authentic, relevant and absorbing.

The idea of using stories and photographs to record and recognise some of these remarkable people occurred to me in 1997 when I went on a life-changing trek in the rugged Kimberley region of Western Australia with the Australian Rural Leadership Program. Two years later, in July 1999, I set out on a camping holiday around the western half of Australia with my husband Bill, planning to collect a few stories along the way. Two months and 20 000 kilometres later, the plan had changed dramatically. My germ of an idea appealed to the National Council for the Centenary of Federation, who kindly granted project funding, but wanted me to write a book that would be published commercially. Venturing into the world of publishing was no small challenge for a first-time writer. I am immensely thankful to Lansdowne initially and later to New Holland Publishers for believing in my idea.

After months of interviewing and photographing in each state, on the very night I finished the last interview and was flying back from Brisbane, feeling immensely relieved and excited about the next stage of writing in undistracted solitude by the sea, my mother had a heart attack. The deadline for my manuscript loomed as stark hospital corridors and frustrating negotiations with doctors replaced the soothing sound of waves and my imagined serene unfolding of stories. Armed with a trusty laptop computer, boxes of transcribed interviews and a fierce determination that both Mum and the book would survive, I became a nomad moving between the rainbow worlds of my storytellers and my mother's dark world. Mother and book both survived.

How did I select the storytellers?

I wanted to show a small slice of the rich diversity of rural Australians beyond the popular media images of brawny stockmen on horseback turning bullocks, down-at-heel farmers kicking dirt in drought-bleached paddocks and mums in aprons pulling trays of scones from wood-fired ovens. My storytellers are women and men from across Australia, of different ages, Aboriginal and non-Aboriginal, some from other countries, some who have been connected to the land for several generations, others with a tribal tradition stretching back at least 40 000 years.

I searched for people who were tackling important issues such as suicide, reconciliation, changes in agriculture, Aboriginal health, balancing conservation and resource management, renewing country communities. In this year celebrating the centenary of Federation, I also wanted to recognise living pioneers who are not in the public eye. Half of the storytellers I already knew as friends and work colleagues; the other half I found through networking and thanks to my gregarious husband, who would always strike up a conversation with anyone who looked interesting while we were 'on the wallaby' around the outback.

You may wonder what connects an immigrant pioneer of the prawning industry and an Aboriginal man building a healthier community; what links nurses chasing leprosy in the Top End and a group of Benedictine monks revitalising Australia's only monastic town; or a helicopter pilot cleaning up Northern Territory cattle and a woman fighting for the emergence of other women in rural Australia. They are all connected by the bigger picture of rural Australia—not the 'basket case' some believe it to be—and the abounding will to excel and to be self-reliant.

I think the subjects of this book share some important characteristics. The first is an abounding zest for life. As tree-grower John Thompson says:

'Like what you do and do what you like.' They are unafraid to tread unusual paths even when others think they are crazy; the dairy farmers in the Margaret River area laughed at Di Cullen when she planted the first vines there. They are persistent and determined in setting and pursuing their own goals: as Marlene Farrell says, 'You never give up.' They are open-minded, constantly learning and using their experience, no matter how old they are or what kind of education they did or did not have; Aboriginal health worker Jack Little never went to school at all. They are committed to values and ideals, and many, like Margaret Appleby in her quest to prevent rural suicide, have a strong spiritual foundation in their lives. They challenge the status quo, like Joe Ross, Stanley Mirindo and Hugh Lovesy, who see an Australia where black and white work together. Self-reliant and independent, many are adventurous, and empower others to become productive Australians—as does Fran Rowe in her work as a rural financial counsellor. Life is approached with humour and wisdom, calmness and compassion. 'We try to outdo each other in respect for others,' says Dom Eric, a Benedictine monk at New Norcia. Many have been shaped as much by hardship as by joy, as shown by Aboriginal woman Rose Hillman, whose gift for poetry emerged after the brutal murder of her son. And still others are dedicated to a sustainable future for the land and its people: Jill Jordan in community development, Michael and Steffi Eppler in care of the land, Ian Dickenson in preserving and managing native forests, Pat and Peter Lacy in protecting fragile wilderness, and Rod Mitchell in outback health.

Writing such stories is a privilege, and is based on trusting relationships and collaboration with each storyteller. They give glimpses into their lives, their joys and sorrows, their hopes and fears, that they would not usually share with the world. I am fascinated by what makes people tick, how and why they have taken certain paths, and how they see the future. The challenge for me was to observe and question well and to reveal people with insight and integrity. I have not portrayed them as heroes. They are, and want to be seen as, ordinary people. Each storyteller considers his or her story as correct in fact and authentic in portrayal.

Each story gives me hope, faith in the goodness of human nature, and a sense of the power of the spirit to revel and to triumph over troubles. Each storyteller is special, but shielded by modesty and stoicism, they often think they are not. Each life has been touched by beauty, humour and suffering. Each gives a reflection of how humanity can shimmer and glow with a passion for ideals, concern for one's fellows and commitment to going the second mile.

The journey is also mine. I have learned something from each subject, from their characters, their philosophies and their work. I rejoice as my storytellers tell me good news, and mourn for those who have passed away. To me, the messages they give are be true to yourself, fight for what you believe in, care for others and our land, venture without fear into new territory, and never give up, even in the face of apparently insurmountable odds. Ultimately they remind me of the inevitability of change and that one can envisage the future but has to live fully in the moment, for nobody knows what tomorrow holds.

Marg Carroll

Margaret Carroll

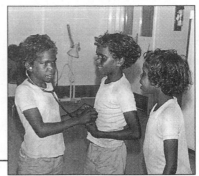

Stepping into New Territory

1 | The Man Who Loves Trees

John Thompson ~
Greening arid lands

My journey to write the stories of inspiring Australians began with John Thompson. I have known him and his wife Robin for many years, and long admired John's abilities. This man spent half his 57 years growing trees—eucalypts, chestnuts, oil-bearing jojobas, tea-trees, coffee, pistachio nuts and olives—hundreds of thousands of trees, mostly in arid areas. He has pioneered the commercial production of many varieties, not for his own gain but for the love of it.

My husband Bill and I have travelled 1000 kilometres from the central west of New South Wales to the mallee-clad South Australian sandhills near the Victorian border, 75 kilometres south of the Murray River, to talk to John. 'When I came here all the hills were moving, because the soil is mostly sand—so fragile it just blows away,' he tells us. It took him ten years to stabilise the sandhills, and he did it with plantings of row upon row of lush green trees that run across the sand dunes and away over the horizon. I marvel at his achievement in this forgotten corner of South Australia. Flanked by swathes of yellow evening primrose is an oasis of 65 000 pistachios sporting clumps of red-blushed nuts. John squeezes open a red shell and points out a fragile tendril inside. 'Here's the nut,' he says. It's a promising spring for pistachios.

With a grin, John tells me that some of the locals called him the 'nut farmer', when more than a decade ago he came to the neglected Kringin Plantation, the largest single planting of pistachios in Australia. He challenged the dusty conventions of agricultural practice to do what he wanted. Now the locals can see that he is far from nuts.

John's leprechaun-blue eyes, auburn hair and fine Celtic complexion are not well adapted to the sun-parched desert, but he treats his body with care, as he does everything else. A long-sleeved shirt and wide-brimmed straw hat are his trademarks. But he looks tired, and his usually energetic body is stooped. Several months before our meeting, he was diagnosed with lung cancer. The pain in his shoulders and back closes in by nightfall; the cancer has spread to his bones.

'When the doctors said he had six months to live, he accepted it calmly,' his wife Robin tells me. 'He keeps thinking it's a nightmare from which he will wake and all will be well, but deep down he knows he's in for a rough ride. He says he has had a wonderful life, with no regrets. He still wants you to tell his story.'

The two-bedroom fibro manager's house where he and Robin live is shaded from scorching summer temperatures by dozens of blue mallee and pink flowering gums John has planted. We stay in visitors' quarters a stone's throw away. On the bedside table are presents: bags of pistachio nuts and John's latest invention, an orange moulded plastic handle for carrying multiple shopping bags.

The next morning three men fly in from New South Wales to take delivery of John's Wilga, a 1956 Polish-made spotter plane. It is one of only six Wilgas in Australia. It looks like a knobbly-kneed dragonfly, and can take off and land almost anywhere, like a helicopter. John bought it for the challenge of flying something different. It is a difficult plane to master, and he has to teach the new owner how to fly it. He has restored the Wilga in Polish military camouflage colours. It is a symbol of his daring and skill, as well as his realism. Methodical and businesslike, he has begun to divest himself of his treasured possessions. The sale of his plane shows his courage in facing his situation.

John's life set out along the path of prestigious boarding schools producing well-educated, well-connected businessmen. From an early age he challenged the status quo. His independence began at the age of eight, when his parents' marriage broke up. He was sent to boarding school at historic Tudor House in the Southern Highlands of New South Wales. It provided the perfect incubation for an energetic boy from the city with a taste for adventure, and John led a band of mischief-makers on many an intrepid escapade.

At the age of nine he built a boat in carpentry class. He and another boy sailed 'around the world'—48 kilometres along the Wingecarribee River from Bowral to Berrima. 'We had to tow our provisions on tyres behind the boat and paddle against the wind. Everything broke,' he recalls with a grin. 'My mate went on to join the Navy.' Then John constructed a homemade bunger gun that fired ball bearings. One day he told his mother he was off to get a duck for dinner. Decked out in a Davy Crocket hat he made from rabbit skins, he lit the bunger and took careful aim at a duck paddling on a lake. The bunger went off and the ball bearing hopped across the water, hitting the unlucky duck. John waited for the wind to blow the body back to him then proudly bore it home for his astonished mother to cook.

His ability to design and build practical contraptions came from his father. John laughs as he tells how his father built a house on steep ground near Sydney's Middle Harbour and erected a pulley system to run wheelbarrow loads of rock from the bottom of the block to the top. One day a man who had been studying this through binoculars could contain himself no longer. He leaped into his car and drove around the foreshore to meet this superman who could run up a cliff pushing a wheelbarrow of rocks. What he hadn't seen was the pulley system, with a rope between the wheelbarrow and the family car. John's father would whistle to his wife Pat to wind it up by driving their car down the road.

As a student at the King's School, Parramatta, John loved to run, training in boots he had fitted with lead soles. In the 1961 Greater Public Schools Athletics Carnival in Sydney, he ran the last leg in the 440-yard relay. Removing the lead soles, John 'flew', helping his school to victory. That win broke a 30-year athletic drought for King's.

When his parents split up, his mother married a farmer, while his father stayed in Sydney. John says he had the best of both worlds—school holidays on a farm at Ivanhoe, in western New South Wales, and term time in Sydney. 'It shaped my life's directions. I knew I didn't want to stay in the city.'

An unquenchable need for action propelled him out of an economics degree at Sydney University in 1964 and into studying at night at Sydney Technical College for a certificate in agriculture, and by day working with the CSIRO in the Royal Botanic Gardens. He had always loved planes and flying, so at the same time he trained at Bankstown to fly light aeroplanes.

Armed with a pilot's licence he went to central Queensland, flying and mustering cattle for stations around Hughenden in the early days of aerial mustering. John remembers winning a bet of £100 to muster and yard a mob of Brahman cattle using a beautiful old 1934 Leopard Moth with huge fabric-covered wooden wings. 'It used to backfire when I pulled the throttle off, like firing a machine gun behind the cattle. I brought them in about 20 miles, edging them along at a steady trit-trot as Brahmans do. There were no doors on the plane. I had a dog in with me on a short chain. It leaned out the open window and barked at the cattle. I landed near the yards, taxied the plane behind them, jumped out and ran over to shut the gate as they went in. That hundred quid was a fortune.'

The intrepid pilot saved up to buy a small Auster for spotting and mustering cattle. Aged 23, he flew 2500 kilometres from central Queensland to Sydney using visual navigation, with no radio. He spotted some hilly country west of Port Macquarie on the New South Wales coast and later returned to buy it. This was the first in a string of rundown farms around the state that John bought, revitalised and sold. Starting from meagre savings he doubled his money on each farm, cleaning up other people's agricultural messes.

Between farms, he worked for academics in the Botany Department at the University of Sydney, sampling wheat crops in central and western New South Wales, and continued a keen involvement in the Sydney University Citizens' Military Force. The Army had taught this loner how to work in teams and how to bring out the best in others. He believed in passing on knowledge, and spent his spare time teaching young recruits.

John is an innovator. A self-taught designer, he has a practical yet brilliantly inventive brain. 'There's plenty of time to think going round on a tractor, but you've got to put it into practice,' he says. Wherever he has seen a need he has invented something to fulfill it. The severity of the 1972–73 drought shook the faith of many farmers. John designed a 'Licka Drum' a revolving plastic drum that dispensed molasses and urea as supplements to hay for starving cattle. This overcame the corrosion problems of steel designs. He recouped his costs in the first months and sold thousands worldwide. Australian Consolidated Industries (ACI) Nylex now manufacture the original design, for which he still receives royalties. The 'Tuckertruck', a simple mobile system for feeding cattle, followed.

John's life now is trees and his close family. More than 30 years ago his first date with Robin, whom he married in 1970, was to look at chestnut trees he had planted at Bundanoon in the Southern Highlands. Their children James and Julie were born in 1974 and 1976, at Molong, in central west New South Wales during his first experiments growing eucalypts. I had married a farmer, Bill Carroll, and moved to Molong. I first met John Thompson when Bill and I discovered that our new neighbours were my old school friend, Robin, married to John and living over our back hill. In a few short years they resurrected that farm.

John's first large-scale tree-growing venture—100 000 blue mallee eucalypts at 'Cugong', near Condobolin, in the central west of New South Wales—was in 1979. Family and friends would visit him on weekends. Planting eucalypts and distilling their oil was a new field. John, who had previously tested leaf samples for distilling, selected the best trees for oil and designed and built a unique portable stainless steel oil distillery. The pure eucalyptus oil was top class, and was direct-marketed by the Thompsons for 20 years.

John put all the money he had saved from restoring and selling four farms into the Condobolin farm. Next, in a brave new venture for Australia, he decided to trial jojoba, another tree crop which fascinated him. He saw a niche market opportunity. The killing of whales for oil had finally stopped, and cosmetic companies predicted that jojoba would replace whale oil in their products. The plants are native to the deserts of Arizona and California, and cultivating them was pioneering work in Australia. They had proved tricky to produce commercially because they have male and female plants that are only recognisable as such when they blossom, years after planting. John experimented and found a way of producing blossoming plants in greenhouse conditions after just nine months, which improved jojoba's commercial prospects dramatically.

It was still a long-term venture, and he needed additional capital. So he invited in two partners. They couldn't agree on future directions, whether to sell or continue developing it and the venture collapsed. A ten-year legal battle from 1984 to 1994 resulted, with the partnership dissolved and the bank foreclosing. In the end the bank and the court held the two partners responsible, but by then John and Robin were left with no land, no trees, no money and bitterness about partners.

Never one to give up, John built a consultancy for large-scale developments in coffee, grapes and tea-tree oil. Just before the Gulf War broke out in January 1991 he answered a newspaper advertisement to work in Saudi Arabia, and was invited by Bedouin sheik Mubarek-al-Suakit, head of a tribe of 30 000 people, to advise on underground fossil water use and salt management. John learned in Saudi Arabia that given the right conditions, desert land can grow trees. So when the opportunity arose to help resurrect the Kringin Pistachio Plantation, he took it.

o o o

We drive through the plantation, a series of plots meticulously laid out with fine tubes of black polypipe drip-lines snaking along the rows. Circling the pistachios are ragged-trunked mallees and wildflowers— yellow, purple and white.

'Where did pistachio nuts originate?' I ask John.

'They are native to Iran,' he says. 'They were one of the original stored crops that enabled early man to move from hunting and gathering and form villages.'

The nuts thrive in hot, arid conditions like those at Pinnaroo. Kringin was one of the earliest pistachio nut ventures in Australia. It started on 200 hectares as a tax minimisation scheme, capitalised by hundreds of small investors. The project had defeated three previous managers. The trees were vigorous rootstock onto which another variety of prolifically fruiting pistachio had to be grafted. They were unstaked, and only 3 per cent had been grafted when the company called in John Thompson for a six-week rescue mission. He trained a team of eight local people to graft the trees, after which 72 per cent of trees produced nuts in 1992.

Within three years, all the 65 000 trees were producing the delicious lime-green nuts.

John tells me the key to success is water. Kringin has an annual rainfall of only 275 millimetres, but water has accumulated in an ancient coral reef 100 metres thick, deep beneath the earth. 'It is replenished by run-off from the Grampians in Victoria,' John says. 'We had to install an irrigation system of seven bores, each drawing up 100 000 litres an hour. We laid 900 kilometres of drip-lines through the plantation, the distance from Sydney to Melbourne.

'The sand has a wax coating,' John explains. 'It's difficult to wet.' He had to work out how to water each tree, a practical problem that had baffled many scientists. Through trial and error he filtered the water and applied it via drip-lines. He next had to figure out how to feed the trees, as the sand contained no nutrients. His solution was to inject small amounts of vital nutrients into the drip-lines. Kringin now works along the principles of a giant hydroponic farm.

The method of harvesting pistachios remains unchanged since ancient times. Pickers beat the trees with rods, knocking the nuts onto tarpaulins underneath. Speedy delivery—four hours' drive—to the processing plant in the Victorian town of Robinvale for dehulling is essential or the nuts will deteriorate. Kringin nuts are lightly salted and dried. My favourite recipe using John's pistachios is Indian-style lamb covered in the nuts, ground and mixed with yoghurt and spices. As the meat roasts, it is permeated by the distinctive flavour of pistachios.

Local attitudes to the 'nut farmer' changed as nuts went on sale in the Pinnaroo BP Roadhouse. Discerning consumers beat a path there. The investors came to field days to see how their trees were growing, one woman driving 1000 kilometres from Orange to be photographed beside her favourite tree.

The growth of Kringin Plantation has been astounding. From no production in 1991, output has doubled each year as more young trees bear fruit. When all the trees mature, the potential production is 300 to 500 tonnes per annum. John sees a bright future for pistachios as the Australian market has been growing by 10 per cent per annum. Australian nuts could well replace imports from Iran and California, and may even be exported. 'It was only possible to start such a large operation by using investment dollars, and with tax incentives,' he says. 'It is vital to maintain *more*, not fewer, tax incentives for rural Australia. They drive innovation and research, particularly for new ventures, and channel business money into the farming sector.'

John's latest venture is olives; the South Australian government has earmarked the Pinnaroo district for olive development. In 1998 he travelled to Italy to investigate growing and processing. By May 1999 he and his team had planted 38 000 trees, completing the project two months after he was diagnosed with cancer. He expects these trees to be producing in three years, to be making oil in five, and eventually to be large enough to justify a processing facility.

The nut farmer continues to live where he loves living and do what he loves doing. Cancer has slowed but not stopped him, says Robin. His circle of friends and family comes to him at regular intervals, amazed at his continuing fascination with the world around him and how he never complains. On my second visit, I ask whether he would like to learn meditation. He is interested. That night he and Robin sit quietly marshalling their mental and spiritual forces. This is a far cry from our first visit when he was pessimistic about being alive in six months' time for the nut harvest. Morphine and radiotherapy help with pain, but he doesn't waste energy wondering, 'Why me?' He is determined to work for as long as he can. Important goals have been set and reached: his daughter Julie's wedding in Queensland in October 1999, Christmas, his and Robin's thirtieth wedding anniversary, and his son James's 26th birthday. The first mechanical harvest of the pistachios is completed in autumn 2000 with the help of his son-in-law, Andrew.

The night before Julie's wedding John was desperately ill in an Adelaide hospital, with excruciating pain in his bones. A determined Robin rounded up the doctors and nurses and begged them to help him get to the wedding. Half an hour before the plane was due to leave for Brisbane John walked out the hospital door, supported by a doctor on one side and Robin on the other, armed with pills and potions. He was able to give the bride away.

He always returns to the trees. 'My greatest reward is doing something that will last a long time. The pistachio trees will last for 60 years. With good management, so will the eucalyptus trees I planted in New South Wales. And the olives will live for 100 years.' The longevity of his trees is important to John. 'It's satisfying to do something that you know will last, like growing trees. Like what you do and do what you like. I love these trees. I know them all by name!'

o o o

Postscript: At 7am on 5 August 2000, the man who loved trees died in Calvary Hospice in Adelaide, surrounded by his family. Robin described their last 15 months together as being 'intense, like a honeymoon', despite the horrific effects of lung cancer. On 5 August 2001, according to John's last wishes to return to his favourite childhood haunt, Robin and some close friends scattered his ashes into the surging sea of Lord Howe Island's Old Gulch. John Thompson will long be remembered for his incredible courage, his daring, creative mind, and his ability to enrich the lives of all who knew him. His legacy to the world is more than 200 000 trees, which continue to green arid lands.

2 | Maleny, an Empowered Mob

Jill Jordan ~
Co-operative community development

It is drizzling the April evening I arrive to see Jill Jordan at Maleny. The small town nestles among the green, bosomy hills of Queensland's Blackall Range past the sheer cliffs of the Glasshouse Mountains, two hours' drive north of Brisbane. This is a story of how Maleny rejuvenated itself and of Jill Jordan, who played a pivotal role through her conviviality, strength and ability to draw disparate people together. Reluctant to claim much credit, she says she is one of many players who have contributed. I first met Jill in 1996 when I was drawn to Maleny by stories of how its community spirit was built from the inside out by co-operatives, instead of relying on outside help and government funding.

It seems a pretty typical Australian country town, except that I'm looking for a jam session at the Upfront Club, a co-operative boasting

500 members. On a damp Monday night in any other country town of 1500 people I know, you could fire a shotgun down the main street. Here it looks as if a party is in full swing. Cars and people line the street and the lively sound of a jazz band splashes out the door of the club across the footpath. I soon spot Jill, 'chief cook and bottle-washer' for the evening, sliding through the crowd bearing plates heaped with lasagne. She has a beaming smile and red hair curving smoothly around her jawline. Some people drain others' energy; this woman gives it out like flashes of electricity. She greets everyone as if this is her home. It almost is. The club is her latest 'baby'. Jill and 54 other volunteers are rescuing it from a financial hole, donating time and expertise to run it.

She gives me a warm hug and shows me to a ringside table with other visitors from Tasmania. No time to feel like an outsider here. We get a substantial meal for $6, a glass of house white and a smorgasbord of local talent. The audience enthusiastically applauds haunting melodies played on an Indian string instrument, a jazz saxophonist in full flight and a troupe of sinuous belly dancers who turn out to be local schoolgirls. The dangle of earrings, swish of plaits, and exuberance of the dancing brings back a whiff of a 1960s hippie scene, only now the hair is greying and the atmosphere is mellow.

Jill sits down with the visitors, snatching time to eat.

'Is it always like this?' I ask.

'Oh yes, every Monday,' she says. 'When we started it five years ago, the hospitality professionals told us, "You can't run this co-operative with volunteers. You've got to let professionals do it." We believed them, and almost lost the club because of wage costs. By next year it will be making money and we'll be able to appoint a paid manager again, but I would never recommend getting rid of the volunteer role. It gives the club humanity and ownership. Before, it had no heart. I've poured in a lot of energy. That feeling of pouring energy into a black hole is hideous. I can remember coming home one night, and crying my heart out, thinking, "We're going to have to close it". Then just laughing at myself, thinking, "Come on, Jill, this is what you're meant to be doing". Members now say it feels different, like it's "our club".'

I can feel the vitality and palpable pride among people in the street, in shops, in interviews. 'Magic Maleny,' says one. 'I love it,' echoes another. Here you can enjoy an excellent cup of coffee and cuisine from any corner of the globe, take your aching back to any number of alternative healers or a conventional doctor, feast your eyes on exquisite Australian arts and crafts or find support for a new idea.

People told me Maleny has always been a 'co-operative town', starting as a creamery co-operative in 1904. Dairy farmers had moved on to range land after rainforests of cedar, hoop and bunya pine were logged in the late nineteenth century. By the 1960s a collapse in world butter and cheese prices led to farmers abandoning dairying and changing to beef cattle. Less intensive agriculture meant fewer farm workers, larger holdings and empty cottages. The early 1970s brought alternative lifestylers to Maleny, searching for a sense of belonging, and remnants of wilderness. They moved into disused cottages for cheap rent.

Jill Jordan was one of this new wave in 1970, desiring a less material-istic lifestyle away from the busyness, pollution and noise of Brisbane. She had heard of this beautiful place in the hinterland. With a laugh Jill says she 'dropped in', not out. 'Maleny has always had a charming setting,' she says, 'but then it was a depressed farming town with closed shops and the main street half the size it is now.' She and her husband Tony bought a former dairy farm on heavily cleared hilly country in Frog Hollow outside Maleny as a weekender, and planted an orchard. Later, she wanted to live in Maleny, and Tony wanted to stay in Brisbane, so they parted company and Jill moved there alone.

Her home is a former milking shed, each room lovingly converted from a cow bale where the cows were milked. We lunch in this living museum of the last 30 years with its red-painted doors and concrete floor, surrounded by photos of local identities, events and phases of her life. Jill lives with exactly the creature comforts she needs—a couple of chairs around a pot-bellied stove, a fresh-air-ventilated composting toilet in the garden on one side of the house, a perspex-surrounded shower on the other side. Through the open door I see a brush turkey speed by, and a tiny leech loops its way across the doorstep towards my foot. Up the hill lives Jill's sister Ann Jupp, a nurse, and her husband Howard, a wood craftsman. Dotted around Frog Hollow are the nine households of other community members. Rain sheets down through the surrounding forest planted by this active community to revegetate the once-denuded valley.

In 1951, as a sickly child with lung problems, Jill was the reason for her English parents' immigration to Australia's warmth. 'They loved it, thank heavens! And I came to where I needed to be,' she says. 'As a kid I didn't have as much connection with my father Jack as I wanted to because he was a travelling salesman and away a lot.' Her mother's influence prevailed. Jill says she was 'a great businesswoman, an intelligent woman who had few opportunities to show that'.

She describes herself as 'a sassy kid who had to be the best at everything'. Jill's well-developed self-esteem was shattered during the vulnerable teenage years by her principal at Townsville Church of England Girls' School, a nun, who advised her to be 'less appreciative of her own abilities'. She rebuilt her confidence using role models of teachers who were happy and loved what they did, two characteristics that she also models.

At university she studied psychology, but felt it was 'just snipping around the edges of what was important, not getting to the essence of human behaviour', she says. So in 1974, disillusioned with Western psychology, and wanting to see how the rest of the world lived, she studied Buddhist psychology for two years in Thailand. 'I immersed myself in understanding consciousness, the value of non-harm, and right thought, word and deed. My Thai teacher taught me about developing wisdom in everyday life. It made sense because it talked about the whole person and what drives us.' Travel and the Thai experience had affected her so deeply that when she returned to Australia, Jill realised that her greatest desire was to live in Maleny, but she had no idea why. 'I didn't know it would become my life's base, the path where I would do my best work.'

Jill has strong views about how the prevailing economic paradigm of complex technology and powerful institutions causes individuals to feel powerless and develop a 'welfare mentality', expecting government to look after them. Likewise she says our economic activities lead to pollution, degraded land, and depleted resources. Turning her back on that paradigm, she wanted a different life although she didn't know how she would make a living. She had a strong gut feeling to leave her already strained marriage, bought out her husband's share of the Maleny farm and moved there in 1976.

'We newcomers were brutal in our criticism of how farmers managed their land, and that set up a confrontationist attitude towards us,' says Jill. 'They were suspicious of us and looking back on it, we must have been insufferable. They were just doing what their fathers and their fathers' fathers had done, what they thought best.'

The new arrivals ate different food from the locals; 'hippie food' such as lentils and soybeans, another 1970s settler, Jan Tilden, called it. The place she rented back then for $6 a week has now become a Swiss-owned resort. The hippies decided to provide their own wholefoods and, at the suggestion of an American woman who had been involved in a food co-operative in California, set up the Maple Street Co-operative in 1979. Instead of bulk-buying just for themselves, they took a risk and rented a shop in the main street so anybody could participate. None of the newcomers were shopkeepers; they had university educations. They started out small, selling wholesome, reasonably priced food, providing an outlet for local growers and acting as a focus for other newcomers, with an information board on housing and jobs.

Jill became the Co-op's first manager, in a voluntary capacity. 'It was deeply satisfying,' she says. 'It used all my business and interpersonal skills. At the beginning I didn't know it would be community development.' Gradually, conservative locals began to patronise the Co-op as they realised that they, too, could sell surplus produce. The Co-op brought like-minded people together. It prospered and was able to pay Jill wages by the second year. She says she does what she loves doing and that she has always earned enough to live.

Baskets of organically grown fruit and vegetables and the aromatic smells of homemade soaps fill the Co-op. Nine hundred members run it as an ethically based, non-profit organisation. No cigarettes, Coca-Cola, or genetically modified foods here. Manager Alan Harrington, a 'refugee' from the Taxation Department and small business in Canberra, has brought in business management skills. 'The effectiveness of co-ops depends on how well they are run,' he believes. He likes the challenge of not just solving a problem according to normal business dictates, but to everyone's satisfaction as the hundreds of members require.

After food, the new university won money. In 1983, at a conference in Tasmania, Jill learned from permaculture co-founder Bill Mollison about the ethical investment movement flourishing in the USA, which harnessed local capital for local residents. Inspired, Jill suggested the idea of a credit union to recycle local savings. The co-op members were enthusiastic, though the wider community was non-committal. 'We thought, "We've got nothing to lose,"' says Jill. The Maleny and District Community Credit Union began, with Jill as volunteer manager.

One of its present board members, Peter Pamment, tells me that on the first day investors removed $53 000 from the only bank in town to deposit in the credit union. It was not yet ready to receive so much, and had to redeposit the money in the bank. 'A lot of money went round in a circle that day,' he laughs. Eighty-five per cent was loaned to community members, many of whom would have been ineligible for a bank loan. Within three years assets stood at more than $1 million, staff were paid wages and loans enabled people to buy their own land, build houses and start businesses. The credit union set up a community development fund to support worthwhile local projects, such as funding a group of unemployed young people who wanted to grow organic produce (they are still in business), and a community assistance fund to help members and non-members in times of hardship. By the year 2000 Maleny Credit Union had 5000 members representing the hugely diverse community. It has financed more than 100 new businesses and has built up assets of $13 million. Jill describes it as 'the lifeblood of the community, the most empowering strategy, because people become disempowered about money'.

One of its most innovative customers was Crystal Waters, the first permaculture village in Australia, which contributed $1 million to the credit union from land sales in the late 1980s. The village started in 1988 with 83 residential lots. Now all are sold, housing more than 200 people. Located half an hour's drive from Maleny, the settlers of Crystal Waters value living close to nature. 'Care for the earth and care for people,' say residents Annette and John Powell. They show me buildings made of natural materials, north-facing to catch maximum sun and using low-energy systems such as solar power and composting toilets. Rammed-earth domes, straw-bale and mud-brick houses cluster on half-hectare blocks around large dams that double as water supply and recreation venues. 'Green' businesses such as mail-order seeds and plants, herbs, arts and crafts, massage, acupuncture and healing therapies such as natural vision improvement, are based in Crystal Waters. Many residents grow their own organic fruit and vegetables. No pesticides, cats or dogs are allowed. Native birds and a massive population of kangaroos and wallabies roam freely through corridors in this wildlife sanctuary.

Good physical design does not necessarily make a good community. Resident Val Oliver works in the Oceania/Asia office of the Global Ecovillage Network (GEN), which supports the development of sustainable settlements and links 'intentional communities' like Crystal Waters across the world. GEN describes ecovillages as small rural or urban communities that seek to nurture the full development of human beings and explore how people can live in harmony with each other and nature. They exchange information on how to sustain the land, people and culture. Val shows me around her rammed-earth house, made by husband John, a builder, and her flourishing permaculture garden, where chickens scratch vigorously.

'What's special about living here?' I ask her.

'I think we have a strong "family" feeling, a sense of belonging,' she says. 'We are not an "all-eat-and-dance-together" type of community, but more of a support network.' She cites the case of resident Dave Johnston, aged 89, who broke his hip, had cataracts removed from his eyes and a pacemaker installed in his heart. His neighbours regularly took him to rehabilitation and put in a concrete path so he wouldn't trip over. He is still able to live at home and look after himself and there is no talk of a nursing home.

Val Oliver says that when you live in a big community where everybody is an 'import', and not related, you soon learn to listen, even though you may not agree with them all. 'Most came with ideals and dreams of saving the earth,' she says. 'Annual general meetings used to be colourful events, sometimes going on for days as people tried to resolve differences.' Now the community elects 'elders' who mediate if conflicts arise.

The next revolutionary concept introduced to Maleny was LETS (Local Employment Trading Scheme), based on the premise that community wealth lies in its goods and services, not its money resources. Jill went to Canada in 1987 to research the idea and imported it to Australia. It is based on an extended barter system: members trade in goods and services using a unit called a 'bunya', named after a local nut. One person may provide pumpkins to another, who in turn provides desktop publishing for a third. Traders negotiate on a fair price for a service. One little girl whose service was brushing older people's hair was sorely missed when her family left town.

LETS appealed to Jill as a powerful economic and social tool, capable of building a community: 'Older people who have a lifetime of skills can pass them on and earn credits that allow them to employ energetic young people to do physical work they can no longer do for themselves,' she says. Maleny's list of services covers an eclectic range, from spiritual healing to farm labour, roof thatching, reliable pet-minding, didgeridoo lessons and fine leather crafts. LETS helped many self-employed and unemployed people who were talent-rich but cash-poor to get on their feet. 'Best of all, it encourages generosity and an attitude of abundance,' says Jill's sister Ann Jupp, a LETS trustee voted in by members to be responsible for the scheme. The concept has spread from Maleny around Australia, with more than 300 LETS operating now.

By 1987, when Maple Street Co-operative, the Credit Union and LETS were all established, Jill Jordan says it hit her that 'there's a process here'. The renowned Austrian philosopher and educator Rudolph Steiner considered that organisations have a life force, like a person. He believed they go through the same developmental stages: infancy, teens, maturity, sometimes senility and then death. 'I think I played a mother role, and hopefully now that of grandmother,' says Jill. 'I was the manager of many co-ops we set up, and when one was established I would move on to the next one. My idea was to help them start, get them to a certain stage and train someone else. When they're strong enough they don't need a mother (who may be a man or a group of people) but aunts and uncles.'

Permaculture teacher Lea Harrison draws an analogy between the stages of a project and the natural succession of vegetation. First comes the weed stage, she explains. They are rugged individuals who initiate projects. They cover and mulch bare, inhospitable ground and build up the nutrient status so that other species, the shrubs, can then come in. This second stage represents team people who get things up and running and eventually shade out the weeds; if the weeds remain dominant, the project may flounder. Then in comes the third stage, the trees, or people who like the routine of maintaining the system or project.

Jill says: 'Our process is bringing together half a dozen people in a room and building something out of that, getting community support, then having three of those people move on to the next strategy. They in turn gather three more people, and those six people build the next strategy. It's like a yoghurt culture, really, feeding more and more. The principles are simple. It's all about need. If there is no need for an organisation, it won't be successful, no matter how good the idea is. Getting that momentum going is the challenge in start-ups. It's about having common values, building up trust, and then dealing with contentious issues. Trust is really important. Most communities have half a dozen "movers and shakers". But in Maleny, with a huge range of organisations, it's a rare person who is listed more than once in the community directory.'

Maleny has 17 co-operatives, the second largest number in the world. Only the ethnically distinct Basque town of Mondragon in Spain has more, developed as self-help initiatives after World War II. The Australian town's co-ops emerged to meet varied needs, and they now impact on many walks of life. In 1989 Wastebusters was started as a joint venture with the council, setting up a recycling depot and repairing whitegoods, electronic equipment, bicycles and furniture. Mountain Fare was a women's co-operative that grew and marketed herbs, established a catering and frozen foods business, and trained women for the workforce. 'It's dormant now because all the women involved are running their own businesses,' says Jill. Its success made it redundant. Black Possum, a publishing co-operative, was followed by Peace of Green, an artists' collective. There is also Barung Landcare group. In an event called 'Bridge the Gap', Barung planted 5000 trees in a corridor across the Bridge Creek valley. Maleny bridged social gaps, mustering 400 people to help a local farmer plant trees. An eclectic mix of music, dance and drama, the Maleny Folk Festival began in 1987 and drew 900 people. By 1989 it was the first venue selected for a national festival outside a capital city, and 17 000 came. By 1994 it offered music, dance, theatre and children's events, and was generating $3 million of annual spending in the local community. Originally held under canvas, it had outgrown its venue and the organising group wanted to buy land. Jill facilitated a plebiscite of residents in that borough, which found that 73 per cent wanted the festival to stay there. However, the organisers couldn't find a block of land, and stiff opposition from more conservative locals who described long-haired, hippie participants as 'white trash', meant it was moved to a permanent site at nearby Woodford. In 1999 the Festival drew 86 000 and generated $7 million. It was Woodford's gain and, sadly, Maleny's loss.

In 1991, Jill was elected to Caloundra City Council for a three-year term. 'We instigated community consultation and development and an awareness of environmental issues, with changes such as open council meetings, permission for privately owned water tanks and user-pays water,' she says. 'But that council was attacked by the radical right wing. People would ring me at three o'clock in the morning and ask if I was asleep! Fear tactics. I hated the polarisation in the community. A lot was dismantled quickly after that period—the water tanks, open council meetings, the Environmental Department.' Although hurt by such tactics, Jill shows compassion to opponents and reminds herself of whose problem it is.

During the three years Jill was on council, the district had an annual growth rate of 8 per cent, a legacy of previous council policies. Within five years the population had doubled. 'That was too fast. We were creating more and more jobs, but going backwards,' she recalls. 'When people move into an area, only about 30 per cent of them can be absorbed by the growth in economic development. The other 70 per cent have to create their own jobs. It changed from a sleepy village to a bustling town. In one sense that's extremely healthy for economic activity, but sociologically it's been harder. Some of the older residents say they don't know anybody any more. Lifestyle needs to have sustainable economic backing.'

She is now involved in LEED, Local Economic and Enterprise Development, which started in 1997 to help people become self-reliant by providing micro-credit up to $4000, business planning and mentoring. 'Small businesses commonly fail because they don't have support. LEED is helping businesses such as a horse trainer, a lingerie maker, and someone making baby slings, to "fly" and succeed.'

Jill contends that people live in a community because they love it, but they spend 90 per cent of their time fighting about the 10 per cent they don't agree on. 'Instead of ignoring social problems when people can't cope with change, the Maleny community faces them squarely. Here people care. Despair is the opposite of empowerment. A lot of terrible things happen in the world. Unless you allow yourself to feel that despair, but don't despair over it and then come up with your full working energy, you will stay in that despair. I think that's the mood in a lot of rural Australia today. People don't feel listened to. They feel powerless, as if they've got no choices.'

She has embraced the movement begun in the US called 'Heart Politics', which looks for bridges between people, rather than focusing on the things that divide. 'It's the politics of inclusion, not exclusion. You do well by doing good.' From this, a new group has sprung up in Maleny called

'FACE of the Hinterland', which stands for 'Family and Community Empowerment'. It assists people who have little support, such as single parents. Jill says it is recognition that in a land of plenty there are still people who are marginalised.

Lea Harrison observes that Maleny, with its many recent arrivals, 'is like a chessboard with a black and a white set of pieces. They intermingle on the board, but they are separate sets. They have different value systems.' She is referring to the different worlds of old and new cultures she sees, including a middle class of retirees and 'trendies'.

'Once it's a success, people want to live here,' says Jill. She tells them that this sort of community can be developed anywhere if people have the desire to do it. She sees her path in the world as being an activist and an agent for social change. 'For me, it's a journey in personal development to do creative work and not harm the planet, but the challenges haven't been without incredible heartaches. Having a central role makes me a target. A few people have tried to bring me into disrepute, out of jealousy maybe, because I take up a lot of space. I understand from my psychology training and Buddhist background that unfinished business is the biggest drain on people's energy. The more we can clear those past hurts, the more energy is available for the present. The more people are satisfied with what they do and the more they develop their skills and relationships, the happier and more fulfilled they are. I love Maleny, its diversity, and my roles in the community. There is something here for everybody. That diversity is so important.' She cites the 1999 Maleny Community Fair, where stallholders as different as Neighbourhood Watch and the spiritual community, co-operatives and the Chamber of Commerce happily rubbed shoulders. She thinks of Maleny as an organism with a life of its own, more than the sum of the people in it. 'It has a great future if it remembers *who* it is and how it came to be. For me the next job is helping more people to find satisfying lifestyles, by earning their living doing what they love to do. What inspires me is having a mob of empowered people around. Community spirit has infused this town. In the local weekly newspaper, the *Range News*, people are always thanking others for caring, or you might read, "Would the person who borrowed the horse blanket from my ageing horse in X paddock please return it?" followed the next week by, "Thank you so much for returning the blanket!"'

In 1995 Crystal Waters was recognised by the United Nations Habitat Committee for its 'pioneering work in demonstrating new ways of low impact, sustainable living', and it has since been listed on the UN Best Practices database. In 1999 the Credit Union won an award as best national small credit union and the non-profit LETS scheme exchanged Australia's second highest LETS monthly average, 25 000 'bunyas'. The Blue Mountains LETS, west of Sydney, had the highest.

The paradox is that growth can destroy the peace, space and community spirit of a place—the very things that attracted people to it in the first instance. Jill says the current council has tried to be development-oriented, but citizens have said, 'No, we are different. We want to shape our own destiny.' 'Small is beautiful here,' she says. 'Huge growth destabilises the feeling of place. A sense of identity comes from being quiet and still in a place. The Aborigines understand it. Many people on the land understand it. It comes from understanding deeply what has shaped the place—the birds, the animals, the people, the stories.'

The district has been rejuvenated by co-operatives, from Barung Landcare to the Credit Union, from the Upfront Club to Wastebusters. It is a far cry from the conventional thinking that economic development relies on new outside businesses or government initiatives to stimulate growth. In Maleny, the rich mixture of people has created a cycle of demand for a vast range of goods and services, and they in turn have developed the businesses to supply that demand. Here many share dreams for real community spirit, where people co-operate, giving instead of taking. They value self-reliance, support local initiatives and plan for a truly sustainable tomorrow. Clashes occur, as they do in all communities, but there are honest attempts to recognise and resolve conflict, even to the point of running training courses in conflict resolution.

Jill Jordan believes she became quite dependent on Maleny as her source of inspiration and happiness. 'Then in the early 1990s I was working on Flinders Island in Bass Strait—beautiful climate, great people, good initiatives. I thought, "I could live anywhere and be happy because everywhere you go there are magnificent people who love where they live and want to do the best by it." At that stage, I let go of Maleny.' After pouring heart and soul into her community for 20 years, she no longer had a desire to push it one way or the other. The ties are love: 'My family's here—some are blood relations, such as my sister, who is also my neighbour, some are family in the wider sense, and my "kids" are my co-operatives. I have a sense of my tiny place in the universe and the spirituality of that. I believe in karma. What I do matters, what everybody does matters,' she says, as she dashes out the door to her reviving 'baby', the club.

The green landscape clothed in morning mist is soothing to troubled souls. In the small town teeming with life, bright, flowing skirts mingle with moleskins. I watch the Anzac Day parade as it progresses down Maple Street. Wrapped in garments of the past, people display the spirit of Maleny. Schoolchildren march by in their neatly pressed uniforms, followed by returned servicemen and women, and then what you could only see here— the Fifth Regiment of the Light Horse, four men and women in full military regalia, silhouetted against the blue awnings of the Upfront Club.

3 | Modern Kimberley Pioneers

Pat and Peter Lacy ~
Taking the good with the bad

The Gibb River Road is a mecca for latter-day adventurers to the Kimberley in Western Australia, a last frontier of dusty potholes and corrugations capable of bouncing you from Derby on the west coast to Wyndham on the north-eastern fringe. It's a region of great extremes: storms and flooding from 750 to 1500 millimetres force its closure in the Wet from mid-December to mid-April. In July my husband and I work our way north from Derby through the limestone razors of the Leopold and Napier ranges, past clear waterfalls that leap into cool pools over rocky terraces. Mt Barnett Roadhouse, the only stop on the 700-kilometre dirt road, stocks everything from fishing lines to fast food, including the most costly diesel fuel in a 20 000-kilometre trip. You pay for isolation.

A few vast cattle stations now open their gates to a curious world. The first of these was Mt Elizabeth station, owned by the Lacy family. It is a 200 000-hectare cattle station 365 kilometres from the nearest town, Derby. The air has noticeably cooled with the gradual climb to the homestead, 210 metres above sea level. Nature's avenue of slim white-trunked boxgums funnels us from the gateway on the Gibb River Road to a clearing. Ahead is a long, low house made from pale-pink slabs of hewn limestone, with a side road leading to wooden stockyards, machinery sheds and a cottage. Beyond the cottage, camouflaged by tropical palms, is the camping park.

A tall, willowy woman in her forties, with smooth ash-blonde hair, comes to the homestead gate. She measures me up.

'Are you a journalist?' Pat Lacy enquires warily.

'No, I'm collecting bush stories for a book about ordinary people who lead extraordinary lives,' I tell her. 'I asked Peter if you two would be one of my stories.' The atmosphere warms.

'Oh, that's all right then,' she grins. Our communications have 'gone west' somewhere between our roaming life, largely beyond telephone range, and their hectic life running the cattle station and annually catering for 2000 travellers.

Pat has married into a family of adventurous pioneers in the north Kimberley. She tells me her husband Peter is one of those people who is unfazed by anything. I hear his good-natured chuckle and quiet voice as he comes into the garden talking with Brett, a 21-year-old version of his father. Peter, a sturdy man in his fifties, with a twinkle in his eye, looks at our battered four-wheel drive with amusement.

'My dad pioneered up here in two-wheel drive; now it's four-wheel drive only!'

Peter Lacy's father Frank came from New Zealand when he was in his twenties. Between 1919 and 1939 he crisscrossed the Kimberley, droving cattle on the mighty Ord and Fitzroy rivers and sailing around its treacherous coastline. In the Wet of 1937 he did the last mule pack Royal Mail run between Halls Creek and Fitzroy Crossing. In *Rivers of Time: Frank Lacy, Kimberley Pioneer*, Marion Nixon's self-published story of Frank, he described it as 'probably the worst job I ever took on', having to unpack and repack the precious mail so it wouldn't be swept away in turbulent currents as he and his cantankerous mules forded numerous flooded creeks in the 320 kilometre journey.

'Dad first saw this Mt Elizabeth land when droving in the 1930s, and fell in love with it,' says Peter. He had a government contract to deliver 1000 head of cattle from Wyndham to Walcott Inlet, a remote and rugged area of 11 metre tides where three major rivers surge into the sea. It was the first herd moved from coast to coast across the Kimberley. 'He became pally with Fred Russ at Gibb River station, who talked him into applying for this lease, which he got in 1945. Dad would go droving each year to buy a few cows for the station. One day he delivered a mob to Broome and went to have a feed in the hotel. He had a delicious steak and kidney pie and wanted to meet the cook. Mum was cook. They must have clicked.' Pat can remember Mum Lacy saying, 'But I didn't say "yes" the first time!'

Peter's mother, Teresa Lacy, came from Thangoo station, south of Broome, born of an Aboriginal mother and a white father. Frank and Teresa's family was two boys, Frank and Peter, and two daughters, Mavis and Ann. Peter spent his first year of life droving with his parents and brother. Only a year old when he came to Mt Elizabeth, he used to sit in a beer crate playpen watching his father work cattle. 'My elder sister Mavis, who was educated at Forrest River mission, taught me by correspondence, but any activity outside was more interesting.' He went away to school at the Australian Inland Mission in a former gold-rush town, Halls Creek, in the east Kimberley, but left at the age of 14. His father couldn't afford an education for both Peter and Ann. Peter returned home to do a man's job because his father suffered from asthma, and was running the stock camp with only his brother and an Aboriginal man named Scottie.

'When I was 8, police patrols collected up bush natives to be taken for leprosy checks. The men who were inclined to run away were chained neck-to-neck,' Peter recalls. When a patrol overnighted at Mt Elizabeth his father saw Scottie's family and asked the police to leave them at the station for checking. They were the first members of the Aboriginal community on the station, and still live at Mt Elizabeth. Unlike most stations in the region, the community still forms the stock camp.

'We've had the same group for 50 years,' says Pat. 'They shine at cattle work. When award wages came in a lot of stations couldn't afford to keep big Aboriginal populations so they moved on, but because we're so isolated, the community wanted to stay. The older people got pensions and we paid the stockmen, who shared their money with relations. Peter excised land for the community and taught them house-building and fencing. He understands and can speak their language, Ngarinyin, and has a strong affinity with them. When people ask him what it means to be an Aborigine, he says, "I just be who I am, Peter Lacy."'

Peter thinks he missed out on social life and sports like rugby as a boy, but he did learn how to catch barramundi, a fighting fish. 'We had a solitary life, only brothers and sisters, hardly any other kids.' Their nearest neighbours were at Gibb River station, 32 kilometres to the east, where the mail was dropped. 'When it was dry, Dad and Mum used to drive over and back in an old two-wheel drive Chevy truck, but during the Wet it was a three-day event to pick up the mail on packhorse with a mule.'

I ask how they communicated. 'Smoke signals!' Peter quips. 'We had the old pedal radio, but prior to that you would ride to meet someone, or talk through the Flying Doctor. Dad used to tune in to radio news every night, ABC and other worldwide stations. In the old days you were lucky to see one stranger in 12 months. If anyone came on your property it was to do you harm rather than good, or to pinch cattle.' At the front gate of some stations, signs warned 'Trespassers Will Be Shot'. Now Mt Elizabeth's sign welcomes visitors, but warns against shooting!

Peter followed in his father's pioneering footsteps. 'In 1963 my brother Frank and I put in a 220-kilometre vehicle track from Mt Elizabeth to Walcott Inlet, the same direction Dad drove cattle in 1931. Old-timers, including Dad, said "You'll never get a vehicle down there. It's too rugged."' We didn't have any machinery, just crowbars, pick and shovel. We rode first to find the best way through the Edkins and Harding ranges, high sandstone country. That took three weeks. It was fun all the way. We lived off the land, lots of beef. I wonder how we did it now.' Pat says her husband has great bushmanship and an unerring sense of direction. There were only survey maps, not accurate for creeks and hills. They headed west, following the setting sun. Now it is Aboriginal-owned land called Munja and the Lacys have access for safari tours.

Like his father, Peter also went droving. 'With eight guys, 20 horses and six pack mules, we could cover ten or 20 miles a day, depending on whether it was mountain or sandy country. We used to look forward to it. We took turns riding around the cattle at night, making a constant noise by whistling or playing a mouth organ. Any sudden sound on a quiet night, someone coughing or tripping over a billy can, would startle the cattle and you could have a stampede. One year I had a contract to muster Walcott

Inlet and take wild cattle 230 kilometres to road trains. We had two stampedes on that trip. A couple of guys would go after them in the dark to try and pull them up. It was pretty hairy. Some terrain was so rocky we had to string them out head to tail. You couldn't push them too hard, they'd get lame.'

Pat is as adventurous as her husband. She came from a small country town, Wickepin, south-east of Perth, where everyone knew everyone. She started nursing training, but wanted to teach. Looking for excitement, in 1969, when she was 18, she applied for a position as a governess through the WA Pastoralists and Graziers' Employment Agency. The next day instructions came to start immediately at Mt Elizabeth station. Apprehensive, she caught a plane the following evening. 'I didn't know where I was going,' she says. 'I had never flown before, got into Derby at 5.30 am, then caught a smaller plane to Gibb River station. All I could see was red ground and black faces. Peter and his nephew were there. They were very shy. Mrs Russ from Gibb River station eyed my best woollen dress and said, "You're going to be covered in grass seeds on the way home, dear." As we travelled through ten-foot spear-grass in an old Land Rover without windows, I became a pin cushion.'

Peter remembers that Pat Burton's arrival 'got the heart racing'. She taught his sister Mavis's daughters, aged 7 and 13, daily tuning into the School of the Air at Derby. There was no glass in the schoolroom windows. 'At first the younger one would jump straight out the window and off if she saw Uncle Peter and horses,' says Pat, 'but they learned to respect me, and she would come back.' Pat's teaching helped the older girl win a scholarship to boarding school the following year. After nine months as governess, she returned south. Peter pursued her. The old Aboriginal people told him she was right for him. They became engaged, then married in 1971. I asked if there was anything she missed from her previous life when she moved to Mt Elizabeth with Peter. 'I used to hang out for a tin of beetroot,' she laughs. 'Whenever I had money, I would buy a tin. The hardest part was not seeing my family for three years. The Lacys only went to town once a year, for the Derby races. It took ten hours. We used to jump in every waterhole because the car had no air-conditioning.'

The whole family moved to a new site and nobody lives in the original homestead. It is still in good repair, as cool as a cave, made of river stones joined together with crushed antbed broken from anthills and pounded with water to make a natural mortar. Its floor is also made of compressed antbed covered with special tar. For six years the young couple lived in a tin shed in the garden, the louvred windows providing relief from summer heat. 'I loved it,' Pat recalls. 'Peter's mother was a great home maker, gardener and mad keen on fishing. She saved seeds and grew mangoes, oranges, pawpaws, and vegetables. We bought little, apart from sugar, tin jam and flour. It was 50-pound 'bagged flour'. By the end of the Wet, it was full of weevils and tasted awful. Peter's Dad used to say, "Eat it up, it's good for you." There were 500 goats, shepherded by the Aboriginal women. We had kerosene fridges which when they worked, worked well, and old Tilley lamps run on kerosene. We've only had 24-hour power for the last four years and the phone for the last nine years. We relied on the windmill or had a bucket brigade with everyone carting water from the river. There was no septic toilet, only a dunny pan. The Aboriginal women would take me walking for bush tucker or diving for water lily roots. They shared their way of life and beliefs. I helped look after their kids and taught the girls sewing, gardening and cooking.'

Eventually Peter took Pat to pick a site for a house. She told him it all looked like bush and he should choose. 'I've been cursing ever since. It's all rock. We broke it with a pick, carted soil and planted trees. Peter has built everything here.' The rock he levered from a creekbed 130 kilometres away for the house, and cut it with a modified cutting disc on a chainsaw.

The year 1983 was rock bottom in the Lacys' lives. Peter tore a foot off when he rolled a bull buggy (a cutdown jeep) chasing cattle. The bone was sticking into the ground, the sole of his boot twisted up. 'I could see the boot sole and realised my foot was still in it,' he remembers. 'I wrenched the boot back on. Luckily one of Pat's friends was a nurse and gave me a morphine injection from the Royal Flying Doctor Service medical kit. That numbed it a bit.'

Pat says she felt sick when she saw his foot. She kept her cool until she put the medical report in to the Flying Doctor, but once she had given the details, shock set in. 'The Flying Doctor was here in an hour. He put the leg and the foot, which was hanging by a piece of skin, into an air splint to stabilise it for the flight. The surgeon had to stitch everything back together, then slowly get skin grafts to take and patch up the gaping wounds.'

'It developed gangrene. At one stage I nearly lost the foot,' Peter says. 'Peg Leg Pete! They rushed me to Perth and got me onto antibiotics. Pat was on the station working out what to do with the cattle. She sold some and called it quits for the muster. Ever optimistic, Peter played down the horrific accident and at first maintained he had just broken his ankle and would be back home in a few days. He was stunned to find himself in hospital for 12 weeks. What helped save the foot was a movement machine that rotated day and night, backwards and forwards, round and round to keep the muscles going. 'I was nine weeks on my back in the Charles Gardiner hospital and for a few weeks after that hobbled around on crutches. Eventually I threw them away, and I'm still hobbling around.' He is laconic about continual pain and a slight limp. 'I couldn't ride any more. It's constant agony, but I've learned to live with it.'

In the same year Peter's father died and so did Pat's father. She was coping with two small children. 'I was always run down, but I had to remain strong to keep going.' She remembers her hair falling out and going to a hairdresser in Derby, who asked Pat's sister-in-law what was wrong. 'I think Pat must be under some sort of stress!' she said. Pat's dry humour often disguises her own strength and courage.

In 1984, a week after Peter had thrown away his crutches, a mate called in during the Wet and they decided to fly to Derby. 'On the way back, we were over Mt Barnett, descending for Mt Elizabeth, when we ran out of fuel. We were coming down in the hills,' he recalls. 'The wings were hitting trees. We said goodbye to each other.'

Pat was at the station airstrip waiting for them. When they didn't arrive, she returned home in time to hear 'search and rescue' on the two-way radio saying a plane had gone down in the Mt Barnett area. 'I knew straight away it was him,' she shudders. 'The country was so rugged and never in my wildest dreams could I imagine they would survive. I went down to tell his mum and she lost the plot. Then I set off to find him. I had the two kids telling me, "We'll take a loaf of bread for Dad, Mum," and "Don't worry Mum, the doctor's plane will come and fix Dad up." What should have been a 50-minute drive took me two hours. I don't recall driving that slowly, but I didn't want to get there. When I arrived, Peter met me saying, "Where the bloody hell have you been? I've been worried sick about you." "You've got a cheek!" I said.'

The pilot had kept his cool. 'We landed in the only spot to land,' says Peter, 'but the Cessna 185 had half a wing torn off, the other buckled and the belly pushed up. I had bought our daughter Tanya a kid's comb set at the local store, for her birthday, so I flashed the mirror at the search plane to say we were alive.'

Pat says they both had nightmares for a long time afterwards, waking up screaming. 'Peter was supposed to go out on a boat a month later. I said, "There's no way I'd be taking you." He ran into Father Lorenz, the Catholic priest in Derby, who said, "Listen here my son, you've used up your lives." "It depends which way you look at it, Father!" Peter replied. "I reckon I'm having a pretty good run so far."'

Peter says a lot of people give up too easily on what they want. He loves the challenge of each day holding something different, 'of setting ourselves a goal and sticking at it'. By the mid-1980s, a new goal started to emerge. Mt Elizabeth was a midway stop along the Gibb River Road for government workers and travellers. 'Kimberley hospitality is "come in, have a bed",' Pat says. 'It was a thrill to see people, but we couldn't keep feeding them. So we put in some accommodation.' Peter started fishing safaris to Walcott Inlet, a fisherman's paradise where great barramundi and small mullet surge in their hundreds into the remote inlet on the twice-daily 11-metre tides. 'The neighbours thought we were mad,' he laughs. 'I thought it might come and go, but it's built up. Showing people the station way of life and Aboriginal rock art goes a long way to lessening the gap between Aborigines and other Australians.'

o o o

An hour's grinding drive away from the homestead my husband and I strip for a swim in a series of placid pools wreathed in paperbarks and pandanus palms. Climbing down beside a waterfall and around a brown snake sunning on rocks, we come upon a magical site, Wunnumburra. On the rocks are painted mouthless white faces with red-ochre halos from which radiate lines. They have large eyes ringed by lines like long eyelashes, prominent noses and rounded shoulders clothed in radiating lines like capes. These strange, compelling faces are Wandjina, an art form unique to the Kimberley. 'They are the spirits in the clouds. Their headdresses represent lightning. Special people are appointed as custodians and are allowed to retouch the paintings,' Peter later explained. To me they look like a group of ancient goddesses, powerful and mysterious, guarding the gorge against intruders from their overhanging rock wall. 'I'm encouraging our Aboriginal community to show the rock art and tell the stories,' says Peter. 'In that way we hope to protect the art sites.' Pat wants to train and build the confidence of young people from the community to work with visitors.

Tourism has changed the Lacys' lifestyle. Non-stop from April to November travellers camp or stay in the house enjoying generous family meals and day tours. 'You either do it properly or not at all', is Pat's philosophy. Unlike Peter, his children have grown up surrounded by people. Pat is concerned about the impact of eager tourists on this fragile country and the pressure on facilities. She thinks numbers will have to be controlled or pristine wilderness areas may be degraded.

The isolation can still close in on them, sometimes at the hands of unaware bureaucracy. In 1998 the ABC ended its shortwave radio service due to budget cuts. Outback people who relied on it protested, but to no avail. In February 2000, as the Kimberley drowned in a huge Wet, the Lacys were about to step onto the mail plane from Derby to flood-bound Mt Elizabeth when the Civil Aviation Safety Authority decreed no further passenger transport. They had to charter a plane, at six times the cost. 'We are going backwards,' concludes Pat. 'There are not enough of us to matter.'

Peter's life is devoted to his 3500 cattle, which he is gradually upgrading from Shorthorn to Brahman. They are shipped live to South East Asia and the Middle East. The meatworks at Broome, Wyndham and Derby have now closed, unable to compete with live exporting. The mustering begins during our visit. Rays of the rising sun catch in dust swirling up from horses' hooves as Brett and six Aboriginal stockmen saddle up. The Lacys muster with horses as they always have, but now a helicopter flushes stock from rough country. The horsemen round up a 'coaching' mob of cows and calves, which they shepherd along to quieten wild cattle brought in by the helicopter. Mustering time has halved to six weeks with the choppers.

Back home, Pat is packing supplies for ten days from a well-stocked storeroom into Superb Baker's Flour drums. Food, fuel and swags are neatly stacked into the back of a lumbering old army truck driven by a now snowy-haired Scottie. His wife Maisie is the stock camp cook. 'I used to take a Land Rover with small swags for six horsemen. You've got softer and the swags bigger since helicopter mustering,' Pat teases her husband.

An hour's drive from the homestead, the helicopter whirrs overhead, bringing belligerent Brahman bulls in to the 'coaching' mob. The horsemen ring the mob like centaurs. Peter drives an Avgas-fuelled bull-buggy with tyres strapped on the front, chasing breakaway cattle. He takes off at great speed through scattered trees, trailing blue smoke. A bull tosses its head at the buggy, trying to reach Peter's unlikely offsider Dennis Taylor, a bible translator who lives in the Aboriginal community. Peter quickly reverses, turns and bowls the bull over, cushioning its fall with the tyres. Dennis grabs a leather strap, leaps out of the buggy and hobbles the angry bull's back legs with the strap. It hops about, still tossing its horns at the men. Eventually it quietens down, then it is unhobbled and runs back to join the mob. It is fast and risky work. We watch from safety atop the truck.

Pat tells me that once when they were mustering, Peter got off his horse to throw a beast, grabbing it by the tail and throwing it off balance so it fell over, but it unexpectedly sprang up and horned him in the groin. 'He applied pressure to stop the bleeding, then dug out a needle and some catgut normally carried to stitch up horses horned by charging bulls and proceeded to stitch himself up. As there were no vehicles in the stock camp, he then rode 30 kilometres home and called up the Royal Flying Doctor Service doctor on the radio. The doctor reassured Peter that he had done all that needed to be done and to call back if the wound got infected and get a prescription for antibiotics.'

Peter is incredibly tough, and like all those in isolated places doing potentially risky jobs, he needs to be. 'After some narrow misses with savage bulls, he got a revolver,' Pat tells me. 'Another time Peter jumped off his horse to throw a beast, but he slipped on the damp grass and lost his grip. The angry bull spun around punching the ground, trying to rake Peter who was lying there. Its horn ripped his shirt. He was not able to reach his revolver, but an Aboriginal stockman acted as a decoy, teasing the bull from behind a nearby tree to distract it so Peter could get up and escape.'

Peter Lacey is one of those unassuming, courageous people who takes the good with the bad. His wife Pat says she often wishes she could be like him. I think she is. They are two of a kind—modern pioneers reconciling black and white worlds, tradition and technology, family and work, in harmony with their magnificent environment.

4 | Hey, Sister!

Margaret Carnegie-Smith ~
Bush nursing in the Top End

It is five o'clock in the morning. A red Kimberley sun lights up the Carr Boyd Ranges that fringe Lake Argyle in Western Australia. Like a scene from one of her books about station life in the Top End, best-selling author Sara Henderson drops in by helicopter from her station Bullo River, over the border in the Northern Territory. It is 1997, and 30 of us are recovering from ten days' hiking through rugged mountains and gorges on the first adventurous 'leg' of the Australian Rural Leadership Program. We watch her aircraft circle and settle on top of Point X. Sara, a director of the program, has come to inspire us with her philosophy of strength and survival. I ask her who inspires her. She replies, 'The bush nurses who tracked leprosy in the Top End during the 1970s'. Leprosy in Australia? This was news to me.

My search for such people takes me to Katherine, a tropical town roasted by the Dry of July, and to Margaret Carnegie-Smith. A slight, sweet-faced woman, she greets me over coffee as if we have met before. What is most noticeable is her grace and dignity. She is no chatterer, but states her piece in a matter-of-fact way. Her story is a testament to the rigorous and selfless work of a small band of people who, with skill, compassion and determination, succeeded in containing the spread of leprosy.

I meet Margaret's fellow nurses Barbara Tynan, former leprosy control sister in the southern region of Northern Territory and Margaret Cooper, public health nurse in the Katherine Centre for Disease Control. I imagined a trio of tough pioneers but found gentle women whose enthusiasm for their work and delight in the people kept my writing hand running hot.

The experience is still alive for them as they speak of escalating health problems among Aboriginal people going through great changes from tribal to Western ways during the 1960s. Their words reflect deep understanding and heartfelt concern. The nurses dealt with the impact of overcrowding as these people moved or were brought into 'communities'. Often semi-nomadic, small family groups didn't know how to live congregated with many others. Traditional larders of bush foods were soon depleted, replaced by unfamiliar rations of Western foods. Poor sanitation led to hookworm, which caused anaemia. People were confronted with unfamiliar diseases against which they had no resistance. Barbara Tynan says that by 1969 in some parts of the Territory 'an Aboriginal child was dying almost every day of diarrhoea, vomiting or chest infections. Children went so quickly. Even bonny babes would suddenly die.' Relatively minor ailments such as colds can kill when coupled with poor nutrition and heavy parasite loads. The Health Department acted, sending out bush nurses to support the overstretched Aboriginal welfare and mission staff and the station women. Margaret Carnegie-Smith (then Margaret Eldridge), joined their ranks in 1968.

Margaret Eldridge grew up in the east coast cities of Newcastle and Sydney. 'Since I was knee high to a grasshopper, I wanted to be a missionary nurse among people with leprosy,' she says. She left school at 14 after gaining her Intermediate Certificate, and in 1956 her parents joined the Aborigines Inland Mission and moved the family to Darwin. For her father it was a courageous leap from bus conductor to missionary. Stan

Eldridge became pastor and later superintendent of the inter-denominational community church of the Aborigines Inland Mission and held regular services at East Arm Leprosarium on the outskirts of Darwin, a community of 200 people. He built a church there with the aid of patients. Margaret remembers a happy place with people who loved the missionaries' children.

After five years of working in a bank in Darwin, Margaret felt the call to be a nurse. At Darwin Hospital she found studying a struggle, and some of the sisters struck fear into the students' hearts. In Sydney on her first holiday she sent home a telegram, 'I'm not coming back'. Her father replied urgently, 'Second year will be better'. She did return, because she loved practical nursing and her patients, especially the Aboriginal people. In 1967 she graduated with three certificates, giving God credit for helping her through.

Her bush nursing career began when, with three other nurses and a doctor, she was seconded to an infectious typhoid fever outbreak on Elcho Island, off the north coast of Arnhem Land. Margaret thrived on the challenge and decided to continue bush nursing instead of taking charge of Darwin Hospital's children's ward.

Mobile nursing was not for the faint-hearted. Margaret and another nurse covered the Territory from Darwin east to Borroloola. They travelled for a month at a time, their Land Cruiser loaded with boxes of medicines, ointments and dressings, fuel and water, food and sleeping bags. 'We had to be self-sufficient, because we mostly slept at cattle stations where there were large Aboriginal populations and few medical services,' says Margaret. Station wives would talk to them until all hours of the night, starved of women's company in a man's world.

Calvert Hills station, south of the Gulf of Carpentaria town of Borroloola, was her first port of call as a mobile sister. 'The Aboriginal people were out bush in stock camps, so immunisations had fallen behind. I had 20 children to do. After the first few days of jabbing children with needles, they cried automatically when they saw me. Months later when I returned, the station people wanted to name a horse after me. They couldn't decide whether to call it Sister Margaret or Sister Needles!

'It was exciting. I remember our vehicle broke down in the East Alligator area, now Kakadu. In one direction we saw a buffalo so we walked the other way. As we rounded a corner another buffalo emerged, angry, hoofing up dust. We looked around for trees to climb.' Instead they sprinted back, locked themselves in the vehicle and waited for help. Again in East Alligator, driving up a steep gravel road they stopped to photograph a stunning sunset, only to find the brake wasn't holding. Margaret dived to pull on the handbrake as the vehicle rolled back to the edge of a cliff. 'We missed the sunset' is all she says.

Some roads were just station tracks not marked on maps. In one day they were covered in mud as they pushed the vehicle out of a bog, had to hoist the spare tyre from the roof before changing a flat tyre, then set off again, only to collect a well-camouflaged wire strung across the road to act as a gate. During the Wet they coped with flooded creeks. In the Dry they ploughed through sandy creekbeds and sank into patches of bulldust.

They had to pitch the radio aerial over a tree to communicate at their regular call-in time. The bush tuned in. 'Nothing was secret,' Margaret said. Their official Health Department title was survey sisters as they worked their way through entire communities, screening station and Aboriginal people. First babies, then school-age children and finally adults were checked from top to toe for infected eyes and ears, decayed teeth, skin complaints and other health problems. They were treated for hook-worm and tested and immunised for diseases such as tuberculosis. Difficult cases they referred to the doctor who flew into stations every six weeks.

If they noticed thickened eyebrows, clawed hands and feet and patches of skin without feeling they suspected leprosy, and sent skin scrapings to Darwin for testing. 'Leprosy first entered Australia in the 1880s with the Chinese gold miners flocking to Pine Creek, near Katherine in the Top End,' says Margaret Cooper. The disease spread its tentacles from the Top End south after World War II as Aboriginal people travelled more. By the late 1950s and early 1960s the incidence was very high in some Territory communities, affecting mainly Aboriginal but also some European people. Six hundred cases were diagnosed, mainly in the Top End. Many more were at risk through prolonged contact.

The bush nurses had to find people with leprosy and persuade them to get treatment early so the disease would not take hold and spread in their overcrowded conditions. Specialists like Barbara Tynan, a dedicated nurse trained in anthropology, whose job was to detect leprosy, proved valuable allies. When Barbara wanted to study anthropology Health Department officials told her, 'Nurses go to college, not university'. Undaunted, she applied for and won a Public Service scholarship. Covering the southern half of the Territory, her anthropology training paid off in the meticulous way she traced patients and their contacts, mapping entire families and their whereabouts. With this baseline data, on each trip she could follow up and ask, 'Where's so-and-so?' Among hundreds surveyed, those with leprosy were usually in the last ten, reluctant to leave their families.

In one Top End community Margaret Cooper remembers seeing older women whose hands were gnarled and missing fingers. She suspected leprosy. 'Oh no,' one woman told her. 'These my fighting fingers.' At times they fought each other with nulla-nullas or wooden clubs, sometimes knocking off parts of fingers.

Enter Dr John Hargrave, hero to nurses and patients, who came to the Territory as a district medical officer in the mid-1950s. Federal Health authorities sent leprosy-affected people to Channel Island in Darwin Harbour then, and some never returned home. Dr Hargrave won the battle to allow patients to return home by convincing the authorities that patients were no longer infectious after sulphur drug treatment and with regular checkups. He became a world-renowned leprologist, and his ground-breaking work was crucial in stemming the spread of the disease in the Territory.

Margaret Carnegie-Smith trained for a month with Dr Hargrave at East Arm. 'He was an excellent teacher and skilled surgeon. I saw one of his first operations, when he transplanted a tendon from a healthy limb into the arm of a man with a leprosy-affected hand. Marvellously intricate microsurgery. I saw joy on that man's face when the little plaster casts came off and his fingers could move. Even now people say, "Dr Hargrave, he fix my hand." They worship him.' He also initiated the training of Aboriginal people who had had leprosy to return and work in their communities as health workers (see Jack Little story, chapter 5).

In 1971 the young Margaret Carnegie-Smith studied at London's Hospital for Tropical Diseases and went from there to a hospital in Zambia as sister-in-charge for two years. When she returned to Australia in 1974, Territory Health sent her to Borroloola. In her absence its population had swelled from 200 to 1000 to accommodate Aboriginal people displaced from surrounding cattle stations. The introduction of an award wage for Aborigines in the pastoral industry had put many stockmen out of work, as stations could no longer afford to pay them and keep their families.

The Wet was in full swing, with its oppressive heat and constant storms. Life revolved around the Macarthur River. The township consisted of an old pub-cum-store, a few tin buildings, fewer houses, the large Aboriginal camp and some caravans. A van, quaintly called a silver bullet, became home for the town's new sister. Its lighting was powered at whim by a cranky generator. The generator pull-cord was so heavy she had to wait for stronger-armed help or light the hurricane lamp.

'As soon as I put out the lantern and crawled under the mosquito net, I would hear the "plop, plop" of a frog inside the van. I couldn't settle until I caught it and put it out. Away in the long grass was a toilet and shower, which I shared with snakes, frogs and the Works Department blokes.' When Margaret first arrived, she got locked in the clinic toilet after hours. Green frogs hid under the toilet bowl rim, leaping out with each flush. 'I didn't fancy spending the night in there,' says Margaret. There was nobody around to hear her cries for help, so she climbed up the wall to escape.

After her first day at work, Margaret returned to the silver bullet to find everything soaked. 'I hadn't closed the top vent and rain had flooded into the van. I didn't know that I should light the fridge after attaching a new gas cylinder, so it defrosted. When I opened the door, water poured out.' Thirty-three and single, Margaret had to be self-reliant. 'I was too busy to be lonely,' she says, practical and frank in her approach. 'I accepted isolation as part of the job, but in that small community I made lifelong friends.'

During her first three months at Borroloola, Margaret was the only nurse and permanently on call. 'It was difficult and tiring, but I learned to cope.' Later another nurse arrived, and a new demountable clinic replaced the primitive room behind the 1880s police station. Forty-hour weeks were unknown. 'If someone was seriously ill at night we would sit up with them until a plane could come from Darwin the next morning to fly them out. It was before airstrip lighting and night flying facilities were available.' Once in a three-day period Margaret delivered three babies who all needed hospital care. One mother haemorrhaged, another had a retained placenta and one of the babies had a deformity. Sometimes two nurses were needed, one to clear the baby's airways, the other to look after the mother.

When she was on mobile in 1968 Margaret didn't see any alcohol problems, but when she came back to Borroloola in 1974, she found many people affected by alcohol. 'My heart was saddened. When Darwin breweries went on strike for several weeks, I noticed a distinct change in the people. They were happy and eating good food. I asked them, "Isn't this better without the grog?" They said, "Sister Margaret, we're much healthier and happier".

'In August 1974 my father was killed in a car accident. I was working over the border in Queensland. My boss had to tell me over the radio, and the nurses heard.' Margaret remembers her disbelief. 'I had seen him just the previous weekend in Darwin. He was so proud of his nurse daughter working out bush. My last sight of him was waving goodbye.' The Health Department sent an Aerial Medical plane to take her to Darwin to be with her mother. On Christmas Eve she flew back to Borroloola. On Christmas Day, Cyclone Tracy struck Darwin. 'My mother was in Queensland staying with family. I couldn't contact her to let her know I had left Darwin. The weather had closed in on Borroloola and it was pitch black. The airstrip was closed. Eventually, to reassure Mum, I was able to send a telegram from Macarthur Mines, 50 kilometres away.'

In Margaret Carnegie-Smith's seven years at Borroloola, people learned to trust her and come to her for health care. Yanyula and Garawa people paid Sister Margaret their highest honour. 'When you earned their respect, they included you in their family group and community giving you a "skin name". I didn't expect it when someone came into the Clinic and referred to me as "Nangala". Children would come up and take my hand and say, "You're my auntie", or whatever relationship. Even when I moved to Katherine, a long way from Borroloola, people would still call me by my "skin name". It meant a lot.'

In 1981, the Health Department asked Margaret to help extend the Aerial Medical service to the Katherine region. She worked with them for 15 years, becoming sister-in-charge, then moved to the Katherine Centre for Disease Control. In 1987 she married Brian Carnegie-Smith, an ambulance officer she had met on an emergency flight into Katherine.

Margaret left Borroloola as she came, in the Wet. The heavens conspired to keep her out bush. 'I had just bought a new car. I came to a floodway, walked halfway across, decided it was okay and then carefully drove in. The car spluttered to a stop. I saw water coming up through the lovely new carpet. I composed myself.' Rain poured down as she walked an hour to Tanumbirini station, thinking she had drowned her car. They towed her prized possession to safety and next day escorted her in style through the trouble spots.

Margaret Carnegie-Smith and Margaret Cooper went back to Borroloola recently. 'People love Marg,' Margaret Cooper tells me. 'She is respectful of their culture, yet holds the dignity of her own culture. If you could see how they scrubbed up to see her,' she laughs. Margaret Carnegie-Smith was also excited to see her old friends. After 20 years she has retired from bush nursing in body but not in spirit. She and her former colleagues warn against complacency about the spread of leprosy.

As one of only two infectious disease control sisters covering a quarter of the Territory around the Katherine region, Margaret Cooper continues vital work started in the 1960s by bush nurses such as Margaret Carnegie-Smith and Barbara Tynan. An excellent communicator, she paints a vivid picture of the present situation. 'People forget history. Leprosy lies dormant. In just one of 19 Aboriginal communities around Katherine, there are two active cases and 30 "contacts". Most cases are coming in with immigration. They can scatter anywhere. There are potentially hundreds. We advocate more rigorous surveillance and screening, and specialised training so that health professionals can spot leprosy.'

'In the 1970s,' Barbara Tynan says, 'we found that the key to forestalling the disasters of disabilities, deformities and amputations from leprosy was to get in early and reduce the spread. We didn't know how well we were going until the incidence was down to one case a year by the 1980s and East Arm was closed in 1982.'

Margaret Carnegie-Smith fulfilled her dream to be a bush nurse. 'I'm thankful to God for His guidance in my life and for keeping me safe. My satisfaction is the deep relationships and trust I forged with Aboriginal people. They don't forget you.' We were walking down the main street of Katherine one February morning, when an Aboriginal woman waved and called out from across the street: 'Hey, Sister Margaret!'

5 | Jack's Dream

Jack Little ~
Overturning the odds for Aboriginal people

While I wait for Jack Little in the practical two-room health centre at Bulla camp in the Territory Top End, nurses visiting from Timber Creek argue about his age.

'54,' insists one. Jack appears.

'When were you born, Jack?' they chorus.

'1929. I'm 71,' he says.

One woman hurries to check his records. It's no wonder they are astonished. He is an upright, vigorous-looking man with a wicked laugh. He chortles at her complete disbelief.

Jack strides over and shakes my hand. His deep brown face is strong, intelligent and good-humoured, his grey moustache neatly clipped. He stands tall, smartly dressed in white shirt and grey trousers. We meet here so I can see one of the achievements of his life, the Jack Little Health Centre at Bulla, opened by Jack himself in 1991. It is one measure of a life devoted to improving the health of his people.

As I had driven into Bulla, on the East Baines River near the Western Australian border, bulbous baobab trees extended their strangled boughs in welcome at the entrance, clustering around a sign proclaiming a 'dry' community where no alcohol is allowed. Community members were curious and helpful, directing me through clean streets past large houses to the health centre.

I have come to interview Jack about his recovery from leprosy when he was a young man. Instead, as we sit in the whisper of shade on the health centre veranda, I discover that he is a walking history of Top End cultural change from his early days as a cattle ringer or stockman, through suffering leprosy to becoming the Territory's first Aboriginal health worker, and over the last 25 years building up a new community, Bulla. We watch neatly dressed, squealing children rushing to school, young men emptying garbage drums on their regular run, mothers stirring up their cooking fires, older folk sitting on their verandas enjoying the morning sun—everywhere people taking pride in their community. 'You can see for yourself, something happened here,' says Jack.

'Tell me about your early life, Jack,' I say.

Jack begins, 'As a boy living in a humpy with my father and mother at Humbert River station, south of here, my early life was real hard. Aboriginal people couldn't get a good education. My only bit of experience came from Charlie Schultz, the owner of the station, who taught us that we wanted to live a better life. I grew up with Charlie, he was like my father. Charlie's wife Bessie loved Aboriginal children. She would take us into the house and we would play with their children.

'At the same time I used to listen to my parents for things they had learned and passed on, like how to go hunting. We go through ceremonies, learning how to obey parents and respect elders. That was our teaching, our school. My father would take me hunting, make me a little spear. When he caught a kangaroo, we cooked it in the ground with bark and hot rocks and shared it with close relations. We'd hunt a lot of things—turtle, goanna, crocodile. I never had a fishing line, just dived in and grabbed fish. The first time I saw my father spear a freshwater crocodile, he jumped on a log and paddled to where the croc was, grabbed the spear and pulled the croc back to the shore. Croc's good eating, similar to chicken. I still eat croc, my medical food!' he laughs heartily. Two young mothers, babies on hips, arrive at the clinic and join in the laughter.

We walk across the road to the open-sided Bulla church made of tree boughs. Jack continues, 'When I was 16, I made my own wooden spear. It's hard to teach kids the way we've been taught—too much motor car, too much grog. They can't understand our background. They don't want to listen to the old ways. When I was a kid my father would take me walking hunting, now it's motor car hunting. Bush walking makes me strong and healthy.'

Jack's mother cooked in the homestead kitchen, his father was a ringer. 'He taught me. Big flogging teach me to ride a horse, cop the lot. Charlie Schultz, he wanted to make ringers understand his way. If it wasn't for him, I wouldn't be a good stockman. I thought it hard at first, but realised I had to learn.

'We left Humbert River station when I was about ten and went to Waterloo station, where I worked as a ringer. I would go hunting with the young people, never stay still, moving from station to station. The stock camp was a wonderful life. We were all Ngaringman, same language group. We'd get up at five or six o'clock and go out mustering bullocks, get bronco horses, brand cattle. We had just our bare hands and a horse.'

Jack tries to get comfortable on an unyielding chair. He tells me of an old injury that still causes pain. 'We had broken arms and legs from horse accidents. Sometimes the horse hits a hole when you're chasing a cow. Once I was thrown over the front. The seat of the saddle hit me in the back, knocked me out. It nearly broke my back. They flew me to Wyndham.' His back hurts if he sits for long, so we continue to talk while walking around the community.

'We lived on damper and corned meat. No money at all and real hard work. The whitefellas were paid, we were satisfied with what we got. When we were mustering bullocks for the meatworks, we had no sleep. Day and night mustering. There were 17 Aboriginal stockmen and five whitefellas. We only came back to the homestead to get fresh horses. One day me and another fella were riding together in a big storm. We were hit by lightning. The power came at me and grabbed me in the leg, like a white band. I thought I was split in half.' He quickly recovered. Jack was younger than the others. 'We were strong, smart, healthy. We had meat, never greasy food. It was before alcohol.'

I ask about his parents. 'My dad "finish" when I was 15. Parents, why do they die? Maybe not eating the right food or living in a humpy, or maybe to do with Aboriginal custom. Dad was a tribal person. Some young people don't like the way the elders try to discipline them to lead a good life. The lore is tough if someone makes a problem. They are punished in the bush and the elders talk to them to educate them in right behaviour. With European law a fellow goes to jail. Nobody talks to him. What comes of it? When he comes out he might do the same thing again.' Jack is referring to the complex and unchanging system of tribal rights and obligations in Aboriginal lore that involve all aspects of life, including relationships with different people; European law, in comparison, can be changed by parliament. 'With blackfella lore you don't come out with nothing. You come out a different person. When I was about 17, I was a wild man,' he rolls his eyes at the memory. 'With our lore you come out with a respect for the elders, for older women, for everybody as a family. I went to the bush a wild man, I came out as Jack Little. I don't believe in jail much, lockup maybe. In Timber Creek lockup, relatives can visit so the person knows someone cares.'

Jack Little's life took a dramatic turn in 1958, when he was 29. He tells me how his right hand went numb. 'Dr Hargrave came and saw me at the station. I went to East Arm Leprosarium hospital in Darwin where they took a smear from my ears and eyebrows and sent it away to check. Results came back positive—leprosy. I lost the tip of my little finger from rope damage because I couldn't feel it. The nerve was buggered up. I never used the hand. Dr Hargrave transferred a skin graft to cover a crack in my hand. I said, "I can feel something. I can move it." This hand, a hand of help. It can do anything now.'

I notice Jack's hand is bandaged. He assures me it is just a cut. I ask how he felt, moving from station life to East Arm for five years. 'It break my heart, different country, different people, but then I really enjoy it when I got used to it. Good food, play football, made a lot of friends. There were over 200 Aboriginal people. We had little separate houses, two or three people in each. When you believe that sulphur drug treatment can work and trust the person treating you, you overcome it quicker. Leprosy is a real scary thing for others, not for me. You can be born with it. I probably got it from my mother. She also came to East Arm, same sickness, a year after me. I was very happy to see her.'

Jack met his promised wife at Kildurk station, west of Katherine, and she came to East Arm hospital to work. 'In 1970, our daughter Marjory was born. Not many children at East Arm. She was in contact with leprosy when she was a little girl but she had sulphur injections and now she's fine. We have one grandson. He makes me proud. Sometimes gives me a headache!' More chortles here.

In 1963, after five years in the leprosarium, Jack decided to do something for his own people. There were hundreds with leprosy, especially from Arnhem Land. Some had lost hands and feet. 'I thought, "My people need another Aborigine to try and explain." ' He was 35 and had never been to school. Jack trained for eight months with Dr Hargrave in Darwin in physiology, anatomy and hygiene. He specialised in leprosy care, so he could go back into the community and also work on stations with Aboriginal populations and look after people returning from East Arm. 'If it wasn't for Dr Hargrave, I wouldn't know how to look after my own people. I'm proud to be taught something new in health by him. They even took us to the mortuary. I didn't eat for two days. People were cut up like a bullock and their guts taken out.'

Jack was one of the first Aboriginal health workers in the Territory, and 29 years later became one of its longest-serving. In 1971, his first post was to Katherine to help people returning from East Arm. 'I would go out to their camps and treat them there instead of bringing them in. We would look for causes of sickness. The main thing is to clean up regularly and keep showers and toilets clean. I really enjoyed it because I did it for my own people. Aboriginal people were excited to see Aboriginal health workers coming to their communities.'

Jack and his assistant, Hannah Brumby, starred with nurse Barbara Braddock in a film called *Bush Nurse*, one of a series made by an independent film maker for European distribution. Hannah was shown driving to camps to hand out tablets, and Jack was shown doing daily dressings. They covered a large region and all diseases—heart, high blood pressure, scabies, diarrhoea, immunisations and new cases of leprosy.

Our circuit of the nearly 200-strong community brings us back to the verandah of the Jack Little Health Centre. The family line of Aboriginal health workers continues: Jack's niece Betty Laurie, sole parent to eight children, studies public health in Katherine and has now taken over health work from Jack's wife and daughter, who followed Jack into health work in the 1990s. People come and go all day at the centre.

'Dr Hargrave had a fair idea training Aboriginal health workers to work with nurses and doctors, especially between them and Aboriginal people. I never saw a doctor doing such wonderful things to help Aboriginal people,' Jack says, settling down on a bench. 'Not only that, he can talk half a dozen languages, my language too. We call him by a blackfella name. It opened up the way to see Aboriginal people working with government departments and turned around attitudes to medication.'

Jack recalls the Katherine years. His mother died, he was a 'Ngaringman blackfella' working with different language people, and he discovered alcohol. 'I was earning big money and trying to balance too much work, too much alcohol, and family life. Which comes first, family or alcohol? I got mixed up. I said, 'It's my problem, it's up to me to deal with it. I've got to have strong mind, strong will.' I was sick in my spirit. One day I said, "Is that can [of beer] my boss?"

'My wife said, "Yes." So I kicked that can out the door.

"Not my boss any more!"

'I couldn't see any help for me in a dry-out centre so I went to the church. I still had the problem, but in the church I could see what the Lord done for other people. Then I think, "He can do the same for me."'

In 1975 Jack was ordained an Assembly of God pastor in Kununurra. His parish was enormous—from Katherine to Fitzroy Crossing. He was an Aboriginal health worker looking after physical illness and a pastor looking after the spirit. 'I was wild. I stop all that. I met Arnold and Margaret Con-goo in Kununurra and stuck with them.' They were missionaries from Queensland. Both their grandmothers had been full-blood Aborigines; Arnold's father was Chinese, Margaret's father was a Filipino pearl diver. Jack points me towards the Con-goos' house, next to Bulla health centre, while he has lunch. A neat curly-headed woman pops out of the door, followed by a man with a round, genial face and a beaming smile. The Con-goos regard Bulla as their life's work. It is a good subject to discuss over a cup of tea.

'In 1975, Bulla was scrub, a few old people living in humpies. We worked as a team with Jack, who was spokesman for the traditional owner, Bobby Widdaburra,' Margaret begins. 'People from the stock camp at Auvergne station wanted some land for a holiday camp so four of us went up to Darwin to see the politician, Bob Collins. Jack said, "Look Bob, I'm a Labor man too. We need your help." Bob Collins got out a map and said Aborigines were entitled to land along the East Baines River. The owners of Auvergne station, the Fogartys, gave Bobby Widdaburra 30 acres when he was pensioned off to "sit down" from being a ringer. He was a great man, old Bobby.'

Margaret Con-goo describes how people gave up their tribal law, killings and payback. 'Others would say, "What's Arnold doing with the Aborigines at Bulla? Is he making them white men, without their own culture?"'

'Arnold said, "No, there are two cultures, the good and the bad. We are fighting against the bad one, but they still have their good culture." The Ngaringman tribal elders wanted Jack to carry on with tribal law after his father died, but Jack told them he was a Christian. They said Jack could be a missionary. Otherwise he could have been killed for defying tribal law.'

Jack comes to join us. 'This land was here since the beginning for Aboriginal people. We should look after it. People lived in tin shacks in the 1970s. Hot as hell,' he says. One day Dr Hargrave came from Darwin and saw Jack sitting under a tree at Bulla. He asked, 'What are you doing here?'

Jack said, 'Relaxing.'

He said, 'You want to be a health worker like before?'

'Yes, where?'

'Here.'

The community had grown from six to 200 people by then. Jack was employed by Territory Health Services and had to take on the health problems of children and old people. Bulla had alcohol problems and a lot of fighting. 'He served medicine to all these people out of a caravan, a silver bullet,' Arnold tells me as Jack looks modest. 'No fridge, just an old tin trunk for medicines. He did a marvellous job. Eventually he got a medicine box and a two-way radio.'

Jack asked the officials from the Department of Aboriginal Affairs, ' "Where do you put your family? If they all live together, they all get sick. Too many dogs, too many people. They get scabies and colds." The mosquitoes, man—enough to carry you out of your swag. Now there are only a few mosquitoes because we clean up rubbish every second day. It wasn't easy to fight for better living conditions. I didn't give up.'

Margaret Con-goo observed Bulla growing. 'In 1980 the first house went up, then the lights with electricity from the generator, the airstrip, the school and the clinic. Before that, they had school under that baobab tree where the church now is.'

Jack said to the Northern Territory minister of education, 'Give us a fair go, we need a better school. Look at the kids running wild.' They got a brand new one. Earlier I had seen children huddled over computers in the well-equipped two-teacher school. The Timber Creek nurses were testing all children for trachoma, a contagious eye condition common in Aboriginal communities. They found none here.

Bulla is an alcohol-free community. 'But some of the young fellows sneak in grog,' Arnold says. 'Sometimes people flare up, but they calm down and work together again.'

Jack continues, 'There was too much mess and fighting because people wanted to drink all the time. It's hard to stop. I tried to help them slow down because I've been a drinker myself. A dry community doesn't happen overnight. It needs the leaders working together.'

The Community Development Employment Program funded by ATSIC and Centrelink to employ people on community projects, in a similar way to work for the dole programs, is the reason young people get up in the morning, Jack believes. 'We keep Bulla nice and tidy. If you want your place not to be sick or dirty, you have to work together. Funding comes into our community. We try to make it work where needs are. If there was not someone strong enough to fight for it, it wouldn't have happened.'

We leave the Con-goos and set off towards the school. Army-built houses raised off the ground for coolness, and large enough to accommodate extended families, have supplanted tin shacks and communal pit latrines and showers. Young men clean a huge barramundi just fished from the river. An itinerant saleswoman sets up hangers of clothes from her van.

'You'd look smart in this shirt,' she kids Jack, holding up a loud Hawaiian special.

He laughs and points out a shed planned for women's activities. 'We need the right person for that job. More jobs for our people. I've never been on the dole myself.'

In 1990 Jack was given a World Health Organisation Award in appreciation of his services to Aboriginal health. 'I couldn't go to Darwin to receive it because there was no lift. Dr Hargrave also received one. That made me feel good about it.' He seems prouder of the Tidy Towns awards Bulla regularly wins.

I ask Jack about native title. 'I stick to health, that's where my heart is,' he replies. From 1995 to 1998, Jack managed the Katherine Institute for Aboriginal Health, training Aboriginal health workers to care for people in their communities. 'It was good to have Aboriginal people in charge.'

Jack is vice-president of Katherine West Health Board, one of the first Territory all-Aboriginal boards given responsibility for making important decisions for the region. 'For the future, I'm looking at self-management, self-control, self-determination,' are Jack Little's parting words. Given his own fierce determination and drive for his people, I have no doubt he will succeed. He waves cheerily and walks off after his pig, which has escaped from under the house.

Overnight at Timber Creek Wayside Inn I am blasted by the strains of 'Sta-a-a-nd by Me' played by a New Zealand band to a noisy, mostly Aboriginal clientele. Bonny, a sturdy barmaid missing a front tooth, grabs troublemakers by the scruff of their neck and throws them out the door. It is only 60 kilometres away, but it is a world apart from Bulla, where two hours before I sat in the bough church and listened to the children singing their hearts out. I was taping the singing and the swell of joy and confidence as each child sang made the little machine crackle. Jack's daughter Marjory sang too, while Jack hung on to his lively grandson. Jack Little was right. 'Something happened here' indeed. The legacy is the shining faces of the children from Bulla and the laughter that echoes around the community.

○ ○ ○

Postscript: Jack Little's wife passed away on 5 August 2000 at the age of 53 from a heart attack brought on by diabetes—yet another tragic casualty contributing to high Aboriginal mortality rates. In accordance with Aboriginal custom, her name has been removed from this story in order to let her spirit go. Jack was 'very down in the dumps'.

6 | Beetlemania

Michael and Steffi Eppler ~
New answers to old problems in the
Ord River Scheme

'When I was 20, I saw an advertisement in a German farming magazine for young farmers to work in Australia for six months,' says Michael Eppler. 'That was enough for me. I didn't care where, I applied. I came to the Ord for six months and was hooked. There were opportunities here, whereas in Germany, if you didn't inherit or have a lot of resources, farming was impossible. In Kununurra I saw that with a lot of hard work, even starting from scratch, I could do it.'

Michael Eppler is part of a new wave of innovative pioneers to the oasis of the Ord River Scheme in Western Australia's East Kimberley region. He and his wife Steffi emigrated from Germany in 1987.

I envisaged a tall, blond couple, tanned and athletic, and here they are, just as I imagined. Early this July morning Ceres Farm is an antbed of activity. Ceres, the Roman goddess of the harvest, has surely blessed this fertile patch of watermelons and pumpkins. Steffi welcomes me to a slice of their 12-hour harvest day after she has climbed down from a large, new tractor. Dressed for paddock or office work in faded jeans and open-necked shirt, she is a pert-faced woman with easy-care short hair and a ready smile. I feel her direct gaze summing me up quickly as she introduces Michael. He invites me into their busy office tucked in the corner of a huge packing shed. He has finely chiselled features and an unexpectedly deep voice, which reverberates around the room as he chooses English words carefully. The couple are alert and in tune with each other and young workers coming and going to the office to get the day's instructions.

'Farmers in our society are totally undervalued. Farming is a noble profession fulfilling one of the basic human needs—to provide food,' Michael says. It's a surprise to hear a farmer proclaim he is proud to be a farmer and that agriculture is a profession on par with other professions, instead of the usual self-deprecating response of: "Oh, I'm just a farmer".

Steffi negotiates by phone to market freshly picked butternut pumpkins. A long road train arrives outside. In the shed, staff wash seedless watermelons and grade and pack produce into large cardboard boxes. I watch Michael forklift the boxes brimming with luscious giant watermelons onto the road train for trucking to Melbourne markets. Ceres Farm is a national leader in watermelon production, marketing a massive 2000 tonnes of the prized seedless variety into the major eastern Australian markets in 1999 and selling 40 000 boxes of butternuts over four months.

Over the whole harvest period of five months 200 people, mainly backpackers, work on the farm. Dotted through the endless green rows like workers in an Asian rice paddy, they toss ripe melons along a line for loading onto trailers. A woman drives by on a tractor, mechanically clearing the orderly rows against the backdrop of the purple Durack Ranges. Never have I seen a farm so neat and tidy, not a weed in sight. 'Our German heritage,' says a slightly apologetic Steffi.

Six months later I fly in during the Wet. A different scene greets me. Muddy streams break through the folds of green ranges. Rainclouds hang low. The Ord River is a serpent decorated with clumps of waterlily, winding its way through walls of cane grass. Michael and Steffi look relaxed. He leads the way to their three-bedroom demountable house, sloshing barefoot through the flooded lawn. After the seven-days-a-week, non-stop, sunrise-to-sunset cycle of the Dry, the pace of the Wet is slower. There is time to catch up with maintenance, bookwork, 'spending money on new machinery', and resting.

Neither of the Epplers has a farming background. Michael developed his love of nature on weekend visits to his grandparents' farm, near Germany's picturesque Black Forest. It was just eight hectares in area at a time when 'get bigger or get out' was the catch cry. The farm was swallowed up by the expansion of surrounding farms. Michael's parents worked in factories. 'I loved to read about exotic places with space—Australia and Canada. I went into farming because I love the outdoors, driving tractors and producing things,' he says.

Michael also loved rock climbing, ballooning and flying gliders. He gained his pilot's licence in Germany and took his first solo flight when he was only 16. 'If you get nervous driving a car, you can pull up on the side of the road. With flying, you are on your own,' he says, 'You don't get a second chance, but I'm not a risk-taker. I know my limits. I like independence, the age-old dream of flying like a bird, not being tied to the land.'

Michael then devoted his next 15 years to being 'tied to the land'. That advertisement for an Australian working holiday brought him to the farm belonging to Wilhelm and Gabi Bloecker, a German couple in Kununurra. Six months of hot, hard work on the other side of the world convinced him that there was a future in tropical agriculture, although he had to return to Germany to study it when his Australian work permit expired. The Bloeckers recognised his talents and soon offered him a position as their farm manager. 'I had three years to go in my degree. It was the hardest decision of my life, because I would have loved to finish studying.' Michael asked his parents for advice. Instantly they replied, 'Go! This is a once in a lifetime chance.' So he left university and came to Australia.

Steffi's family lived in Selk, a small German town near the Danish border, where they had a grain milling business. Hard times taught her to be careful. 'I am the one reluctant to let go of money,' she laughs. As a home economics student she was apprenticed to a German family who decided to emigrate to Kununurra. Steffi chose to finish her apprenticeship with them and came too, aged not yet 17. 'Everyone at home said, "Australia is flat and always has blue sky." As I flew in over the hills, it was pouring with rain. I thought Australia was great—wide open spaces, friendly people and as a nanny, I went everywhere with the family.'

Steffi might have 'drunk from the Ord', as locals say. She returned three times to Kununurra and met Michael briefly at the Bloeckers' farm, where she was a nanny, in 1986. They swapped addresses. As their work visas had expired they both returned to Germany, where the relationship blossomed. 'Come back to Australia with me,' said Michael as soon as he was offered the manager's job at the Bloeckers. Steffi agreed and they married in Kununurra in 1990. The Immigration Department said they had to have witnesses that they were living together and had a genuine relationship for Steffi to qualify for a permanent resident's visa. 'They even asked us to produce love letters!' Michael remembers.

Those early years in a new country were difficult, especially for Steffi, while Michael worked long days on the farm. 'I would think, "Why does he have to be out there working 14 hours a day?" People would say, "What does your husband look like? Do you have one?" I was looking after our three kids, Johanna, Raphael and Franziska. When he came home, I would think, "Why not go to the movies tonight, or the pub, or visit friends?" but he would be worn out. I love kids, so I applied to be a family day carer in a childcare program where you look after children in your own home. There was hardly anything here for little children, so I also started gymnastics classes.' The lithe young bodies of their own children show the results, as they swing from trees and race around the house.

Michael loved the challenge of adjusting to totally different farming in a tropical environment. 'The Bloeckers chose me because I am adaptable, hardworking and don't blame anyone else if something goes wrong. I learned the ropes from them. I had $1000 when I came to Australia. After eight years, we were desperate to have our own farm, but we would never have had the opportunity with so little money.'

The Epplers leased 380 hectares of virgin bushland on Packsaddle Plain from the Bloeckers, who had bought it as an investment and who remain silent partners. 'It wasn't like moving to Paradise,' says Michael. 'We had to borrow money and always there was the risk we might fail hanging above like a dark cloud. When you are employed it's so easy. You work and pick up the pay cheque.'

For Steffi it changed everything. 'We were pulling on the same string. I was not feeling left out because we were working together, and Michael could see the children. Before that he was up early and home late after they went to bed.' Steffi's parents lent them money to get started, to buy an old tractor, implements, fertiliser and seed. They invested it all in the first crop of 80 hectares of watermelons, which they sold to Sydney and Melbourne markets. 'It was primitive. We packed melons in the open on pallets. If it had been a disaster, that would have been our first and last crop. But it was a success.'

In 1964 I visited the Ord for the first time. On a stage of bare paddocks split by irrigation channels in preparation for a brilliant agricultural future, I vividly recall seeing a pair of brolgas dancing their graceful ballet. The Western Australian government had invested $20 million in a diversion dam across the Ord River near Kununurra in 1963, and $22 million in Lake Argyle in 1972, to irrigate nearly 80 000 hectares for agriculture. George Gardiner, chairman of the Ord District Co-operative, explained to me that the Australian government's original idea was that agriculture, particularly cotton, would put the Ord on the map and cover the infrastructure costs. But by voluntary agreement in 1974, farmers decided they could no longer afford to plant cotton. They were applying up to 40 sprays of chemical every three days over the season to try to control insects.

More than two decades later the Epplers were also caught in the insect/chemical spray deadlock. Michael describes how when melon growing started in the Ord Valley, no-one sprayed with insecticides. 'Then ten years ago someone started spraying every ten days to be on the safe side, then seven years ago every seven days, then two years ago every second day. 1998 was a disastrous season for aphids on melons. We sprayed every second day. We realised we couldn't keep doing that.'

That was when they looked at integrated pest management, an approach using all available tools to control pests—natural and biological ways and, if necessary, chemicals having the least impact on the environment. 'It was trialled on cotton,' says Steffi. 'Michael said, "Why not try it with melons?" They discovered Bugs for Bugs, a Queensland business breeding beneficial insects. These insects had turned around the citrus industry in Mundubbera by eating the pests. The Epplers decided to import live larvae of native lacewing beetles from them. Flown over weekly, packed in rice hulls and accompanied by sterilised moth eggs for food, they are dispersed in pest 'hot spots' from a container like a salt shaker. Larvae are voracious hunters, camouflaging themselves among the aphids by impaling corpses of victims on spines along their backs. They consume huge meals of 60 aphids an hour.

'We were the first to use them,' says Michael. 'We had to experiment because the company said to spray them as eggs, but ants ate them. Now that we distribute lacewing larvae, which hatch quickly at a rate of 1000 per hectare in different parts of the farm, we see fewer aphids. It is hard to eradicate the aphids, but we try to keep them to a minimum. A natural system in balance means you need some pests or the predators won't survive. After starting with native lacewings we have used only the occasional spray, and then it is a biological or natural insecticide. Insects don't know about fencelines, so it only succeeds when everyone works together. We are lucky being at the end of the irrigation area.' They leave lucerne strips among the melons as 'trap' crops where the beneficial insects can hide and spread. Michael is always in the crops, sleuthing for insects.

The Epplers are an extraordinary team. 'We try to keep the business out of family life,' says Steffi. 'When we talk work over the kitchen table, the children soon tell us. I think because we have been good partners in marriage, we work well as partners in the business. At first we didn't talk much about our visions, but when we did a Farming for Profit course we discovered that we see in the same direction. Even though we work together, we have our own departments—Michael produces and I market. We don't fight or interfere with each other. We sit together and discuss what we will grow. I will say, "We can't market that then," and he might say, "That crop won't grow at that time of year." We think on the same wavelength.'

Michael is an avid reader of agricultural publications, always searching for new ways of solving old problems. There was no bookshop in Kununurra until 1999, so he mail-ordered and now uses the internet for global information. In a remarkable five years, Ceres Farm has become a highly profitable business. 'You can't be green when you're in the red,' says Michael. The farm is established and the family debt-free. Michael and Steffi no longer use a pallet for a worktable, but have a modern operation with two large sheds and six tractors.

Now they are consolidating and wondering, 'Is this the right way to go?' On my first visit, Michael described conflicts as broadacre farmers moved into Packsaddle Plain driving tractors 24 hours a day. The noise, dust and use of pesticides caused an outcry among some hobby farmer neighbours. I suggested he invite critics and other farmers to an open day on Ceres, and Michael took the idea and ran with it. 'We had farmers, environmentalists, tour operators and others, including our critics, to show and tell them what we do here,' he recounts enthusiastically. 'Not a traditional field day where you show them all the nice crops and it makes you feel good. We showed them everything, even the problems—paddocks with erosion, insect pests, what we've tried to change and what we're trying to achieve in the future. It cleared up some misunderstandings and brought us closer.

'We can't change overnight. We aim for environmentally friendly ways, and if an idea looks promising, we will trial it. We try to improve spraying techniques with a big, new rig using air pressure. It looks like a monster, but reduces chemical use. We reduced our aerial spraying by 98 per cent by reducing off-target drift. We use green manures of a legume crop called lab lab, and forage sorghum to build up earthworms and return energy to the soil, and we plan to change from wasteful flood irrigation to trickle irrigation. We don't want to rape the country. We want to leave it better for our kids,' he says.

Michael recognises that there are bad practices in farming, but thinks the responsibility for a good environment has to be shared by all of society. 'We used to grow cotton, but we weren't happy with gene-manipulated varieties with inbuilt resistance to insects. Genetically modified organisms are a complicated issue and the biggest threat facing agriculture, I think. I'm not overly religious, but it's human beings playing God and manipulating evolution with as yet unknown consequences,' he says. 'The environmental impacts are not yet understood, and it's far too early to know the effects on humans. Multinational chemical companies control more and more of the seed companies, which in turn swallow up the smaller seed-breeding companies, so they control the whole length of the chain, right to the supermarket. Fewer companies, more monopoly.'

Over breakfast in Kununurra, I meet Leon Mugmin, the Epplers' agent. They form an integral part of a national marketing group set up in 1996, now called Select Melon Australia. It is a co-operative of 20 seedless watermelon growers from different producing areas across the country. Ceres farm is one of the biggest producers and well advanced in its approach to biological and organic farming, but each member is equally important in fulfilling the group's aim of year-round supplies of top-quality melons to the southern markets. Mugavin says, 'Steffi and Michael want to know how the produce arrives and what's wrong if there's a problem. Other growers in the valley watch and ask, "What's Michael doing now?" They are highly regarded for introducing new ideas.'

The Ord also has prospered, generating a staggering $55 to $60 million annual revenue in 1999. 'We grow what the market wants; we don't try to sell what we grow,' says Michael. 'We have a bright future here providing clean, green food. I get a great sense of satisfaction seeing road trains going out of Ceres with trailers of watermelons or pumpkins. It's not just the income, although that also makes me feel good; I am proud that we have produced those things. It was a good decision coming to Australia. I want to be remembered as a caring person, as someone who contributed to sustainable farming practices in this corner of the world.'

'And a wonderful husband and father!' adds Steffi.

She reflects on the pull of their two homelands. 'People help out here, like when I had a car accident.' Steffi was pregnant with their second child when the car skidded off the road early one morning and was destroyed. Steffi and baby Johanna, who was in a baby capsule, were greatly shaken, but had minor injuries.

'I love Kununurra, but we can't deny our heritage,' she says. 'We return to see our families in Germany every four years. We still think in the German way. Things have to be perfect, especially for Michael, who takes after his father, aiming for 150 per cent perfection. When we are invited to a party, the hosts tell everybody else 7pm and us 7.30pm, because we are so punctual!'

Michael says that farmers visiting Ceres like to joke about the six Eppler tractors parked in a neat line. 'They ask "Do you use a measuring tape?"' he laughs. The packing shed floor is so clean you could eat breakfast from it. However, Michael thinks the laidback attitude of Australians has rubbed off on them. 'Ten years ago I would jump up and down and get upset about a dispute with staff or other small matters. Now I just shrug my shoulders and walk away.'

It's a hot day. The family promises me a swim in their favourite waterhole. Michael edges the truck along a sandy track. Suddenly down we go, bogged to the axles. 'Oh, no,' he groans, and trots 5 kilometres home while we continue on by foot to Packsaddle Creek. An hour later he returns with a big tractor. While he debates how close to go to hoist out the truck, the clean tractor also sinks into chocolate-pudding mud. This time his laidback Aussie side surfaces, and Michael just laughs. As I fly over next morning I spot an even bigger tractor pulling the first one out on a 100-metre chain. Michael and Steffi Eppler are well and truly tied to the land.

Challenging
Stereotypes

7 | Bloom Where You are Planted

Cathy McGowan ~

Women in agriculture emerge

A crisp spring wind is blowing on the day I journey to Cathy McGowan's hilltop in the Indigo Valley of northern Victoria. Her round, inviting house moulded into the hill looks like a child's favourite cubby, with stones piled on stones and a lid of corrugated iron. The breeze enters the hallway with me, lifting papers. More papers and reports are strewn on a desk. Nearby a bright blue computer screen shows a long list of email messages. Cathy beckons me in while jotting down phone numbers. 'What do you think of my view?' She motions towards large windows overlooking the valley that sweeps down towards the Murray River.

Cathy McGowan leads a subtle revolution for the emergence of women in agriculture. As president of the community-based Australian Women in

Agriculture, and head of the Federal Government's Regional Women's Advisory Council, she is well placed to influence change. Increasingly, men in agriculture seek her carefully researched views. The tools of agricultural revolution in the new century are not ploughshares but personal networks and technology. The blue computer and the internet provide her daily connections with women and rural and agricultural groups all over the world.

Cathy is one of a growing band of single women who farm. On her 45-hectare hilltop she grows fine wool merino sheep and walnut trees. 'The nuts are so slow-growing, they are my superannuation,' she says. Her riding boots, blue jeans and tousled hair are dusty from tree planting. She pushes her glasses up a snub nose to take an appreciative look at my gift of home-grown lamb, and puts on the kettle for tea.

Now in her late forties, Cathy McGowan is a confident, energetic-looking woman who has taken on the macho world of agriculture with intelligence, humour and a big heart. She has a square, determined chin, a ready grin and an exceptional ability to reflect deeply and, if necessary, to reinvent how she thinks, acts and even looks. Eight years ago, when I first met her, she considered fashionable clothing and becoming make-up supremely unimportant. What you saw was what you got with this action woman. After six months in the Australian Rural Leadership Program in 1996, a corporate woman had emerged, with red coat and matching lipstick, black high-heeled shoes and an air of elegance. My jaw visibly dropped in surprise on the first occasion I saw this transformation, at a meeting of dairy women with the New South Wales Dairy Farmers' Association. She laughed, assuring me she was the same person as she proceeded to chair with aplomb this first meeting of women farmers within the male-dominated organisation. Her challenge was to build leadership skills and confidence among women who had always left industry decision-making to their menfolk. 'I want people to listen to me. They listen better if I look smart,' she says. More importantly perhaps, Cathy shifted her focus to listening to others, starting from their viewpoint, not her own frank and strongly held opinions.

From growing up in the Indigo Valley, Cathy McGowan's path has taken a loop through wanting to leave as a teenager and study in Melbourne, to working in the nation's capital, travelling around the world and returning to live and farm in the same valley two decades later. 'I am a daughter of the community,' she says. 'I have deep roots in this country.' Her ancestors were Cornish miners and Irish Catholic immigrants who came to this part of Australia in the early nineteenth century. Serving their communities was paramount. Successive generations of her extended family were shire presidents and fire brigade captains, members of the Country Women's Association and sporting teams. 'We visit their graves here and the land where they worked,' she says. Cathy feels woven into a long tradition of belonging to an extended family, which helps her understand her role in the community. 'I know their stories. I build on what other people have done, and I know others will build on what I do.'

The Irish tradition of living a happy life and making the most of each moment drives her wish to leave this world with a rollicking wake. 'I love being here. I love the location and the fact that my ancestors have worked here and made the community what it is. I feel connected to the landscape and to the people in the valley where I was born and where some of my extended family and friends now live. The hills and valleys and sky and bush make it a very Australian place.'

Cathy was the fourth of ten girls in a family of 13 children. 'I grew up surrounded by women,' she says. 'My parents loved and appreciated girls. They supported us to become what we wanted.' She acts out a conversation with her mother when she was a teenager, playing both mother and daughter.

'But Mum, you're a farmer.'

'She'd say, "No I'm not, Dad's the farmer."

'Yeah, but you farm. What about all the work you do with the chooks, and the vegetable garden? Dad works with cows, but you work with livestock too. It just happens to be different livestock.

'She'd say, "Go away, Cathy."

'I'd persist. "But you grow things." She had a huge vegetable garden. "If you grow things, then you're a farmer."

' "No, no," she would reply.'

Cathy came to understand that real farming happened beyond the back gate. Anything inside that was seen as 'domestic stuff', not real agriculture or production. Her recollection was that her mother made a huge contribution to the family's sustenance, but never as paid work.

In the 1950s, the state school bus wouldn't pick up the McGowan tribe because they went to the local Catholic school. 'Mum had to organise the kids who were still at home, or Dad had to stop milking to take us eight kilometres to another bus stop. We all learned to be organised.' She remembers walking down the drive chatting and telling stories with her sisters. When the last child left secondary school, they threw a party for their long-suffering mother.

In such a large family, the children had to earn their keep. All 13 obtained university degrees. Cathy's was in Arts/Economics at Monash University in Melbourne. She received a generous studentship in return for teaching with the Victorian Education Department. At 24 she applied to teach economics and was sent to a country secondary school at Nhill, in the Wimmera district of western Victoria.

They said to Cathy, 'We want you to teach typing.'

'But I can't type,' she said.

'Well, that's what women teach,' the principal told her.

Her first class was a group of Year 9 and 10 girls. 'I was reluctant to teach what I didn't know, but as a country woman I had an affinity with those young women. I thought the real work was teaching economics. It wasn't. The real work was the blossoming of those young women.' She taught for four years, worked off her bond, then decided to try something different.

Cathy was fascinated by politics. For four years she worked for the local Member of Parliament, Ewen Cameron, spending six months in Canberra, and six in Wangaratta learning the political ropes. Then in 1980 she made her crucial decision to put down roots in the Indigo Valley. 'I wanted to settle down and own land, so I decided to buy a farm to grow sheep and walnuts. I went to a bank for a loan. I was 28, had a well-paid job and felt I could make the repayments. The bank refused to give me a loan and insisted I get a guarantor. I went home to my parents, distressed that I was not recognised in my own right to borrow money.' The family offered Cathy money and stood security for her. She quickly paid off the loan. It made her determined to demonstrate that women could buy land and succeed as farmers. 'I wanted to prove that the ability of farmers is related to their skills and management expertise, not their gender,' she says.

Her father had set up a business as an agricultural consultant to bring in extra income. Cathy followed in his footsteps, setting up a rural consultancy, an uncommon career move for a 32-year-old woman. 'What I'm doing now is modelled on his experience, combining farm, family and consultancy. I made a conscious decision to seek work in rural Australia and make my contribution, particularly to the women,' she says. One of her first contracts was negotiating with Commonwealth and state governments for the Flying Fruit Fly circus to establish a circus training school in Albury/Wodonga.

She lives half an hour from those two towns straddling the Murray River, designated by the Whitlam government as its first national planned growth centre. 'I learned about planning and was excited to find people could knowingly create good environments, as opposed to just letting towns happen. I remember working with some social planners from the city whose job was to welcome newcomers to Albury/Wodonga. I said, 'Could we get my uncle and aunt involved in welcoming people?' The planners just laughed. They had met some of these relatives, and thought they were conservative farmers who wouldn't be interested in welcoming newcomers.' The farmers themselves weren't keen to be part of it. Cathy saw a gap between urban and rural people and thought she would make sure country people had access to the same level of services such as childcare and information as city people did. That has become one of her missions in life.

She thinks hard about each step of her life, not tumbling from one experience to the next. A male farmer recently asked her, 'You're intelligent, you're beautiful, you're fun. How come you're not married?'

'Just lucky, I guess!' was her droll response. She is fiercely independent and believes opportunities have come her way *because* she is single. 'Our Irish Catholic tradition has always had maiden aunts. There has been space in my family for people to be unmarried,' she says. 'Being an unmarried woman hasn't been seen as a lesser existence, but an honoured role.' All her sisters have families. 'Not being pressured into being married has helped me reach my potential as a woman,' she says. 'I have a special place in my family as "the aunt".' She describes the satisfaction of returning home and reading email from a young niece: 'Cathy, when you come home, can you ring me please, 'cause I'd like to come over and visit you.'

'I rang her and she walked up the hill to see me and have a cuppa. I love that sense of connectedness, of growing up together with my nieces and nephews, being able to share our lives,' she says. She takes them travelling; a niece went with her to Western Australia recently for a women in dairying meeting. 'It's a big adventure for them.'

In the mid-1980s, during the United Nations Decade of Women, Cathy was consulting with rural women for the National Women's Advisory Council. To her amazement she found little confidence among women who were competently managing farms and families. 'They had enormous skills, but thought they were less than I was because I had a university degree. Nurturers and carers were not recognised.' Marilyn Waring, who entered New Zealand's parliament in 1975 as its youngest MP, wrote about valuing women's work in a book *Counting for Nothing*. It strongly influenced Cathy and helped her understand the real importance of women's work in the care of the land and people, and why women as well as men have to participate in decision-making.

In the 1980s farm women were important in the domestic sphere, but had no public face in agricultural circles, at farmers' meetings, around boardroom tables or in saleyards. Cathy realised she would have to travel elsewhere to learn how to assist farm women. In 1990 she applied for and won a Churchill Fellowship to Canada. In Ottawa she met farming women actively involved in a network, then a newly coined term. They lobbied to improve rural services—health, education and childcare—and to have a voice in agriculture. For the first time she heard women claim their place in agriculture and proudly say, 'We produce fine, healthy food.'

'I was so inspired,' she recalls. She wanted to share the knowledge and motivation, so she took the courageous step of a speaking tour around Victoria. Women responded because she spoke in a way they understood. 'I was surprised to find there was a growing rural women's movement and I was part of it.'

Momentum was gathering for rural women to have a voice in decision-making. The Victorian government took the initiative to fund the first Rural Women's Network in Australia, based in its Office of Rural Affairs. The network was a program to improve the communication between rural women and government. Cathy was working as an adviser for the Office of Rural Affairs and became involved in the network. In 1991 she invited Marilyn Waring on a speaking tour of regional Victoria. Women flocked to hear Marilyn. Many of them shared a dream for an organisation to unite and raise the profile of women in agriculture, and in 1994 Australian Women in Agriculture (AWiA) was set up with Cathy as its foundation secretary.

Her people skills and experience were developing. Her style, in turn fun-loving and brash, drew others to her, but she felt lacking in strategies for change. 1993 was a key year. Her mother died, she turned 40, and she decided to study as an external student for a masters degree in systems agriculture at the University of Western Sydney. It proved a milestone in putting a theoretical framework around what she intuitively knew about gender issues—how people learn, how communities work, and how to best work with women and communities. After she finished her degree the university put her on staff to work from her Indigo Valley home using email and phone to support postgraduate students. Through word of mouth, she has encouraged students to enrol. Now half of the farmers enrolled are women, some on scholarships.

The next step she took was to test her skills among males in agriculture. She chose the two-year Australian Rural Leadership Program, which seeks out, inspires and develops leaders from across rural Australia. Cathy was one of only six women in the third course of 31, in 1996–97. Important things happened to her in this prestigious scholarship program. 'I started to understand the skills needed to bring about change at a policy level,' she says, 'and other participants challenged me on my work with women. One man kept referring to farmers as "he".' Not one to accept this submissively, she confronted him and realised she was setting up a gender battle rather than using her persuasive powers. 'Affronted, he told me I might win the battle, but I would lose the war because I would always be surrounded by angry people.' This made her ask herself why she worked with women, not men, what women had to offer and where they fitted into agriculture. She wanted to know why agriculture was mainly a male occupation. Why did men leave women out of the picture, even when they were married to them and knew how much their womenfolk did on the farm?

'Over the next few years, it became clear that my work with women and the change needed in rural Australia was not about competition and making men change, but rather about working with them,' she says. 'Men and women are like the two wings of a bird. Without one or the other, it cannot fly high. In the world of agriculture, we women don't need to be "look alike men", but play our part in nurturing the land and its people.'

Cathy started to think about ways that women could find their voices. She went back to her roots, the extended family. 'The women in my family and others throughout rural Australia had been important in creating and making communities strong and vibrant. They built swimming pools, schools, churches, the essentials for community.' She found older women in the Country Women's Association, and asked them, "How did you get organised? How did you work with the men? How did you get your voice heard?"'

'What I'm coming to understand is the virtue of grace,' she says. 'The women admired and respected in my community build relationships based on graciousness. I think women's voices will be heard when we have something to say, and we can say it with graciousness.' She thinks the temptation has been to be strident. 'Is strident the opposite of gracious?' The other characteristic she notices among these older women is patience. 'When I was younger I thought we had to hurry. Now I'm coming to understand that the world will go on for a long time and there is no great rush to bring about change. It is more important to do it well.'

When she bought her farm Cathy joined the Indigo Valley Landcare group. 'I was inaugural secretary and later president. Anyone who wants a go can be president in country organisations. Most of the committee then were women.' From these women she learned the practical skills of working with a community, running meetings, making people interested in coming along to meetings. 'They helped me tone down my brashness, my sense of being in a hurry,' she laughs. 'They would say, "Go slowly, visit people, have a cuppa."' She became part of a team, accepting everybody, not just doing what she wanted.

In 1994 Cathy and a colleague were asked to an international environmental conference in Moscow to present a paper on 'environment and activism', using women in Landcare as an example. 'Our Landcare group organised a farewell party for me and sent greetings to the women in Moscow.' When she returned home, the women wanted to understand what she had learned. She realised that she had had opportunities often denied to women with families, and could play a role as an advocate, having a voice.

The former USSR had only recently opened its borders. Cathy listened to five days of horror stories on the environmental costs of poverty, salinity, pollution, Chernobyl and nuclear waste dumps and the illnesses of children, and knew she didn't want Australia to have these problems decades hence. 'If it's left up to governments or big business, then the health of people and the land won't win over profits. I can remember on the long flight back, thinking, "I can be part of whatever is happening in Australia. I've got a choice. I can go along with traditional farming and environmental methods, or I can become actively involved and work towards something better." But I had no sense of my own power. I thought, "Who am I to stand up and say or do anything?"'

What changed her mind was something her mother told her as a child. 'She said, "It is important to bloom where you are planted. As women you may not get a choice about where you live, but you can choose what your life is like. Your responsibility is to do the best you can wherever you are."

'I thought, "I'm planted in rural Australia, and it's my choice whether I bloom or not. I might be a cactus, but I'll be a gorgeous cactus." We may complain that the ground is rocky, or we got transplanted as kids, but it's up to us to reach our potential. We don't have to be the same kind of plants. In fact the greater the diversity, the more attractive the garden will be. So that sense of blooming where we are planted, particularly for women, and doing the best that we can wherever we are, will stop Australia suffering like Russia.'

In July 1994 Cathy struck a chord as she spoke of 'Blooming where you are planted' to 850 delegates from 40 countries at the first International Women in Agriculture conference in Melbourne. The phrase has become common among rural women searching for inspiration.

Cathy says she would never have dreamed of such different things happening in her life. 'For instance, at the end of two years in the Australian Rural Leadership Program our group came up with a shared vision for rural Australia. We struggled and were committed to working our way through our different perspectives. We persisted in keeping our relationships intact, which led to strong bonding within the group. I am proud to work for our vision of "a prosperous, caring rural Australia, alive with opportunities for everybody". I'm keen on the "caring" side, because prosperity for the sake of it, without caring for the environment and people, is not much chop. My little bit is to achieve this with women. I do it, confident that the others are doing their bit, whatever sphere they are in.'

It gave her the confidence to step up to the then Federal Minister for Primary Industries and Energy, John Anderson, in 1996, as he was closing the first Women in Agriculture and Resource Management conference in Canberra. He was talking about women's role in marriage and with families. Cathy asked if he was prepared 'to work with women in agriculture for better, for worse, so long as we both shall live?' Completely taken by surprise at her boldness and wit, he laughed somewhat sheepishly and said, 'Yes!', to resounding cheers from the 200 women and men.

He has kept his word. In 1999, Cathy McGowan was appointed head of Deputy Prime Minister Anderson's nine-woman Regional Women's Advisory Council. I suspect she is still surprising him as her team recommends broadening traditional economic models to revitalise rural and regional Australia. To complement the focus on constructing roads, railway lines, capital works, and telecommunications, they said to him, 'How about building human infrastructure at the same time?' Cathy puts it simply. 'It comes again to women, mothers, community builders. They know a community needs a tennis court, but they also know the community needs social skills, so they teach kids how to play tennis, be good sports, and socialise. A tennis court is not enough. Human beings don't automatically know how to do the rest.' The council has the important task of reporting back to the Deputy Prime Minister on what makes rural communities succeed.

In 1998 the Rural Industries Research and Development Corporation commissioned a study, 'Missed Opportunities', which found that women contribute 48 per cent of total real farm income, worth almost $14 billion in 1995–96. $4 billion is in on-farm work, over $8 billion in household work and almost $0.5 billion in volunteer and community work. According to Ferguson and Simpson in the 1997–98 edition of *Australian Agriculture*, one-third of the farmers in Australia are women, double the proportion of 15 years ago. Their off-farm earnings have increased from 24 per cent to 68 per cent of farm cash income since 1984. Women in the agricultural workforce have a higher level of tertiary education than the men, but a much lower level of representation on industry boards and committees.

'In trying to manage change and new ways of thinking, traditional leaders rarely factor in women or communities or kids,' says Cathy. 'So when the plan doesn't work according to their models, they are confused. In my experience, if you've only got men making the decisions, you'll get a male-type answer. If you've only got women making the decisions, you'll get a woman-type answer. The two are different. You've got to have discussion and compromise, the male way and the female way. If you've got that balance, like the bird needing two wings, you'll get good decisions.'

She admits to feeling enormous frustration with outdated attitudes, but has mellowed in recent years and doesn't worry too much about the occasional skirmish, because the bigger picture is what's important. 'I don't take criticism as personally as I used to. I'm much more aware of situations and relationships that take my energy away. I say to myself, "What's happening here?" then make a decision about what I'm going to do. That stops the drain, because I make a choice.'

Cathy cites a frustrating Australian Women in Agriculture meeting. 'I was complaining, but I had a choice to be there and be miserable or to participate. I ended up saying to myself, "This is the organisation I want to be involved in", and put up my hand to be the next president, but it was a big decision.' In deciding to step out of the group and into a leadership position, she felt she was putting herself on the line. 'I was pleased to be elected, but I think we women have great difficulty with the competitive win/lose side of elections.' It is a continuous challenge to build teamwork in an organisation spread across a huge country with often poor communications infrastructure.

Another downside is occupying the presidency voluntarily, which means significant income loss when she could be doing more paid work as a self-employed consultant. 'Why do I have to do all this as voluntary work?' she questions. It's a thorn in her side. 'When the mainstream farmers' organisations are more representative, then I hope we won't need a separate organisation for women in agriculture.'

In May 2000 Cathy spoke to the executive of the National Farmers' Federation (NFF) on how it can include women. 'There were no elected women representatives around the table,' she recalls. 'We said to the president, Ian Donges, "How can you say NFF represents us women?" He conceded we had a point, because it was obvious that women were an integral part of the whole rural and agricultural scene. But the fact that someone has to jump up and down about it amazes me. Such a waste of time and energy!' She negotiated and won their support for a combined sub-committee of Australian Women in Agriculture (AWiA) and the NFF to address these inequalities and improve the way women are represented in agriculture.

The good news is that rural women have come a long way in ten years. An example is the Women in Dairying project on which Cathy has worked for four years. One of their initiatives is an email discussion group linking 150 women all around Australia. 'They talk about the realities of dairy deregulation, what different states are doing, milk prices. It gives me such satisfaction to know that women can use technology to communicate and bloom and grow, all in the safety of their own home and at little cost.'

'What do you want from your life?' I ask her.

'I want to do more of the same,' she says, 'learning the lessons and becoming better. I want to make sure other women come along so when I disappear, a large number of other women can keep a strong network going and support each other.' She is adept at giving other women a hand, as I know from her suggestions to me to go for a new position in 1992 co-ordinating the NSW Rural Women's Network and in 1996 helping me apply for the Australian Rural Leadership Program.

She has a strong sense of finite living, influenced by her sister's death in a car accident many years ago. 'I can only do farming and all the active women's business while I'm healthy. I'm grateful for every moment I'm alive and well.' In September 2000 Cathy McGowan was honoured by her Australian Rural Leadership Network colleagues with the inaugural award for Outstanding Network Member for the year.

Cathy McGowan is sustained in her work for the emergence of women in agriculture by her faith, the spirit of the land, and the support and encouragement of her family and community. 'I've got all this family growing up around me, my nieces and nephews, brothers and sisters, uncles and aunts. I don't have a sense of passing on through my genes as I don't have children. It's more my contribution as a part of the community and the movements I am part of. My life couldn't be better!'

'How do you bloom?' I ask her.

'Like a bunch of spring flowers. Eclectic!' she laughs.

8 | Two Worlds

Stanley Mirindo, Rose Hillman and Joe Ross ~
Weaving threads between Aboriginal
and Western worlds

On 10 October 1960, two Aboriginal men were born within two hours of each other on opposite sides of the Fitzroy River at Fitzroy Crossing in Western Australia's Kimberley region. Forty years later, they are leading members of two of the major language groups. The first is Djunawang Mirindo, Stanley to his many whitefella friends, of the Gooniyandi people. His father founded the Bayulu community on land excised from Gogo station, and he has followed in his father's footsteps as leader of his community. He lives in the same well-kept house his parents did, a house that is painted the blue of a Kimberley sky.

Stanley is an actor and dancer who appeared with Bryan Brown and Ernie Dingo in 1997 in his first film, *Dead Heart*, the powerful drama of a clash between tribal Aboriginal and Western law in a desolate settlement west of Alice Springs. He played Tjulpu Tjangala, last of the desert people, but the real Stanley has developed cross-cultural programs to help mainstream Australians return to a simpler life and understand Aboriginal values. He is a striking figure, long and lanky, his wild black hair contrasting sharply with his quiet dignity, and graceful hands that express his feelings about his land and culture. His legs, long and thin like a brolga's, are made for dancing and tracking noiselessly through his traditional land.

Stanley is married to Raelene, a talented artist of oil paintings of ochre-dotted crocodile, turtle and fish swimming in blue seas. He has a 10-year-old daughter, April. Raelene's round brown face constantly crinkles into laughter at the antics of Stanley and the steady stream of relatives who settle into their comfortable lounge for a smoke, a yarn and a video. Photos from Stanley's plays and movies—*Kings in Grass Castles, Sistergirl, Last of the Nomads*—plaster the walls.

Joe Ross, born in Fitzroy Crossing two hours after Stanley Mirindo, is a leading member of the Bunuba people. His mother was a venerable Bunuba leader; his father, Peter Ross, was sent from Liverpool in England as a five-year-old orphan to Bindoon Boys' Town in Western Australia, a harsh environment where the orphans were the farm labourers. From his lofty height of six foot four, Joe commands respect as well as giving it. He is a fine-looking man of quick intelligence and easy-going charm. He religiously watches Parliament Question Time on ABC-TV, and has the political skills to be an advocate for his people, bringing in much-needed funding for agriculture, health and business ventures. 'I don't have a "dog eat dog" philosophy towards business,' Joe says, 'but I do have a real drive to create opportunities for our people.'

Rose Hillman is a poet from Pitjantjatjara country in the north-west of South Australia. Her 63 years span a childhood on a mission settlement in South Australia, teenage years working on stations, adapting to a suburban life in Whyalla, a return to tribal life after the unsolved murder of her son, and now a new life at Bayulu community. Her serene face and dark brown eyes brim with compassion. Her voice is low and soft, and her words are chosen carefully in each of the three languages she speaks. She is married to Harry Hillman, the father of Stanley's wife Raelene, and lives near the Mirindos. Her pepper-grey hair is cropped short. Women here have spun and plaited her cut hair as a source of strength for her after her nephew was attacked and beaten to death at a party recently. Rose tends the patch of sand beside her mobile home. It has become a green garden of herbs and vegetables.

I had first met both Stanley Mirindo and Joe Ross in 1997, while trekking in the Kimberley, and met Rose Hillman when I interviewed Stanley. I thought the story was about the hidden talent in remote communities such as Fitzroy Crossing, shown through these three—Stanley an actor, Rose a poet, and Joe with his entrepreneurial abilities. But as I got to know them, their stories together painted a picture of Aboriginal life over the last 60 years from many angles—tribal life, urban life, mission life—and how they have each dealt with immense change.

o o o

I arrive at Bayulu community, 20 minutes from Fitzroy Crossing, and look for the blue house with the flourishing garden. Around me is a township with a population of about 350 people in 80 houses laid out around a community store, a hall, a childcare centre, an office, a new church and, most recently, a plant nursery. Stanley Mirindo wanders out in grey shorts and shirt, looking a bit peaky from a long night of partying. With a strong cup of coffee, he soon swings into gear.

As a small boy, Stanley was excited when the circus came to town. He thought, 'I want to entertain people like that.' Then it seemed like a boy's dream; Aboriginal entertainers were scarce in the 1960s. He grew up at Gogo station next to Bayulu community; his mother was a domestic worker, his father the station gardener. His birth certificate gives his name as Yates, not Stanley. 'Maybe it was after the seeds Dad planted,' he laughs, thinking of the Yates seed company. 'My Dad was tall and handsome. I was lucky he had two sisters as wives. My mum was a quiet one, like me. She died of cancer when I was 20. My father married her sister Susie.' In walks Stanley's aunt Susie, neat and trim in a flowered dress. 'This is Susie,' he says. 'She brought me up when my Mum died.' He draws her into the lounge room, a protective arm around her shoulders. Visits from strangers are unusual. Susie welcomes me graciously, with a handshake.

Stanley studied bookkeeping in Port Hedland and community development at the South Australian Institute of Technology and later in Darwin, but more powerful was the lure of drama and dance. 'I wanted to dance, dance, dance,' he leaps up to demonstrate. He had heard of the Aboriginal and Torres Strait Islander Dance Theatre in Sydney, applied to join and in 1989 trained there for six months. 'I did acting to get away from trouble. It gave me confidence to get out of my shell. I was a wild lad, drinking, messing around with my mates.' Susie nods.

His life changed 10 years ago when he saw Jimmy Chi's brilliant musical *Bran Nue Dae* in Broome. It tells the story of an Aboriginal boy trying to find his family. Stanley successfully auditioned for the national tour in 1993. 'I sounded terrible,' he confesses, 'but as a dancer who learned to sing, it was the best thing I ever did.'

Performing in front of live audiences, particularly children, was a real buzz. 'You could see the joy, anguish, surprise—everything we actors conveyed—mirrored on the kids' faces in front of us.' He played a police aide. Stanley, tall and skinny, would come on stage with a short, fat policeman. 'We walked the same way. Audiences cracked up laughing.' He was hooked. When he came on through a smoke screen at the end painted up as a traditional dancer, people said a chill would run up their spine. 'Film isn't the same. You wait for the camera, but it doesn't say anything. Waiting, it's the story of my life,' he says, referring to the problem of boredom waiting for jobs, as well as filming on location. 'On stage if you make a mistake, you get a response from the audience, or your partner gives you a nudge. With the camera, you only get a director saying, "Cut! Do it again."'

'How do you portray Aboriginal experiences other than your own?' I ask Stanley.

'I wouldn't jump in and do all the things that are written down on paper,' he says slowly. 'I'd rather think first and find out from the old people in the area, because that pays respect to them. In some movies, we had an elderly person as an adviser.'

Seeing actors like Ernie Dingo and David Gulpilil inspired him. 'Aboriginal actors are great role models. It shows the local kids a possible future when they see an ordinary fellow like me, son of a gardener and domestic worker, go into acting. We need facilities where kids can go and get trained, say, in traditional dancing.' Stanley Mirindo had his first overseas break in July/August 2000, touring France and Italy with Bugarra, a traditional Aboriginal dance group of three. They performed every day in packed halls, marquees, and street parades. Despite the adulation and invitations to return, he came home to the Kimberley a fortnight early because he was homesick.

'I want to say "bye, bye" to the Community Development Employment Program (CDEP). It's like a work for the dole program where we do community projects and are paid a wage for it. I want to see my daughter, April, and future generations get better opportunities than my grandmother and father and me,' says Stanley. He remembers as a child seeing the handouts to Aboriginal people, one tin for flour, one for tea and sugar. 'Opportunities for acting and theatre work come once in a blue moon, so I'm on CDEP now, but if I can get one foot off the ground, then the other will follow and I can walk a bit faster. Ten years ago I would never have been acting, but now I've met top Australian actors. They want to do something for Australia.'

So does he. 'My mum told me to dedicate myself to what I want to do. I want to give something back to white Australia because I've learned a lot through the European way—to speak good English and get trained. I appreciate that. People in the cities are so stressed. When I take them out bush to know themselves, to rediscover simplicity, I give something back by showing them what I know. It's my aim from the heart,' Stanley says. He is vice-chairman of the Gooniyandi Cross-Cultural Awareness Program. He helps staff at the nearby Cadjebut mine, owned by Western Metal, understand about tribal life and its values through seeing videos and discussing how Aboriginal life used to be. He tells them, 'You are on Gooniyandi land. Use it, but don't abuse it.' Their common reactions are, 'We shouldn't have taken land from Aboriginal people,' and 'How can we work together?'

'We want something from the mine for our younger generation—opportunities, work, friendship,' says Stanley. 'Some Gooniyandi kids are in training with Pacific and Orient Catering at the mine.'

While trekking across the rugged Carr Boyd Ranges west of Lake Argyle on the Australian Rural Leadership Program, Stanley reintroduced me to the beauty and simplicity of life and reminded me to step lightly on Mother Earth, which led me into collecting inspiring stories like his. Around the campfire one night, this quiet man became talkative, telling us about Aboriginal life. One scorching day we got lost and ran out of water. Three years later, he kids me that we would have known the way if we had noticed the direction his feet pointed. Thanks, Stanley! We were hoping to follow his shock of black curls and erect back, swag bouncing against his buttocks, but he steadfastly brought up the rear. Sweating and panting up yet another hill, we had to find water ourselves. It was tough but powerful learning. His eyes missed nothing. He always checked and found something we had left in the campsite. I saw his influence on some of my companions' attitudes towards Aboriginal people, not through forceful words, but through quick wit and thoughtful comments. I wanted to bottle his impact and sprinkle it around Australia.

Stanley's extended family share a chicken salad lunch on Raelene's carefully tended lawn, a rarity in these dusty parts. The national tour of *Bran Nue Dae* brought Raelene into Stanley Mirindo's life. She was a city-bred girl from Sydney's leafy North Shore whose Aboriginal mother had died when she was young. Her father, Harry Hillman, moved to South Australia and married Rose, a Pitjantjatjara woman. After lunch Rose Hillman and I wander a stone's throw away to a gauzed shelter next to her mobile home to escape the heat. She sleeps during the mornings after doing night shift at the Fitzroy Crossing women's shelter. The community comes alive just as she settles into bed. She looks exhausted. 'No, I'm fine,' Rose reassures me. I ask about the incidence of domestic violence. 'It's high, especially with alcohol, but I feel sorry for the men as well as the women,' she comments. 'They also need support and counselling to change.'

Like Raelene, Rose was transplanted to this community through marriage. Her life is rich, washed with sorrow, full of joy. You can see both experiences on her face as she talks. When she was three, her nomadic family was forcibly moved from Twin Well station west of Woomera to Point Pearce Mission, an establishment of 300 people on the Yorke Peninsula of South Australia. Hers was a strict Lutheran upbringing. 'On Sundays, we went to church in the morning, then lunch, Sunday school for the kids and to the cemetery. It was like a ritual, cleaning up and putting flowers on the graves like a busy bee. Afterwards we spent the afternoon at Wadjerton Scrub and cooked sweet roots in the ashes. When I go back, it's healing to watch the sun set over Point Pearce.

'In those days you only went to Grade 7 as an Aboriginal child. A strict elderly couple taught us. We had to march up and down, then stand still with our hands across our chest and chant, "I love my country, the British Empire, I honour King George." I didn't know who he was. The elderly couple didn't know the boys were marching straight out the back gate down to the dam for a swim. We used to cover for them in roll call—Mally my brother, Wally and Nosey. "Present sir," we'd say.'

Rose did well at primary school, but when her teacher recommended she go on to high school, the mission station superintendent was horrified. ' "You can't educate an Aboriginal person. If she gets too much education, her brains will bust, B-U-S-T," ' she recalls with humour and indignation. 'I remember sitting outside on the lawn with another student, Cyril, swinging my legs and saying, "I don't want to go to a whitefella school anyway," and thinking, "I don't want my brains to bust". So we didn't go away because the Aboriginal Protection Board said, "Get that idea clean out of your head." '

She was 12 when she was sent to a Salvation Army training school in Adelaide to do hospital laundry. 'Like a factory, hot and hard, but we made our own fun, like putting too much starch in the nurses' uniforms.' Then she and another Aboriginal girl, Emily Lennon, were sent to a station near Port Lincoln, working 'sunup to sundown' as household help, with no days off and no pay until they left, which might be years later. 'We didn't know any different,' says Rose, until she noticed that jackaroos and station hands had time off. 'I asked the boss lady if Emily and I could have a day off. She said "Why? Where are you going?"

'I said, "We want to go bush."

' "No way," she told us. "We've got shearers coming." '

'I said to Emily, "I'm sick of this. We won't go to work tomorrow."'
Rose did something unheard of by Aboriginal girls in those days; she and
Emily went on strike. When called at 5am, they stayed silent in bed. The
boss lady was furious and reported her to the Aboriginal Protection Board,
who wrote saying she was to do as she was told and work. Rose decided this
was no way to live, so her father, a well-spoken man who knew his rights,
got permission from the Board for her to return to the mission briefly.

One of Rose's poems, *Dusky,* describes another 'boss lady' selecting a
flimsy cheesecloth garment for a young girl to wear to serve the evening
meal to shearers. The innocent girl wonders why these men laugh and look
at her in a strange way.

'Did you know this girl?' I ask Rose.

'Yes, it was me,' she replies in a low voice. 'I was brought up in a very strict
mission. I didn't know why these horrible men were looking at me. I thought
it must be because I was black. I didn't know about other thoughts. Much
later I realised they kept sending me for things because they could see through
my dress when the sunlight shone through.' She is angry, and also relieved
that women can now be educated and are not as innocent as she was.

Rose married a Narrunga man from Yorke Peninsula and had five children.
In a major move, the family went to Whyalla in 1969, where her husband had
employment. 'We were now in a white society. Everything was rush, rush.
There were only three or four Aboriginal families. My children were very
young and came up against a lot of prejudice. We became accepted through
sport, and me being on committees for the kids' sports. My son Buddy played
soccer and in 1972 he went over to England and trained with Chelsea.'

In 1982, this son was hit from behind and killed by two men in Whyalla.
Rose was shattered. She says the case has never been closed under white
law because of insufficient evidence. 'Under tribal law, the elders gather
and discuss matters, the same as white man's law, and then decide what to
do. Aboriginal people fear tribal elders more than they fear the police.
Some Aboriginal boys wanted to leave Whyalla when they knew the old
men were coming to question them after the slaying.' The police never
found the murderers, but whether the elders did and exacted their own
form of justice remains a mystery. Rose is reluctant to talk about it.

She tells me that according to Aboriginal belief, when someone is
attacked from behind and dies, the spirit goes forward and is lost. 'The
elders came to Whyalla to find my son's spirit and settle it down so it could

go peacefully. There was a ceremony to enable the spirit to move on and to comfort the mourners. It was hard for me to let go of his spirit, but I had to,' Rose says softly. She returned to her Pitjantjatjara homeland and went bush with the women for healing. 'I would see the beautiful sunrises and sunsets, and hear the sounds of birds and the stream. I started writing poetry to express my feelings of sadness or happiness.'

She saw changes for her people, health problems, smoking, alcohol and depression due to unemployment and life changes. 'I worked with Aboriginal hostels, Aboriginal health, and flying into Pitjantjatjara communities translating for the Port Adelaide court circuit.' In 1994, she became involved in taking anthropologists to sacred lands around Whyalla to record the sites before BHP destroyed important grounds. Rose is a custodian of women's sacred stories. She took part in negotiations between Bangala and Pitjantjatjara people and BHP to protect special women's sites such as the Seven Sisters, an alignment of hills and rocks where her people held their traditional songlines and dances. She sees it as fate that she went to Whyalla and played the custodian role in preserving Aboriginal heritage.

Rose was taking children on a holiday camp as a volunteer with the Department of Community Welfare when a girl arrived with a letter from the City Council. 'It said, "You've been chosen as 1994 joint winner of the Australia Day Citizen Award for Whyalla,"' says Rose. 'My eyes crossed. I was the first Aborigine in Whyalla to receive it. Some of our people in New South Wales and Victoria were protesting about Australia Day, which gave me mixed feelings of happiness in my award and yet reminded me of past injustices.'

Her murdered son Buddy had a son, Anthony, adopted out in 1973 when he was one month old by the SA Department of Community Welfare because his mother was too young to look after him. 'His father died when Anthony would have been nine. He went to a good white family who loved him.' When he turned 18, he began looking for his natural parents. He tracked down his mother's family, only to find she had died the previous month, aged 35. She had never recovered from the brutal death of Anthony's father and her baby being taken away. She always thought he would come back. Rose spent time with Anthony's mother before her death. 'His mother had seen him on a train one day with some white boys. She sat there and watched him until he got off, hoping to see him again. She never did. She kept going up and down on that train, but I feel she went to her grave happy that she saw him once,' says Rose.

'When we were looking for him, he was right there under our noses near Whyalla. I would have known him anywhere. He looks exactly like his father—his blue eyes, his ways. When he came back to us, we were laughing and looking at each other and hugging. The tears were streaming down our faces. He's happy now being with us. He is 27 now, the same age as his father when he died. He went through a lot of bad things when he was trying to find himself and discovered that he was adopted. Now he's asking, "Why did all this happen?"'

'We live in two worlds, we Aboriginal people,' Rose continues. 'It's not a matter of being clever, but a strain. Many people feel really depressed about it. If we have a bereavement in the family, or even in the mob, everybody feels that same sadness, even if we didn't know that person. We cry and get rid of all those feelings, which you must do. No need for that grief counselling.

'For black and white people to be reconciled is good, but we need to understand each other. A lot of hurt has been done to us, but I don't live in the past. I'm not a prejudiced person. I have non-Aboriginal friends. I've never brought my children up to be prejudiced. They have lived in white society all their lives.

'I'd like to have my poems printed. Those I wrote a few years ago, I thought, "Did that really happen to me?" I'm glad I wrote it down. I can get up and write at two o'clock in the morning. That's the best time for me. I can't write on sunset because that's when we farewell our loved ones. We have a lot of bereavement among Aboriginal people. I'm here in the Kimberley, and my family is in South Australia, so I write messages of condolence. That's all I seem to be writing these days. My family say, "We can feel your spirit with us."'

'But life has been good to me,' she concludes. She tells the story of her life in her poems as a way of coming to terms with terrible experiences. Self-educated, Rose sees the future lying in education so that Aboriginal people can better themselves and run their own communities. She wants to reintroduce traditional songlines and dances to young Bangala people in her grandmother's country.

o o o

Over the river in the new township of Fitzroy Crossing that was built above floodwaters after 1975, Joe Ross's office bustles with people wanting to discuss tourism, cattle or the town plan. Joe heads an Aboriginal corporation, Bunuba Inc, for his 500-strong Bunuba 'mob'. 'We are infamous for the story of

Jandamarra, leader of a band of Bunuba people who tried to stop Europeans opening the country for pastoralism and mining in the 1890s,' he says. Jandamarra was a trusted native tracker called Pigeon by the whites, who in 1894 killed the police constable with whom he was rounding up sheep-stealers from among his own people. After releasing the prisoners, he became an outlaw, at the age of only 20, and trained a formidable guerrilla force of Bunuba men. Through many battles with the WA police force, he would laugh and fire on them from on top of the razor-sharp limestone Napier Range, with his womenfolk acting as lookouts. His hideaway was the catacomb of caves at Tunnel Creek. Jandamarra was eventually cornered and shot by a black tracker before he could escape into the caves. In his book *Kimberley: Dreaming to Diamonds* (1991), Hugh Edwards writes, 'His defiant stand against the whites made him perhaps Australia's most famous Aborigine. Pigeon has often been compared with Ned Kelly, Australia's most famous white bushranger.'

Bunuba Inc is now a major landowner of the old river township of Fitzroy Crossing. Joe's clan are custodians of Geikie Gorge, called Danggu, a vertical-sided limestone gorge where freshwater crocodiles sun themselves on ledges in the Dry, and Fitzroy River floodwaters surge through in the Wet. Jandamarra might smile if he knew that the Bunuba people acquired nearly two million acres of pastoral lease in the 1990s and successfully run 10 000 cattle at Leopold Downs, not far from the place where he fought police for four years in the 1890s and ambushed the first cattle drive into the area.

Bunuba Inc's common room is home to piles of papers, a whiteboard and a small boy sleeping on a beanbag, unperturbed by our interview. Joe's words come easily. He is able to concentrate completely on talking about his life's work and his people, switch to the latest staff query as a head pops around the door, go back to the interview, then gently pick up the little boy who is now crying for his mother.

Joe's peacemaker mother influenced his life. 'She could get consensus by hardly saying anything,' he says. He has seen a lot of conflict in meetings around Australia, 'sometimes down to the wire with a vote. I don't shun conflict, but I try to compromise.'

'And your father?' I ask.

'The old man was a rabid Catholic,' he laughs. 'In a town with no Catholics apart from himself and a couple of others, he managed to convince the bishop to build a church and convent. His philosophy was that if you didn't get satisfaction from the shire worker, then you went to the foreman. You kept going until you got satisfaction.' Joe's father was the local funeral director, ex-shire councillor and 'jack-of-all-trades'. Semi-literate himself, he sent his son away to boarding school, St John's College, Darwin, in Grade 6. Joe learnt it was not a fair society in Fitzroy Crossing. He returned with questions such as, 'Why does the Crossing Inn have a black bar and a white bar?' Police tactics were to lock up troublemakers, so Joe's questioning led to nights cooling his heels in jail. By his late twenties he says he settled down, learning from the elders to bide his time, even when right. No hothead any more, his answers to my questions are measured.

Trained as an electrical fitter and installer, he was one of a handful of local qualified people. When he was 30, his mother suffered renal failure, and for the last six years of her life she was on a dialysis machine administered by two specially trained relatives. So in 1993, Joe left a $70 000-a-year job with BHP Minerals at Cadjebut mine to help her establish her community and start a small-scale tourism venture at Danggu, taking boat trips through the gorge.

The Fitzroy valley was hundreds of kilometres from major towns. It had few jobs or opportunities, a low literacy rate, poor health status, and its people were often in trouble with the law because of alcohol problems and lack of work. Joe was under pressure to help his people. 'Fitzroy Crossing felt a big impact when the Australian Workers' Union brought in award wages in the late 1960s. They thought they were doing the right thing getting wage equity, but there was no preparation for it. There might have been 30 domestics and stockmen and another 70 people living on each property, who got kicked off. Once they were herded into town, there was animosity towards the state government. It impacted on Aboriginal people in this town, so most stations locked their gates and, being on pastoral leases, had the right to restrict access. It's only over the last decade that properties have been acquired for Aboriginal people.'

The population of the Fitzroy Crossing region in the 1990s was 90 per cent Aboriginal. 'There was a yearning to maintain tribal law and culture, but also a facing up to the reality that you can't survive unless you are part of mainstream Australia, having employment opportunities,' Joe says. 'You have to weigh up the values of Aboriginal society and the values of European society. Not many decision-makers know which is best.' He had to negotiate with those elders who viewed offering Danggu boat tours as compromising tribal culture. 'Our only resources are our cultural heritage,' he maintains. 'At what level do we expose non-Aboriginal people to our culture? At the end of the day, it's up to the people who own those stories and culture to volunteer. My strengths are facilitating the project to keep the integrity of the culture and provide opportunities for income.'

In 1995 a proposal was mooted to dam the Fitzroy River and flood the wilderness area of Dimond Gorge for a cotton venture. Joe, who was promoting agricultural development, didn't go along with the dam proposal on the Bunuba homeland. In 1987, he had canoed the 300 kilometres through raging rapids from the Fitzroy's headwaters to Fitzroy Crossing and he dreamed of setting up a rafting venture. This captured the imagination of naturalist John Sinclair, who had saved the pristine wilderness of Fraser Island from sand mining, earning him the prestigious international Goldman Environment Prize, established in 1990 by Richard and Rhoda Goldman for environmental activism. It is hailed as the equivalent of the green Nobel Prize.

The dilemma for Joe was, 'We didn't want the dam, but we did want to create an ecotourism whitewater rafting company that could raise awareness of the wilderness value.' Another school of thought wanted total wilderness, no rafting. Joe's goal was to reach an understanding and build partnerships with like-minded people. He attracted an ecotourism company, Headwaters, with high environmental values. In 1998 Joe, Ross and John Sinclair organised a canoeing expedition down the Fitzroy with 15 wilderness conservationists, including the prominent Tasmanian Greens Senator Bob Brown. The trip succeeded in showing them the beauty of this wilderness area and extended Joe's networks to national allies such as the Australian Conservation Foundation. Their combined efforts stopped the dam project. In 1999–2000 five rafting trips with experienced guides have taken more than 60 people 300 kilometres down the Fitzroy River from its headwaters, testing the best options for tours.

Like Stanley, Joe Ross wants independence from the CDEP. He is shifting increasingly to private enterprise income generated from tourism, having changed his corporation's focus to training and employment for the long-term future of the community. A big problem, he says, is that when Aboriginal people gain skills, they suffer the tall poppy syndrome, get swallowed up into public service or are wooed away from their communities. He has had offers to leave, but Fitzroy Crossing is his land. 'I live here because I belong here,' he says.

A recent graduate of the Australian Rural Leadership Program, he is helping develop a national Aboriginal Leadership Program with a similar philosophy of corporate sponsorship so that scholarship-holders can build networks, skills and experience. It is currently establishing funding for the program, which begins with 25 young indigenous leaders in 2001. 'I don't want to be the richest man in the cemetery,' he says, 'but I want equity, a good quality of life, and having our mob get a fair go here.' He thinks his work will reach its fruition after he is dead, given the magnitude of the issues involved.

o o o

These three—Stanley, Rose and Joe—step like dancers from tribal to mainstream worlds and back again, weaving patterns of connection. It is people like them who are the voices of hope for an Australia with a black and a white soul.

Seven Sisters

Wimboo Wimboo,
Can You see,
If Birra is coming down to the sea,
For we must flee, so to be free

We Seven Sisters shall fly low,
Because we know Birra go slow.
We will travel along the shore
And settle at sunset and not before
Grounded and then we will make a camp
After the tide and the munda is damp.

We Seven Sisters will dance and play
In the twilight till it is no longer day
Tomorrow we hunt food and gather clay
To make it safe for us to stay.

Birra, Birra we can see
You sneaking around under that tree

Inma, Inma white ochre and clay
Women's sacred ground, Fitzgerald Bay.

Rose Hillman, 1996

Birra is the moon, strong and sexual (male).
Wimboo is the Spider Lady.
Munda is the ground.
Inma is a corroboree or ceremony.

9 | First Vines to First Wines

Di Cullen (OA) ~

Pioneering the Margaret River wine industry

Caves Road winds for 110 kilometres through the towering forests of the Margaret River region in Western Australia, from Geographe Bay in the north to the south-western tip of the continent. A limestone labyrinth of caves with such beguiling names as Jewel, Mammoth and Moondyne stretches from Cape Naturaliste to Cape Leeuwin. Tracks west from the road lead to the Indian Ocean surging onto a jagged coastline, a magnetic attraction for surfers. Where the mouth of the Margaret River meets the wild sea, board riders wearing crash helmets catch rip currents out from the shore and skim in over rock platforms. Eucalypts don their February finery of crimson, deep pink and orange blossom.

Three hours south of Perth, the region is a gourmand's paradise of local venison and seafood, cheeses and fresh fruit, accompanied by fine wine from any one of more than 60 wineries tucked among the trees. Yet in 1956, when Diana and Kevin Cullen bought 100 acres (40 hectares) for £100 at The Gallows as a coastal hideaway, Margaret River was an impoverished, depressed area and the population was going backwards. The Cullens ran sheep, cattle and kangaroos, Diana dryly observes. In 1961, they expanded to Caves Road, the site of Cullen Wines, and now own 800 hectares.

It is a balmy summer day cooled by sea breezes. Two-metre high walls of leafy vines at the Cullens' vineyard dwarf its founder. Diana Cullen is as slim and wiry as her vines, from long hours of tending them. 'I love them,' she says, as she inspects leaves for signs of unwanted invaders, mildew or insects. Her pale brown hair, brushed back softly, reveals a face full of character, warm and open. What is not visible is her highly developed winemaker's palate and 'nose' for wine.

Surrounding us are 29 hectares nourishing the raw material for great vintages of cabernet sauvignons, chardonnays and merlots that make connoisseur buyers from around Australia and 22 countries across the globe keep coming back for more Cullen wine. Between the rows dripping with bunches of deep purple or translucent white grapes grow crimson clovers and ryegrass which are chopped for mulch. Towering above are marri trees bursting with creamy blossom. Diana hopes the blossom will distract flocks of marauding silvereyes until the grape harvest is over in a few weeks. These tiny birds with big appetites relish nectar and grapes.

'How did you decide on this place?' I ask her.

'My husband Kevin and I had a friend, state government viticulturist Bill Jamieson, who picked the site,' she says. 'It's very granity, terribly hard to get grapes going. We don't water, which is unusual around here. Well-drained soil and dry farming gives us smaller berries and concentrated fruit flavours. I believe great wine is made in the vineyard.' Her expert eye examines tight bunches of the glossy dark merlot grapes. What makes this place special is the soil, the Mediterranean climate and the unpolluted environment near the sea, she explains.

Overlooking the vineyard is the winery restaurant. A quick walk and straight back belie this energetic woman's 77 years as she leads me through the cool, dark wine-tasting room made of wood and stone, into the sunlit restaurant. 'Call me Di, dear,' she says as we sit by the window and she pours two glasses of clear ruby 1998 cabernet merlot.

'There was nowhere to eat at the wineries in the seventies,' she says. 'In the early eighties my eldest daughter, Shelley, started a trend in the area with a food bar here. She had vineyard platters and in winter, pumpkin soup and pasties.' Its popularity prompted Diana to invest her superannuation in 1995 to upgrade the 1920s house into an up-market restaurant. Laughter and conversation mingle with the clink of glasses and the aroma of delicious food. We taste the wine filled with the scent and flavour of berries.

'Where did you grow up?' I ask.

'I was born in Tasmania a very long time ago!' she smiles. 'I was brought up with the idea that we women have to become qualified, work hard and use our brains.' Her mother strongly influenced her; at the age of 16 she was a suffragette and supporter of Emily Pankhurst, and would climb out a window of her London bedroom to march for women's rights, handing out pamphlets on street corners.

Di's parents met when her mother was singing for soldiers wounded in World War I. Madeline Grace came to Tasmania as a war bride. 'My father wouldn't let her work, which galled her.' She channelled her energy into charity. One day she went to visit a relative of her husband's in a mental asylum outside Hobart. 'I was about eight,' says Di. 'She was courageous. Mental disease was considered a form of demonic possession in those days. Patients were chained to their beds and locked in their rooms with nothing to do.' Horrified at this inhumanity, Madeline visited the asylum regularly and helped by an enlightened man, Dr Brothers, taught inmates to paint and sew, sing and weave. 'She also started a Sunshine Home in Hobart for country children whose families couldn't afford holidays.'

Di's father was director of the Agricultural Bank of Tasmania, and was on the Australian Meat Board. His daughter's first brush with agriculture was visiting soldier settlements with him. The soldier-settlement scheme was an attempt in different states to settle 37 000 ex-servicemen on farms during and after World War I. Nearly 10000 left because of lack of farming experience, severe physical disabilities, land that was unsuitable for settlement and farm size being too small for viability.

In the 1930s, another lasting influence on Di was her secondary schooling in Hobart at Fahan. The education was advanced and disciplined. 'Every morning,' she remembers, 'all 150 children and staff walked halfway up Mt Nelson and ran the half-mile back, rain, hail or snow. We would come back with icy fingers to tiny wood fires in the classrooms, but we were fit and there was hardly any sickness.' She thinks young people nowadays would be healthier if there was more emphasis on physical fitness. Fahan had a hut in the mountains where senior students went on weekends. They had to speak French on Saturdays and German on Sundays, or they weren't allowed to go skiing. Teachers took them on excursions to the children's courts and through factories. 'The Cadbury chocolate factory interested me most!' Di jokes, but these trips also gave her an understanding of other people's circumstances. Her final class of three all matriculated.

It was wartime when she finished school and went to Melbourne University. 'Dad said he couldn't afford my doing medicine, so I did physiotherapy instead.' There she met Kevin Cullen, a medical student from Western Australia living in Ormond College, opposite the Women's College, where Di boarded. 'He would take me to the "bug house" movie theatre,' she remembers with amusement. 'It was cheap.'

Kevin followed her to Tasmania where he did his residency, and they married there in 1946, when she was 23. In 1948, when their first child, Rick, was three months old, they moved to Busselton, a coastal town north of Margaret River, where Kevin started a general practice. 'We rented half a house,' Di recalls. 'Coming from Tasmania with endless water, I didn't realise this house relied on tank water. I used the lot in two weeks washing nappies. Kevin was shocked at how filthy the hospital was, the bedbugs, and no x-ray machine.' The Cullens had six children in 12 years—Rick, Shelley, Stuart, Digby, Ariane and Vanya. Di was a mother during the day and a physiotherapist in the evenings for many years.

In 1957 the family moved to Edinburgh, Scotland for a year so Kevin could study for membership of the Royal College of Physicians. They had five children at that stage. Di remembers the cold and Edinburgh as a beautiful, gracious city. She wanted to study psychoprophylactic methods of enlightened childbirth in the USSR, the only place it was available, but the embassy said it would take a year to get a visa and could give no guarantees she would be able to leave the USSR again. She decided on a 10-day course with a Russian teacher in Paris instead. 'I loved Paris—old world and exciting.'

Di and Kevin Cullen were a formidable team. On returning to Busselton she taught women the psychoprophylactic techniques she had learned in Paris, which reduced the fear of childbirth, and then he delivered the babies. 'I did antenatal and postnatal classes in the evenings and sometimes went into the labour ward with women and stayed with them,' she says. 'Kevin had the lowest rate of caesarean sections in Australia.'

Dr Kevin Cullen became well known through ground-breaking research in the field of preventive medicine. He studied 300 babies, half of whose mothers he counselled regularly, helping them sort out health and family concerns, problems with their children, and doing regular physical checks on the children. The other half he didn't counsel, his theory being that you can change women's attitudes most effectively during pregnancy and soon after birth. When surveyed after five years, the counselled mothers had less depression and illness, fewer marriage breakdowns, and did more exercise. Their children performed better at school, had fewer stress symptoms such as bedwetting and nightmares, and were physically stronger.

Twenty-seven years later, and just before he died of Motor Neurone Disease, Kevin surveyed all the children again, receiving a 92 per cent response rate. The group whose mothers were counselled was more relaxed and healthier, had fewer divorces, played more sport and had a higher proportion of tertiary education than the control group. One of the Cullens' daughters, Ariane, who is also a doctor, published her father's paper after his death in 1994. 'I was always sad that he didn't know it was published,' says Di. 'It was such good work.'

Kevin Cullen was awarded the first doctorate in Medicine at the University of Weatern Australia for a study proving that good hygiene helps keep people healthier. He compared people living in poor housing in timber mill towns to those in Busselton and Perth. In 1962 he won a National Health Institute scholarship to Berkeley University in California to study preventive child health for a year. Again his family joined him. 'We always travelled on a shoestring, but it was easier with children then,' recalls Di.

'How did you get involved in the wine industry?' I inquire as the afternoon shadows gather across the vineyard and Di waves goodbye to late lunchers. 'We had a friend, Dr John Gladstones, who did his doctorate on ideal areas in the world for growing cabernet, I think because he loved cabernet,' she laughs. Based on climate and soil analyses, he found the

Margaret River region was one of the best. Kevin Cullen convened a well-attended meeting in Busselton in 1966, where Gladstones inspired action.

Vines and wine-making were in Kevin's family. In 1890 his grandfather, Ephraim Mayo Clarke, had planted a vineyard at Bunbury and produced port wine, which was sold on the goldfields and at the family store. Italian families had been making wine in the Margaret River area for many years. The Cullens decided to test Gladstones' conclusion, and planted a trial acre of cuttings in 1966. They did well until this farm was sold and the vines were pulled out. Pioneers of the region's first commercial winegrowing after the trial plot 35 years ago were three doctors and their wives—the Cullens, the Cullities at Vasse Felix, and the Pannells at Moss Wood. Back in 1859 the colonial surgeon, Dr John Ferguson, had led the way for Western Australia doctors growing vines when he bought Houghton Estate for the princely sum of £350.

1966 was hectic, as Di planted vines and Kevin began his landmark *Busselton Survey*, which tested the whole town's population for health factors and referred any problems to the doctors. Repeated every four years since, its early detection and treatment regime resulted in the study becoming famous. Meanwhile Di was involved in the community as president of Busselton Parents' and Citizens' Association. Ahead of her time, she took on the WA Department of Education in fighting for the right of girls to learn metalwork and carpentry and the right of boys to learn cooking.

In 1971, at the age of 48, with six children ranging from primary school to university ages and at a time when many women might consider more leisurely pursuits, Di Cullen began a second career. She planted a 7.2 hectare vineyard, driving 50 kilometres each day to and from Busselton and juggling work between school hours. Kevin and the children helped on weekends. She says there is a connection between wine-making and physiotherapy in that each is therapeutic. 'I'm always trying to improve the health of the grapes to make better wine,' she adds.

The local dairy farmers used to laugh at these 'idiots putting sticks in the ground'—meaning the winter-dormant vine cuttings the Cullens planted. Thirty years later the irony is that dairy farmers sell their land to aspiring wine producers.

The Cullen vineyard at Willyabrup is on land that was originally part of the ill-conceived 1920s group settlement scheme to entice English migrants to a new land. The arrivals had expected lush country, contented cows and attractive cottages, but instead they were taken to tin humpies, had to clear tenacious forests for dairying, and pay the West Australian government for the privilege. The 64-hectare Cullen block had belonged to the Robinsons, a family with nine children and 30 cows. 'It was strenuous work,' says Di. 'The husband cleared the forest, ringbarked the trees by hand and then died.'

By the 1970s, the dairies and timber mills in the district could not provide much work. Di employed a husband and wife team for vine planting, and trained other locals. 'One woman asked if she could work here because she couldn't afford shoes for her children to go to school,' she says, adding with a laugh, 'I was trying to get our children to wear shoes, but they wouldn't. Or else they took them off on the way to school because it made them feel different.'

'How did you know about establishing a vineyard?' I ask her.

She is quite frank. 'We didn't know! Nobody had grown grapes down here. We were isolated and had little knowledge. The man drove a tractor digging holes and his wife and I went behind putting in cuttings and tramping them in. We watered by hand from the back of the tractor.'

In 1971 cabernet sauvignon was the only red vine they could plant because of strict quarantine rules. 'That first year we had trained the vine shoots up to the trellis wires and tied them with string, when they collapsed.' Baffled, they talked to Department of Agriculture staff who identified 2-4D weedkiller, but no neighbours had sprayed it. Again the Cullens trained the vines up to trellis level, tied them with string—and the same thing happened. 'We traced it to the *string*, poisoned by being stored next to 2-4D at the supplier's. That was a disaster. We had to re-string all 11 000 vines. It didn't happen to anyone else, but we persuaded the Department to ban spraying 2-4D here.'

In 1972, they planted riesling. Di thinks it is not well suited to Margaret River. 'But funnily enough, the first national trophy for Margaret River was for a 1977 Cullen riesling at the National Wine Show in Canberra. We jumped around in great glee when we heard. We thought they had made a mistake.'

The Cullens always wanted to plant merlot and cabernet franc, because they thought better wine was made with a Bordeaux blend, based on cabernet sauvignon with merlot and other varieties. Due to quarantine restrictions, they couldn't source cuttings for six years. 'At last in 1976 the first imports of these varieties were available.' Di remembers her excitement. 'Seventy-five cuttings of merlot! Kevin said to give 25 each to Moss Wood and Vasse Felix, as he felt we shouldn't have an advantage over them. When I delivered the cuttings, they said, 'Cabernet doesn't need merlot here.' They didn't plant them. We put our 25 in and had the local nursery bud enough to make up an acre. It took years for people to accept cabernet merlot. The merlot makes a fuller-flavoured wine. Customers would say, "We want cabernet sauvignon, not the mer-lotte!" Now it's widely grown.'

In the early years, the only model for trellising was from the hotter Swan Valley, where vines needed shade, whereas the Cullens learned they had to expose grapes to the sun in the cooler Margaret River region. In the 1980s they experimented with different trellises, preferring one called Scott-Henry that opened vines to sunlight and produced grapes superior in colour, sugar, acid balance and flavour. They had to re-trellis the whole vineyard.

'How did you learn winemaking?' I query.

'We read madly, went to seminars, and travelled to wineries around Australia, in California's Napa Valley and Oregon, and around the major French and German regions. People didn't find us a threat because we were so far away, and they gave us information. We both had scientific backgrounds, which helped. We went on taste mostly. You have to have a good palate.'

In 1974 Kevin made the first vintage of half a tonne of cabernet. With daughter Shelley's help they hand-crushed it in a primitive basket press. 'It tasted awful,' Di winces. 'We learned and became better equipped. 1975 was good—a hundred cases, a little acidic as we had to pick it early because of birds.' Kevin sold some and gave most away. 'Our son Rick and his friends were boating down the river on a camping trip with the last two cases when the boat tipped over and the wine went to the bottom, never to be seen again. So we only had a dozen bottles left. It is lovely wine now. We've been trying to buy it back ever since.' It was sold in 1975 for $2.50 a bottle and Di now has to pay over $90 a bottle for it at wine auctions.

In 1976, they produced 500 cases. 'Our 1976 won a gold medal at national wine shows. People wondered where Margaret River was then,' Di remembers. 'I sold a bottle at a time from 1975 to 1978, and then a Melbourne retailer ordered five cases. I nearly passed out,' she laughs. The three original vineyards—Cullen, Vasse Felix and Moss Wood—won gold medals in Melbourne in 1976 which kick-started the region's reputation.

The Cullens hired winemakers Bruce Allen, and then Mike Peterkin, each for two years, until 1981, when Di became the winemaker, a job she did until 1989. She made West Australian wine industry history in 1982 as the first woman to win the most successful exhibitor award at the Perth Show. In 1982, Cullen was in the final three for the Melbourne Wine Show's prized Jimmy Watson Memorial Trophy, won by another Margaret River winemaker, Cape Mentelle. After 1983 Cullen wine sold out quickly. In just nine years they had established a reputation for premium wines. In an unusual mother/daughter combination, their youngest daughter, Vanya, who completed a graduate diploma in winemaking at Roseworthy College in South Australia, made wine with her mother from 1986. Cullen chardonnay has remained in the top ten in Australia since 1994, and their cabernet sauvignon merlot is recognised as one of the best in Australia.

But Di is more interested in relating well to consumers than accumulating awards. 'I think if you are nice to people, they remember that. It's better than having outstanding wines and being awful to customers! If you have a happy lot of people working for you, the wine works better.'

She takes a positive attitude towards disasters, trying to turn them to advantage. 'On 10 December 1997,' she recounts, 'big lumps of hail absolutely flattened the chardonnay. We only got five tonnes from 17 acres. That set us back, but the quality was fantastic because it was so concentrated. We turned it into magnums and sent a few to each of our domestic and overseas markets.'

Another year riesling grapes were raisined due to a long, hot summer. I tasted the delectable amber-coloured sweet wine Vanya made from those grapes. After pressing, the grape skins are thrown to cattle that are run on the rest of the property. In 1980 the cattle were chased out after feasting on fermenting skins, except for one bull that found its way back. 'Next morning, we found him feet up, stone dead, after eating the remaining two tonnes,' says Di. Beef burgundy!

'Not being a trained winemaker I had to do everything by the book,' she says. 'There was more stigma against women winemakers then. I remember when Kevin and I met the head of Roseworthy College, I kept asking questions, because I was the winemaker, but the principal always replied to Kevin. He never once looked at me. I feel you have to think of your own ability, not whether you are male or female. There are now quite a few highly respected women in the industry.'

Vines, wine and the Cullen family are inseparable. They are a family business—all the family have shares. 'Our youngest daughter, Vanya, is managing director. She is a very good winemaker,' says Di.

'You must have been an excellent winemaker yourself,' I comment.

'Oh, not nearly as good as Vanya.' In August 2000, Vanya was voted Australian Winemaker of the Year by *The Wine Magazine*/Qantas. As she accepted the award, she thanked her mother. Another Margaret River winemaker, Di's son-in-law, Mike Peterkin of Pierro Winery, was in the final ten. Di is proud of them both, and swift to point out the benefit of recognition for the region.

'What of the future for Margaret River wines?' I ask.

'The people who brought fame to the area have to continue pursuing excellence,' she says. 'I hope the 30 years of building up the name means that our region's wines will remain world-class and that the area doesn't go down the drain in the pursuit of money.' From a few people putting 'sticks in the ground' in the 1960s, the wine industry has turned the region around, boosting jobs and tourism, and producing about 15 per cent of all Australia's premium quality wines. Di Cullen has been a key player in establishing a regional appellation system, which controls the style and quality of wines, and in 1979 became a foundation member of the Margaret River Wine Industry Association.

Since 1986, the Cullen winery has hosted the annual international chardonnay tasting in which four-year-old wines from France, Italy, America and Australia are compared. 'We pit our wines against the best,' she says. The region performs well, with Leeuwin Estate excelling, and Cullen's winning in 1999. Margaret River maintains its standard with pre-bottling tastings. 'All the winemakers come with their wines in paper bags so no-one knows what's what,' says Di. If there are faults, they can correct them early.

Di is concerned about vast increases in wine planting and production, not only around Margaret River and across Australia, but also in Argentina, former eastern European countries, Russia and China. 'The Australian government should stop tax deductions for planting vines,' she thinks. 'Unless something goes wrong with the 2000 vintage, based on our current markets, growers will produce far more than Australia can drink or sell overseas.'

Our February 2000 interview was followed by bad weather and lower prices for the Australian vintage, slowing the phenomenal growth of the last 15 years in which plantings have almost doubled nationally and exports multiplied a hundredfold, reaching more than a billion dollars in 1999. In an ABC 'Landline' program about the Australian wine industry on 9 March 2000, reporter Ian Henschke said the industry had reached a turning point. 'The pessimists say it is a crisis, the optimists say it is a challenge, but if we are to carve out a place in the world market, it seems certain we will have to produce quality rather than quantity.'

Cullen wines are distinctive. 'We aim for premium wines that go with food and have something different, more flavour and complexity. We get that partly by the oak influence.' Di points out their simple stylish logo of an oak leaf and acorn. 'It is a pleasure to have good wine, and to see people enjoying it. We hand-prune and pick, stressing gentle handling techniques. We are meticulous about cleanliness, for instance steam-cleaning tanks rather than using smelly detergents. It's environmental consciousness.

'The biggest fight humanity faces is to save the environment,' she says with fervour. 'In the 1960s we fought to keep sand mining and oil exploration out of this lovely area. From Cape Naturaliste to Cape Leeuwin we saw pegs along the coast. I found out from a geologist that we should pull them out because if they are there for a month the mining company can claim leases. We madly pulled them out, but a week later the pegs were back! We couldn't keep pulling them out, so Kevin and I and some friends started the Vasse Conservation Council to enlist local support. Finally we joined the Liberal Party to put in a petition and spoke at meetings around the countryside.' Before such protests were common, they decided to march on the West Australian parliament. The day before, the government announced they were putting a Conservation Bill before parliament. 'Three hundred of us marched with placards anyway,' says Di. Her mother would have applauded. 'The power of the press helped change politicians' minds. You have to make an effort if you think it is important enough.'

Di's father became a CBE (Commander of the British Empire) for work with soldier settlements and her mother an MBE (Member of the British Empire) for charity work. Di was awarded an OA in 1999 for service to the development of viticulture and the wine industry.

'So many my age talk about what the doctor said and who has died,' she says. Di is highly unlikely to think like this; she is now launching into a business course. 'It bores me silly, but keeps the brain going, especially now dealing with the GST.' She sees substantial costs and paperwork from the Goods and Services Tax for small and medium-sized businesses such as theirs. Di is philosophical about highs and lows in her life. 'I always think when you go down, you will come up again. Getting married was a high and Kevin's death was a low. I still miss him. We had 48 years together, never a dull moment. Did I tell you I met the Queen at a dinner in Perth in July 2000? That was a high! To my embarrassment, I found myself sitting on her right-hand side. I told her I had felt like sending her a case of wine when she was having troubles with her children. She said, "I wish you had!"'

John Gladstones was right about Margaret River, but its wine industry had to prove it. 'Our winery has had much more international recognition in the last five years,' says Di Cullen. 'I'm sorry Kevin is not here to see it. I want us to be free of debt, but we're not interested in becoming wealthy. Kevin could have made a lot of money if he had specialised, but he only ever charged GP's fees although he was a Fellow of the Royal College of Physicians.

'A passion for wine is number one for us,' she concludes. 'We constantly chase quality.' She unobtrusively hands me a brown paper bag as I leave. Inside is her favourite 1988 cabernet sauvignon merlot, a most generous gift from a gracious lady.

10 | The Salamanca Brumby

Ian Dickenson (OA) ~
Preserving and managing our native forests

The conservation movement in Australia was born in Tasmania around the inundation of Lake Pedder in the 1970s. It gathered momentum over the proposed damming of the Franklin River in the early 1980s and brewed and simmered for more than a decade over the management of Tasmanian forests. In an editorial in September 1989, Tasmania's *Saturday Mercury* stated, 'The population began to divide along diametrically opposed lines. There were those who wanted to continue in the old ways under which jobs and industry were the top priorities. There were also those who wanted the environment, in particular the forests, protected at all costs—even to economic stagnation.'

By 1990 war raged in the forests. Mainland Australians watched the drama unfold on television as conservationists, loggers, farmers, and the community at large battled over Tasmania's vast tracts of forest. Police were called in to unchain protesters from trees, to drag shouting people from in front of bulldozers and to supervise rowdy demonstrations in this previously calm and conservative island state.

Into the turmoil, the Tasmanian government thrust a modest, determined farm forester, Ian Dickenson, 'to achieve peace in our forests', and do it within 18 months. It called for negotiating expertise, wisdom and tolerance, and a whole year and a half of Ian's life. He would argue that he knew his limitations, but took courage from his father's favourite saying, 'faint heart never won a fat pig'.

I knew Ian Dickenson was an achiever. He was awarded the Order of Australia in 1992 for 'his services to agriculture, particularly forestry'. He was the Tasmanian winner in the 1997 National Landcare Awards and state winner also in the 2000 National World Forestry Day Awards. But instead of a high flier, I found a sincere and self-deprecating person who took an unaccustomed weekend off to talk about his life.

Tall and rangy, with the weathered face of an outdoorsman and expressive leathery hands, he is warm and intuitive in his fervent descriptions of his farm, forest and family. His left eye is fiery red from a woodchip that flew up when he was logging recently. 'It looks better from my side,' he dryly observes. I soon discover that this man likes pushing boundaries. In 1973 he took on the business of timber harvesting on his own farm, disappointed by the contractor's performance. It's a dangerous business.

From a rocky goat track high on Old Whisloca, an adjoining property the Dickensons bought in 1989, the view is stunning. Ian points out the towering mountains of Tasmania's ski fields, Ben Lomond, then Ben Nevis and Mt Barrow, which ring the magnificent North Esk Valley. The valley shows the tide of changing times. Plantations of radiata pine and shining gum jostle with the multicoloured sweeps of grazing and cropping that make up Elverton, the 2082-hectare family farm. We return to the house Ian and Rosemary built over four winters, and sit on the lawn looking out over the valley.

Farming is in Ian's blood. As a boy he would gaze out the schoolroom window, checking out the weather and wondering what was happening back home on the farm near Hobart. The family were not well off, but placed a high priority on contributing to the community. His sister died of kidney disease when she was 11. It took him years to come to terms with this, and it made him intolerant of those who complain. He is fond of quoting proverbs such as 'The man with no shoes thought he was badly off until he met a man with no feet.'

On 7 February 1967 the family farm was burnt out in the horrific bushfires that swept southern Tasmania, killing 65 people. The Dickensons lost crops, buildings and fences, but saved the dairy cattle. Afterwards Ian's father encouraged his son to 'play in the dirt' somewhere that had a long-term future. Promising his parents he would be back in one year, the young adventurer packed his swag and went looking for land around Australia. From brigalow country in Queensland to Tipperary station in the Northern Territory and balloted farm blocks in Western Australia, he explored avenues for agriculture. At the end of that year, Ian found his heart was still in Tasmania.

His uncle's developed property was for sale, but the thought of driving in and out of the same paddocks, growing the same crops every year, lacked challenge. He took on Elverton, east of Launceston. It was mostly forest, some of which had been heavily logged. He borrowed 100 per cent of the money for land, stock and machinery, and his parents put up security for the mortgage. Ian had enough money saved to pay stamp duty. 'I had a dog and a large mortgage for company. The dog has long since passed on. The mortgage remains,' he says. He worked alone for five years before marrying Rosemary Sharpe, a teacher from Hobart, in 1973.

Purchasing Old Whisloca at the top of the market to grow more wool was, Ian concedes, 'the biggest mistake'. Two years later, the Federal government removed the wool reserve price scheme and prices crashed. The Dickensons were left with no sale and no options for their 11 000 sheep. The government introduced a subsidy for farmers to shoot their sheep. Ian cannot forget it. 'It was devastating. We shot half of them, five and a half thousand. Just put them in a large trench. It was one of the toughest jobs I've ever had to do. They were healthy animals, and our livelihood.'

Ian and Rosemary were trying to service a debt of $1.55 million as interest rates had risen from 14 to 18 per cent. A man from the Tasmanian Development Authority sat at their kitchen table and said,

'You have 12 months to meet the budget. If you fail, there's no other option but to sell.'

At the same time, Ian was caught in the middle of the forestry debate. He says 'Even when you think all is lost, you need to keep on going. Keep on doing the knitting...' For 18 months Rosemary became mother and father to their two children, Adam and Diana, as Ian tried to help sort out the forestry issues and introduce radical farming changes. He employed a farm consultant to find high-value, small-acreage cash crops to generate income. Interest rates fortunately came down at the same time as he grew barley, oats and later canning peas, seed potatoes and opium poppies on the best soils, moving grazing stock to higher land. For ten years the family just met interest rate payments until timber harvesting provided additional income.

Ian Dickenson looks for balance, the wise use of resources to achieve environmental, economic and social goals on the farm and in Tasmania as a whole. 'It's a vexed question with native forests—do you harvest or keep them for conservation? We have tried to develop management regimes that achieve both. Tasmania has a significant area as World Heritage, and parks and reserves. Forests we are harvesting now have been heavily logged before.' Many farms in Tasmania have commercial forests that used to be burned to promote the growth of native grasses for stock. Ian says that was good for grazing, but not good for the forests.

Forest policy was an issue for government. In 1989 a minority Labor government was formed with the support of five Green Independents. The government asked Ian Dickenson, then chair of the Tasmanian Farmers and Graziers' Association Forestry Committee, to chair a process of looking at both Crown and private forest land with key players—conservationists, the forestry industry, private forest owners, trade unions and government.

The task was to negotiate an agreed supply of high-quality saw logs to industry without coming into conflict with the Accord signed by the Labor/Green government. 'The Accord allowed them to form government. Most of its 15 clauses referred to restrictions on the forestry industry in Crown forests,' says Ian. 'We went through an intense ten days to arrive at what became known as the Salamanca Agreement, named after the Hobart hotel where we met.' As he talks his hands eloquently describe the clashes, breakthroughs and agreements. The Salamanca Agreement guaranteed the continuing supply of high-quality timber to industry and added an extra 49000 hectares to the World Heritage listings. Of greater significance, it showed that negotiation could bring about agreement between warring parties. 'It kept the Labor/Green government alive,' says Ian. That agreement identified the need for the Forest and Forest Industry Council (FFIC) to be established and for a forest industry strategy to be developed within a year. The new government asked Ian Dickenson to chair the FFIC, which undertook consultation with many sectors throughout Tasmania.

'The question was "How much of our forests do we reserve for biodiversity and what will that contribute to our community?", as against "How much do we use for forestry and what will that contribute to our community?" It's finding the balance.' The Council set out to provide a strategy durable enough for successive governments to build on.

'I learned a lot from members of the FFIC. There were strong arguments presented from both industry and conservationists on many issues,' he says. 'Some in the farming community thought I had sold out to the conservationists because I argued the case for protecting rare and threatened species on private land. Some had an attitude of, "It's my land, I can do whatever I like."' He is adamant that you can't do whatever you like on your own land. 'I received hate mail and threatening phone calls. Even then, it was a matter of being honest and realistic about what was achievable.'

Endless hours around the table taught Ian to listen to the whole debate. As chairman he would not tolerate secret agendas, an approach supported by the government. 'Everything on top of the table, please,' he recalled saying, forefinger tapping the outdoor table. The FFIC was instructed to develop a scientifically based strategy by consensus. Ian likened it to staying in the middle of the road, bringing the widest possible group of people on side, not straying into the gravel edges—the extreme positions where you lose control.

All sides had to compromise, but when Minister for Forests David Llewellyn introduced the Forest Industry Strategy Bill, the Greens moved a successful no-confidence motion against the minority Labor government. 'The government went to water and withdrew the Bill,' Ian tells me in some disgust. 'I was in Hobart to pick up a load of fertiliser at the time. I asked the Premier why the Bill had been withdrawn. His reply was that they had no choice. No government wanted to lose office. I said that the community expected this Bill to go through. The media was hovering. One reporter asked me what was happening. I was angry and said, "I've come to Hobart for some fertiliser and I don't know which door of parliament to back up to."

'The community was not impressed. Many of their "fingerprints" were on that Bill.' People demanded to talk to both the government and the opposition. To achieve that, Ian facilitated an extraordinary meeting between politicians and leaders of industry, forestry, trade unions and community groups. They told the political leaders that in a democracy they would not tolerate five Independents dictating policy. 'From that meeting three of us from the FFIC were instructed to talk to the Opposition and the Labor government and find a solution. We secured the life of the government for another six months and the Bill became law.'

Ten years down a sometimes bumpy track, Ian says there is still bipartisan political support for the forest industry in Tasmania. 'We weren't going to satisfy everybody, but we set out to satisfy the vast majority. In 1997, we proved to the Federal government that the figures used for the Strategy were honest and thorough. So we now have the Tasmanian Forest Industry Strategy forming a solid foundation for the Regional Forest Agreement, which is signed by both Federal and State governments. The Regional Forest Agreement and the Strategy brought the forest industry back from the brink. We called the process the Salamanca Brumby because we were all bucked off at some stage. When the Bill went through parliament I presented the Minister for Forests with a set of silver spurs,' he laughs.

Ian underplays his role and insists he is no risk-taker. 'I like to think I'm capable of pulling off what I've taken on.' His honesty and integrity were crucial in navigating the rough waters of environmental politics. Even when vilified on talkback radio and in pubs, he persevered and kept an open mind, but it was a great effort and it had its price. 'Ian was never home,' says Rosemary, who fielded calls and media demands. 'When he was, the phones never stopped. The children didn't see much of their father. Other people got irate, but not Ian. He's unbelievably strong in mind and body. I went to parliament to hear the debates. I didn't ever waver in my belief that they would get the legislation through. Ian has incredible determination. He never gives up, never. I knew they could get the issues sorted out. Everyone asked me if he was going to step into politics after all the public and media attention. They said it was the perfect springboard. He declined.' He decided to step back, recharge the batteries and get his own house in order.

In 1969 Elverton had one employee—Ian—1500 head of sheep and cattle and no crops. The river flats were in their native condition, badly drained, full of tussocks and willows and the forest was degraded. Thirty years later the place is transformed. Ian has removed the willows that clogged the North Esk River and it flows freely once more. He points out the surging stream, now one leg of the heart-stopping annual Ben Lomond Descent. In August 2000, 70 competitors skied and rode mountain bikes down the mountain, then ran and kayaked through Elverton. Ian and Rosemary's athletic daughter Diana and her teammate won the women's section.

The fertile river flats continue to grow the high-value, small-acreage crops, 5000 head of sheep, cattle, and deer graze the foothills and 40 per cent of the farm is native forests and tree plantations. The farm is a model of good management. What impresses me is the predominance of native and cultivated trees, the health of livestock and crops and the importance placed on conservation. The farm supports the Dickensons and four employees, as well as seasonal workers. 'If you have more than one string to your bow, you will ride out lower commodity prices better than somebody in a single enterprise. We have a cash flow from forestry because we're harvesting. We use it to reduce debt.'

Ian learned from the forestry debate that when the community doesn't understand an industry they pressure governments to take action, which can have devastating effects on that industry. 'Unless they understand the full picture, they can go off half-cocked. Then governments get spooked, and spooked governments make bad policy. It's extremely important to educate the next generation and the whole community.'

Elverton participates in the Adopt a Farm program. Four times a year students from St Leonard's primary school, where Rosemary teaches, visit the farm. Each child adopts a tree and learns about farming. Later they want to show their parents how their tree is growing. Children who can't concentrate long in classrooms blossom on the farm. Ian laughs as he recalls one visit when children saw a sheep with cancer of the nose. 'Quick as a flash, the teacher said, "That's what happens when you don't wear your hat in the sun." For the rest of the day they walked around with their hats pulled squarely down around their ears.'

Ian's own schooling was basic, so he listens to others, identifying good farmers and learning from them. One of these was the late John Allwright, a quiet, diplomatic man who headed the National Farmers' Federation in 1988 and successfully carried out the difficult job of amalgamating Tasmanian farm organisations. Ian was also influenced by Zimbabwean Allan Savory's book *Holistic Management: A New Framework for Decision Making* (Island Press, 1999), which considers humans, their economics and the environment as inseparable. 'We're trying to mimic the natural herd behaviour of wildlife. Savory describes how herds of North American bison move into a valley, graze it out in a week, move on, and may not return to that valley for a long time.' When I visited Elverton, large mobs of cattle stood knee-deep in strawberry clover. A week later, they moved to the next paddock so the pastures could recover. 'People either love or hate this idea. We adapt it to our conditions and get good results,' Ian says.

He describes himself as a 'string saver'. 'Our grandmothers hung bags in the laundry to save string. I have a philosophy of recycling and making things last.' He recycles hollow logs as culverts, rejected woodchip logs to make cattle yards and pine thinnings for farm fences. He shows me dead trees sawn off where they stand to form hefty strainer posts for fences, a disused quarry being recycled as a dam, land bridges formed for channelling animals between paddocks. The philosophy carries over to his farming. 'A seed company representative called in recently and asked how long I expected the permanent pasture to last. I told him, "It's permanent!" In developed countries, we often live as if there is no tomorrow.'

The principles of whole farm planning taught him to put the plans in his head on paper. 'It's a great discipline when others know about it, especially employees. For instance, they know that controlling weeds is a high priority here. We each carry bags and pull out new weeds that creep in with contractors' machinery.'

Achieving balance he regards as a community issue. 'We give social, environmental and economic concerns equal weight. If our farm is economically viable, then we can offer employment. Environmentally, we live in the Launceston water supply catchment area, so we have to be careful what we do on-farm to protect water quality.' He fences the streams to restrict livestock access and has noticed how cattle now follow the leader into watering spots, drink and then walk out, instead of loitering and muddying the stream and causing erosion.

'In the next five years we will get the farm as "bullet-proof" or financially secure as we can, and then Rosemary and I can spend more time away,' he says. This is a new phase for a man wedded to farming, who rarely takes holidays. Ian is disappointed that hard times have made his two children wary of taking on agriculture, but admits that 'it's a tough job if you like it, and impossible if you don't'.

He is optimistic about the Tasmanian forestry industry. 'It has a bright future. If we use our resources wisely, we can achieve the conservation goals of most of the community and have a viable forestry industry. We now need to focus on downstream processing and to value add to solid wood and particle board, and continue to focus on using wood residues such as the bark, limbs and leaves for energy production, instead of burning them.' He cites a company, Farmwood Tasmania, trialling small pieces of quickly dried hardwood for export to China as parquetry flooring. 'Australia can no longer live in isolation. Unless we understand world markets, we will continually walk up blind alleys.'

On a crisp autumn Sunday, I lunch at a cafe on top of Ben Lomond with Ian and his family. My head for heights is tested driving up the steep gravel road called Jacob's Ladder, round hairpin bends and past expansive wire nets that stop rockfalls. Ian mentions that he was contracted to grade this road once and the grader blade was wider than the road in some places. I need no more convincing that this man has the nerve to take on what others fear to touch. With a grin, he says he was blessed with a slow heart rate.

11 | One Land

Hugh Lovesy ~

The Money $tory™ crosses cultures

Sixty kilometres north of the South Australian border, we drive into Erldunda, gateway to Uluru. The expanse of red desert is interrupted by a service station crammed with caravans, campers and cars. In the crush of people filling cars at petrol pumps, eating pies, drinking cola, chasing children and rushing to the toilets, one person stands out. He is a lanky man with a broad smile on his tanned face, an English accent and a shock of platinum hair. As men do, my husband gets into a conversation about tyres and fuel consumption, and invites me over to meet Hugh Lovesy.

He is heading for Uluru, formerly called Ayers Rock, and the Mutitjulu Aboriginal community. His four-wheel drive is loaded with the Money $tory™, a pictorial accounting system that is simple to understand yet doesn't lose the complex meanings of financial concepts. We arrange to meet back in Alice Springs so I can find out about Hugh and his Money $tory™, and our 15-year-old Patrol soldiers on to Kings Canyon.

Pangaea, from the Greek meaning 'one land', is the evocative name of Hugh's company. He has a partner, Chris Fraser. Their business in downtown Alice calls for both ultra-modern computer technology and a well-honed understanding of cultural issues to provide indigenous people throughout the Centre and Top End with tools to 'take back their power' by improving the level of their self-management.

From a 1950s childhood in an English village, Storrington, tucked up against the escarpment of the South Downs in county Sussex, Hugh proceeded to immerse himself in different cultures for much of his 53 years. He studied psychology at Trinity College, Dublin, moved to Australia with his family when he was a teenager in 1970, and then learned to understand Indian and Aboriginal cultures.

'When I was in my twenties I didn't have much direction,' he says. 'That was lucky. I had an inner direction to follow the spiritually right things of life, but I'm not a Christian. I believe spirituality is a manifestation of something deep and vast. I look at my life and say, "What do I want to do?" Now I'm doing the most natural thing in the world—living in central Australia. There's still a lot of freedom here. It's easier to be independent.' He has followed his own path and is not afraid to take chances, yet says life is about people co-operating and trading part of their individuality to function in a wider society.

Money has played a crucial role in his life. 'My grandfather was incredibly rich, one of three brothers who invested in cinemas and retired in their thirties, never having to work again. My father went from being rich to poor to rich, but was never happy from his riches. When he died, we found he had no money. I was 17 then and at medical school. I had to leave it to work and never went back. It was a hard time. I learned that riches don't bring you happiness; it's your internal state. That's a lesson I've never forgotten. Conversely, I learned the value of material things in India when people were dying and couldn't afford medicine.'

In 1977, he went to India and learnt Hindi. He was interested in Indian philosophy, and practised and taught transcendental meditation with the Maharishi Mahesh Yogi—famed for his work with the Beatles—living where the sacred Ganges River comes out onto the plain at Rishikesh, 'place of sages', north of the capital, New Delhi.

Flying back to Australia from India, Hugh sat next to a man who offered him work back in India. It turned out to be a disorganised setup, but gave him the idea to start a locally registered charitable organisation called the Society for Rural Development, funded by the Indian government and aid organisations. For the next six years he worked in remote Rajasthani villages in the desert country of north-west India developing programs for women, agriculture, the education of barefoot doctors and social awareness. On issues such as child marriages or people being exploited, he would stage puppet shows, entertainment with a message. 'It was a watershed in my life,' he reflects.

Hugh had to learn self-reliance and how to take hard decisions. He got involved with a family who tried to take over his organisation. 'I was not so experienced then, and I trusted them. I found out signatures were forged to misappropriate society funds. In gathering evidence against these people so we could take legal action, they responded with a trumped-up murder charge and bribed the local police inspector to write the police report. I constantly thought I would be arrested. I took the case to the High Court in India. I didn't run away. I couldn't have lived with myself if I had. I had won almost all the court battles when Prime Minister Indira Gandhi was assassinated in October 1984. In the turmoil that followed, these people made sure my visa wasn't renewed. I wanted to stay, but the government deported me. I had the conceit to think I understood another culture. I learned that there are many different levels of understanding. It's like peeling away layers of an onion and it can be dangerous to assume you've reached the centre.'

In 1984, Hugh Lovesy came back to Australia. He was faced with a career choice: a job with a regional television station or becoming community adviser at Mimili in the Pitjantjatjara lands of north-west South Australia. He chose Mimili, a former cattle station called Everard Park, owned by the Jocelyn family and bought in 1973 by the Federal government for the local Pitjantjatjara and Yankunytjara Aboriginal people. The Jocelyn children returned when Hugh was there. They spoke Pitjantjatjara and there was obvious respect and friendship between them and the people. Everard Park had been their home too, but the historical process was reversing, and now the Aboriginal people welcomed them back.

India had taught Hugh to be sensitive to local conditions. 'If you don't acknowledge those, you won't have success. You can't expect a blanket development program to work. In central Australia you've got different Aboriginal nations such as Aranda and Pitjantjatjara. They seem all the same to us, but it's like the different countries in Europe.

'I loved Mimili,' he says. 'The granite hills looked like they had been squeezed out of a tube of toothpaste, red and rounded. Very red soil. I lived in the old homestead, a huge wooden L-shaped building set among river gums and athol pines. Another community worker and I used to joke that we had to take a packed lunch to get from the bedrooms to the kitchen.' Gradually a community of houses, a clinic and store had been built up around the homestead.

On his first day, four old men took him through the basic ABC of their sacred sites, places they thought he needed to see, told him the 'stories' and explained how this would underpin his role as community adviser. 'They said, "You are here to help us protect our culture." They meant the philosophy and spirituality of their culture.

'I was deeply shocked after India at how poor community development was in Australia. Governments were ill-equipped to work across cultures because they focused on material outcomes, putting in few resources and not encouraging local ownership. They assumed that dealing with Aboriginal people was like dealing with mainstream society, not understanding that extra resources and higher levels of staff skills were needed.'

He arrived at the end of an era. Many older people spoke only Pitjantjatjara. 'It's a hard language to learn well,' Hugh says, but he did learn to speak it fluently so he could communicate with them. Many of the old people died in the next few years. Being community adviser was a key job with a foot in both worlds of traditional Aboriginal and non-Aboriginal culture, responsible for administration of the community. 'Mimili was a wonderful place to work, under relatively less pressure from mainstream society because it was small and remote.

'The pace of change in Aboriginal society is so fast that it causes immense stresses. Many people in mainstream culture see Aboriginal culture as not so different from Western culture, so to them Aboriginal people seem slow to learn and change. In fact, Aboriginal culture is very different, with far greater emphasis on social obligations, for instance. The pressure on traditional culture to change is great. How fast can something change without disintegrating? From the Aboriginal perspective, I imagine such fast and externally driven change must be very unsettling. Aboriginal people have to learn fast just to survive, and it requires a great deal of intelligence, ability and power to survive the stress.' Hugh likens the different perceptions of change to a car travelling a long way away in the desert. 'It seems to be coming slowly until it roars past at 140 kilometres an hour. Then you realise how fast it's going. The people in that car are like traditional Aboriginal culture hurtling along at great speed, but in non-Aboriginal eyes it's like seeing the car a long way off. It seems to be moving slowly. Those who are near the car as it passes have some idea of how fast cultural change is progressing.'

As in India, Hugh was a 'foreigner' coming into other people's country. 'To get on, I had to realise that,' he said. 'Most non-Aboriginal people who go to Mimili take their head space from somewhere else with them, but this is these people's land. Why should they change? A lot of Aboriginal people are very perceptive. They say, "The world is changing, we've got to change, but we want to do it our way." I had to fit into two worlds. White people were a small minority in Mimili, the reverse of mainstream Australian society, where they form the majority. You have to try to satisfy both cultures, but you can't do it. Values clash all the time. That's why it was so full of tension. I used to mix with Aborigines and sit at their campfires more than other whites did.'

After the first six months Hugh could see that money was the most destructive influence on Mimili life and culture. It permeated every aspect. 'Before money, everything was rationed to Aboriginal people on stations. They didn't understand how money worked in Western society. Then State and Federal governments put millions of dollars into communities. If you gave someone a car and they couldn't drive, wouldn't you give them driving lessons?' He is exasperated at such blindness. 'People were, and are, having to make decisions about millions of dollars without the necessary skills. Could the average city person do that? I doubt it.'

Traditionally the old people were the decision-makers, but they spoke their own languages. Hugh says governments put in white people who scribbled figures on boards and spoke English. 'What happened was that the young fellows who spoke English gained control, which put a strain on them, and skewed the social and power structure. It's easy to typecast people. They might be naïve in our world, but we're naïve in their world. These people have wisdom. I thought there must be a way to get through the core concepts of financial management to these people. If you look at competency-based learning, you look at outcomes. Can you fix a car? If you didn't read and write, and could see through pictures how to fix a car, then to some extent you could be a mechanic. That's how I got into the Money $tory™. I was thinking about it so long, it boiled up in my brain.' He is animated at the memory. 'One long weekend it all poured out and basically I had it worked out. The creative process works like that. It possesses you, in a way.'

Hugh was obviously onto an idea brilliant in its simplicity and clarity. He developed a collection of pictures on graphs to illustrate fundamental accounting concepts. For instance, a hand holding up a dollar note represents salaries, a car with a bowser means fuel. The financial year is depicted by seasons relevant to the area. The up-to-date spending on budget items is represented by different colours—blue underspent, red overdrawn, and sad and happy faces summing up the financial situation. It is an exciting concept, particularly for those to whom a standard financial balance sheet is a complete mystery. I can see its relevance to my own small business or a big organisation.

'The Money $tory™ became a cornerstone in self-management,' Hugh says. 'It gave power back to the local people. At first people told Bill Gates the computer wizard that his concepts were too simple and only children would use his icons. Look what happened! Once I'd worked it out, the key was to produce it every month. We had a good accountant, Peter Rowe. All our accounts went down to him at the end of every month. Within a few days he would send back a Money $tory™ every single month without fail. People could see it. They would have to make choices. Once they wanted to get a Toyota. There was incredible social pressure. I said, "I'm your adviser and I've never said no to you. I'm not going to say no to you today, but I advise you not to. I'm leaving the meeting and whatever you decide, I respect that. It's your decision." I thought, "They're going to do it", but I had to trust my faith in what I'd been doing. They called me back three-quarters of an hour later, all laughing, and said, "We're not going to buy it." They had worked through the Money $tory™ to see when they could get the money and had come to the conclusion they couldn't. That was like my Rubicon: to have faith to let go. I was so relieved,' he laughs.

Hugh had good reason to be proud of the workability of the Money $tory™, even under challenging conditions. He found that diesel fuel was an area of chronic overspending, so he added a Money $tory™ for fuel with a weekly, not a monthly target. The Aboriginal community chairman was in charge. When the chairman made decisions on fuel orders, he had to wear two hats: one the 'white man' hat of keeping expenditure under control and not breaking government rules, the other the Aboriginal society hat of being accountable to relatives who had the right to ask for favours. 'He learnt to juggle these and to compromise,' says Hugh.

In a subtle way, Hugh tried to train government officers to discuss concerns with the chairman instead of with him. Hugh sat at a small desk with a small wooden chair behind the chairman, who was at a big smart desk with a big smart chair. The chairman wore R.M. Williams jeans, stockman's boots and a battered old Akubra hat with a high crown. He hardly ever took his hat off. 'He was a careful listener and communicator, and had an even temperament when things got tough. If government officers couldn't talk to the chairman, how could they talk to the community? So in the nicest way I made them talk to him. I learned from Mimili people to be so polite,' he grins.

'My father, a lawyer, once told me about a man who came into his office. "That man is a millionaire several times over," he said, "but he can't read or write. He is smart. He uses good accountants and he comes to me." It made me think. Aboriginal people are smart. They can manage, as long as people present information to them in an appropriate way.'

When Hugh stopped being community adviser and became Mimili store manager, the next person did not continue the Money $tory™. 'The people came and asked me to do it, but I couldn't interfere. However, I think the effect flowed over to other things because people are happier and more self-confident. Petrol sniffing is almost non-existent in Mimili. They are much more sophisticated in dealing with the outside world, but they haven't lost their pride and sense of self-worth. The day-to-day problems are hard.' He describes his own frustration as store manager, seeing the impact of insidious diseases such as adult-onset diabetes. 'A major factor in the high incidence of this disease is the large amount of sugar-laden soft drinks consumed by Aboriginal people. I remember confronting a Coca-Cola salesman and asking him, "How do you feel pushing products that contribute to incredible health problems and death in these remote communities?"' The man just shrugged, amazed at Hugh's audacity.

He feels that many people vastly underestimate the importance, in cross-cultural situations, of making sure they are communicating clearly and are not being misunderstood. 'Along with their normal work skills, they also need to develop good listening skills,' he says. 'Many otherwise intelligent people seem completely oblivious to the fact that clear communication and a shared understanding are the very foundations of getting good results. For instance, some people have the misconception that because someone is sitting in the dirt, eating kangaroo tail and sharpening a spear, and doesn't speak English well, they are unintelligent.

'Once I went to a place where the Aboriginal people wanted to try the Money $tory™. They had really blown their budget. The white town clerk was hopping about. After about ten minutes, this Aboriginal man got up and said, "Excuse me, can I say something?" He clicked to the Money $tory™ straight away.

' "You see 'im red line going too far over that red line going down [year to date budget line], some of those ones they low," he said. "We shift that red line, push them other ones up and then we make 'em more level in other places..." In other words, reallocation of resources,' Hugh laughs. 'I was so pleased because the community people were following him, saying, "Yeah, that's right." '

'The town clerk said, "Can you sit down, please? Now we have to talk about reallocating resources," in a pushy voice, and started using all these long words. Nobody had a clue what he was talking about. He disempowered them and they never used the Money $tory™.'

But Hugh's nature is to focus on the good and positive aspects of people and situations. He quotes former South African president Nelson Mandela, who said, 'After 28 years in prison, I don't have one minute to waste on negativity.'

After ten years at Mimili, Hugh moved to Alice Springs in 1994 to set up Pangaea, based on principles of integrity, openness and respect. It specialises in 'the design and presentation of clear information that inspires understanding between people'. He and his partner, Chris Fraser, whom he met when he worked as a nurse 100 kilometres west of Mimili, have expanded the Money $tories and financial management training to provide Health Stories to groups grappling with the proper management of money.'

I came across a good example of how health issues can be portrayed, and of how far Pangaea's ideas have spread, during my interview with 71-year-old Jack Little at Bulla community in the Top End (see chapter 5). He is vice president of the all-Aboriginal Katherine West Health Board, which administers several million dollars annually. Jack disappeared inside his house and returned triumphantly bearing a laminated picture of the Board's story. Hugh had listened to their issues and illustrated them pictorially. 'Look!' said Jack. 'This is how we community and government people can listen to each other and work hand in hand.'

Hugh Lovesy says the problem for Aboriginal people is 'pressure and more pressure. They must go nuts.' He rattles off a list of 'negatives' that outsiders see: 'Some say, "Your kids are so sick." Others say, "You're not learning fast enough", or "What's happening with the Community Development Employment Program wages?" The message is, "You're not getting it together." This approach is different, asking, "How can I make this information live in this person's head, so they own it and can pass it on and it can be living in that group?" Otherwise what have I done?' Hugh says.

'Two years ago there was a Pitjantjatjara Council meeting. They asked me to do a Money $tory™. I said, "Fine, as long as the chairman, Wilton Foster, does it." Council accountant Mike Donahoo agreed. The chairman gave the Money $tory™ to the people. Whenever he got stuck, he would look at one of us and we would support him. When Wilton finished, everyone clapped, because they had been told the truth in a way they could understand. When there were problems, they discussed them openly, without anger or blame, and looked at how to solve them. It's not just about telling a Money $tory™; it's about bringing a message of hope. "We can do it in our own way and be equally valued." That's a true act of reconciliation.

'We're on a winner when we get in at seven o'clock at night and say to a community, "We'll look at the Money $tory™ in the morning", and they say, "No, no, no, we're having the meeting now," It's a delicate thing going into communities. Usually community members really love the Money $tory™, but to keep things going you also need a long chain of support from white staff and government departments.'

It takes a long time to win the trust of Aboriginal communities, says Warren Bretag, a friend of Hugh's from Mimili days. 'People there think of Hugh as family. Community co-ordinators usually turn over every nine to twelve months. He stayed ten years. They still call him up to discuss concerns and ask his advice. He is like a pool of deep water, strong and philosophical, a moral man.' Hugh reflects that he is motivated mainly by inner goals, but he tries to balance his heart and his intellect.

He says education is important for Aboriginal people, 'but it has to be done right without destroying the core of their identity. We tend to confuse the ability to read and write with the wisdom of life. I see the future working where things are going to succeed. If rain falls on rock, you won't get a crop. Plant in your best fields. You have to think deeply and act simply. It is a fine balance between helping people and encouraging them to become more self-reliant, not getting caught up in the emotional baggage such as the guilt non-Aborigines may have towards Aboriginal people, or over-romanticising them, or ignoring the differences.'

The Money $tory™ has just begun. It is used in 15 organisations in central Australia, three in the Top End and one in Cape York, all of which are involved in Hugh's training. He thinks it has potential to spread around the world. 'Doing things with integrity and enjoying life is more important than success,' he yells over the roar of his motorbike, as he tucks his white hair under a slick black helmet for a dash to the gym. 'In the modern world, how lucky I am to work from Alice Springs. And why couldn't I work worldwide from here? Why not?'

12 | Fighting Broken-down Cocky Syndrome

Fran Rowe ~

Going in to bat for farmers

'It's in the centre of New South Wales,' Fran Rowe told me. I keep driving west from Condobolin as dusk falls. Along 120 kilometres of gravel roads I pass pigs and kangaroos but not a single car, and see the lights of only two houses. The second one is Fran's farmhouse, Bombah. She is indeed isolated. Yet by 1986 she was the centre of a rural counselling service, the Lachlan Advisory Group that covered the whole state. The back roads of New South Wales were her second home as Fran, in the long-suffering family car, beetled off in a cloud of dust to advise struggling farm families. Her management committee was made up of farmers like her who volunteered their help. On Fran's mantelpiece sits a statue of an angel inscribed, 'St Frances of Bombah', a gift from her committee.

The Rowes have just returned from Sydney, a six-hour journey, and Fran is already answering phone calls. 'Watch out for mice. There's a plague,' echoes down the wood-panelled hall of the rambling old house. I check under the lacy white pillows of the four-poster guest bed. An ideal nesting spot. Over the next 12 hours I discover that Fran's life revolves around her phone, her clients and her husband, Peter. She is not easily distracted by incidentals such as food and sleep, but she gives her entire attention to our interview, listening so intently I can almost hear her brain whirr, with thoughtful pauses before replying, frequent husky laughs, her hands stressing points, at ease being photographed. Clients arrive and normal business continues as it does in any professional office—only it is miles from anywhere in a small room of an otherwise remote homestead.

I first met Fran Rowe in 1991, when she gave an inspiring presentation in my home town, Molong. A slight, red-headed, black-suited person hurried into the room, contrasting with the rows of male farmers. She had their undivided attention when she scrawled FART across the whiteboard, her expression deadpan. Those in the front rows smirked. 'What's the matter?' she said, as laughter filled the hall when FART turned out to stand for Financial Advice in Rough Times. I soon learned this was vintage Fran Rowe—grab attention, then deal with the matter at hand. A group of us had asked her to help us set up a financial counselling service for our region's cash-strapped farmers. People queued to talk to her afterwards, to draw strength from her down-to-earth, compassionate spirit and knowledge. She stayed with my family that night, hotly debating issues of the world from her smoker's perch on the back step, glass of red at hand and easily outlasting our other guest, Cathy McGowan (see chapter 7), and I.

Fran was in demand. Embattled farmers, bemused politicians, hard-nosed bankers and inquiring public servants beat a path to her door. Farmers wanted her for financial counselling, the New South Wales government wanted her on the Rural Assistance Authority, and she became its first woman chair. The Federal government wanted her on the Rural Adjustment Scheme Advisory Council, television personality Ray Martin wanted her for the Farmhand Appeal that raised millions of dollars for drought relief, and I, as New South Wales Rural Women's Network co-ordinator, wanted her on our State Advisory Committee.

Fran has been shaped by her battler background. She was born in Melbourne in 1946. Her parents separated when she was a toddler and, unusually for those times, her father was given custody of his two small daughters. Without a mother, her grandmother became her anchor. Her childhood memories are hazy. 'My father had to work,' she says. 'It was difficult for him. I was cared for by my grandmother, and also spent some time in an orphanage before my father remarried. I remember voices singing "Ave Maria" in the Grotto of Our Lady of Fatima at St Aiden's orphanage. I remember holding out my pinny and the older children piling in tomatoes. The smell of ripe tomatoes hit my nostrils. It isn't a time I felt comfortable questioning my father about. He felt great shame. My grandmother, both parents and my sister are all dead, so it's too late for questions.'

Her older sister Maureen later chose to live with their mother. Fran was brought up as her father's daughter and didn't meet her mother again until her teenage years. Fran looked up to Maureen as beautiful and intelligent, but saw the bitterness left by their parents' divorce. 'I saw her die of lung cancer at 52, still looking back. I too had an unhappy childhood, but her anguish taught me that you are responsible for the way you live. Stop wallowing! It's better to try and constructively use those experiences.

'I loved school, but left at 14 because I had to earn my own living,' she says. Unskilled, she made boxes on the factory floor of a Bendigo woollen mill. Fran's circle of friends consisted of teenagers who paired off, married young and had babies. She too wanted a family of her own and was quickly swept into the downward spiral of a disastrous marriage at 17, two young children and depression. 'The only thing I did worthwhile in those years was go to night school and complete my Intermediate and Leaving Certificates by correspondence through the Royal Melbourne Institute of Technology, because I resented leaving school so much,' she says.

I feel privileged to be allowed into this distant world of Fran's sadness and hardship. It is painful for her, but she speaks without regret and with care for the feelings of others. Knowing the trauma of the effects of divorce on children, Fran agonised about leaving her violent marriage. She finally did and moved to Melbourne. There were no marriage settlements then. Desperate for money, better working conditions and a home for her children, she learned to type. 'I was a dreadful typist, disgusting,' she admits. 'I used to take invoices home, type them that night and sneak them back into the office the next morning.' But she learned fast, and it wasn't long before she was promoted from the typing pool to sales co-ordinator. By 1970, working at three jobs, Fran had saved the deposit for a house, only to discover that she needed a husband's signature to obtain a loan. That was her first experience of the injustices that can occur in the financial system and negotiating with banks. The State Bank of Victoria eventually lent her the money without a guarantor.

Meanwhile a gentle and patient man, Peter Rowe, had entered her life. Fran met him in Victoria, but with the memory of her short disastrous marriage and a busy life, including studying for an Economics degree through the University of New England, it was ten years before they went to Armidale, hired two students as witnesses, and walked out of the registry office married. 'The family were never quite sure if we got married,' she chuckles. Peter's parents and the newlyweds owned a farm at Baan Baa, near Narrabri in north-west New South Wales, which the younger Rowes managed. 'It was the first time since I was 14 that I hadn't worked for a wage.' She made a home for her daughters, city-raised Kathleen and Jenny, and had her two 'bush kids', Sarah and Anna. Although brought up in cities, she had always felt connected to the country. 'I soon learned to roll my eyes skyward and ask, "How much rain have you had?" she laughs.

'Life on the farm promised to be free of drama.' It was a fond hope. As Fran became involved in farm finances and learned about balance sheets, profit and loss statements and cash flows, she could see the property was unviable. The family also had to deal with the complexities of being locked into business with an older generation. As Fran said: 'If we stayed in partnership, what would happen if Peter's father died and his share was divided between all children? How would we manage to pay these siblings out? What were his parents' intentions?' Peter wanted to farm his way. The family sold out and Fran and Peter used their share to buy cheaper land in central west New South Wales on the western edge of the wheat belt to grow wheat.

Many farmers and bankers believed that 'after drought years come good years', when you were able to wipe off the drought overdraft. The rules changed with the drought of 1982, bringing a new sense of vulnerability. The following year, 1983, looked promising; farmers purchased additional land or machinery, thereby increasing their debt, and then the season changed dramatically. A wet grain harvest brought poor returns and the combination of financial deregulation, interest rate hikes and a collapse in commodity prices spelt trouble that affected everybody. Government services were geared to urban, not rural problems; farmers shut their strife behind the farm gate. It seemed as if nobody could help, or cared.

In 1984, the Rowes had borrowed $190 000 at 12 per cent interest to buy their 2420 hectares west of Tottenham. They prepared a ten-year plan and projected cash flows for future viability. By 1985 their interest rate had spiralled to 23.75 per cent and annual repayments leaped to $40 000, double their predicted budget. With their large borrowings on underdeveloped land, along came the dreaded letter from the bank—'no further assistance' on the overdraft. Fran recalls her passion for a bit of red dirt. 'I thought, "I am *not* leaving." I believe each experience better prepared me to help those who feel powerless, and that fate or He up there sent me this stage.'

Farmers' organisations, even some other farmers, viewed those in difficulty as being inefficient. At a local NSW Farmers' meeting a lone voice challenged this attitude. With knees knocking, Fran Rowe stood to speak of how 'efficiency' depended on the timing of your last property or machinery purchase and what happened with interest rates after that. She said her husband *was* efficient and how crippling it was to service a debt then at 23.75 per cent. She shared her feelings of frustration, anger and isolation when faced by financial difficulties caused by factors beyond her family's control. Her experience paralleled that of many others; outside afterwards, people quietly thanked her for speaking out. The next day farmers began to call. Fran had inadvertently begun the first counselling service for farmers in New South Wales.

Right time, right person, right place. She was soon swamped with calls from desperate families, often women talking for the first time of drought, debt and their husband's despair. 'Men felt failures, that they were letting down previous generations. It placed real strains on family relationships. My case work was typed on a rickety manual typewriter. Pete had to tie the carriage back on with a leather shoelace. The desk was borrowed from my father-in-law and our personal cash flow groaned under the extra costs of stationery, stamps, fuel and telephone. Now I look back and think "all passion, no skills",' says Fran. Anger at injustice and empathy for others' grief and pain fired her commitment to counselling. She listened as farmers expressed their concerns and gave concrete help in looking at their cash flows, exploring financial options, negotiating with banks and applying for appropriate support and assistance measures.

Farmers were irate in the mid-1980s. Their talk was militant. They dumped wheat and cow dung on the steps of city banks, and hundreds marched on Canberra. 'I learned quickly that many were not going to survive and would face the hardest decision of all—to leave the farm,' says Fran. 'I have seen how eviction tears a family apart. They remain in the past, always looking back at what might have been. I met a man in his nineties who had lost his farm in the Depression years. He moved from crisis meeting to crisis meeting warning farmers, "Don't let them take your farm." He believed that the survivors would be those who hung in there.' There were 45 bank foreclosure notices in Fran's area alone.

On the national front, the pretence that all would be well vanished. The word 'crisis' was allowed out of its box and demanded Federal government action. Fran was invited to Canberra, part of a select group to advise the government. They recommended a national rural counselling program, launched in 1986. After nearly two years of volunteering her skills and energy she was now paid to offer a free service to battling farmers. 'I had a strong bond with clients because I think people "smell" empathy and are then more open to you, and you can help. I saw that if families were supported through the grieving process to make their own decision to leave, and were not forced into it by banks, they could move forward to a better life.

'One young family visited me to talk through the pain of facing the impending death of a child,' says Fran. They were also struggling with drought in the north-west and the financial pressures of meeting interest rate payments. As she listened to them she realised that they felt obliged to continue farming for the family's sake, but really wanted a life outside agriculture. The husband had always dreamed of joining the army. Fran suggested bringing together all those family members with an interest in the farm. It became clear that the husband's parents also felt obliged to keep the farm, thinking their son wanted to stay. They went ahead with its sale and discovered there was life after farming. The young ex-farmer graduated from the army with distinction as best recruit and best rifleman. The counselling experience had helped them communicate with each other, understand their finances and be prepared to adjust to change.

'Back then the majority of farmers didn't budget, didn't maintain financial records, and revered their banker,' she recalls. Bankers felt threatened by Fran as she stepped into their territory. Learning their language and using their tools, she negotiated forcefully on behalf of clients. They would come to see her with their screwed-up letters from banks, and she would look for common ground to show clients where they had power to negotiate. When asked by a Rural Press journalist how he survived the bad years, a West Wyalong farmer replied, 'Fran Rowe taught me to think like a banker.' She is reluctant to accept the accolade. 'Most of the resolutions with which I am credited actually came from farmers driving tractors, thinking through their alternatives. I was the interpreter presenting their proposals in commercial terms to bankers.' She educated bankers to avoid being judgmental, search for options and understand why families might deny the realities of debt and feel angry and frustrated.

Stoicism ruled among farmers, especially the men, in the 1980s. Emotions were a female domain. A worried man came to see Fran. 'I identified strong options for avoiding bankruptcy and adjusting out of farming,' she says. 'I thought he understood. *I* had a warm, fuzzy glow, but he sat there, wringing his hat. "Anything else?" I asked.

'"Yes," he said. "I feel dreadful. I've got BDCS, Broken-down Cocky Syndrome."'

She knew what he meant. He had sought help through mental health services, but they didn't understand that the cycle of grief and loss applied to losing a farm as well as when a loved one died. Fran spent time explaining to these urban-trained service providers what farmers were going through and that they needed support to deal with the loss of an occupation, a lifestyle, a home and heritage. 'They began to recognise a rural face to poverty and to see that the "front" of a solid house and acres didn't necessarily mean riches,' she says.

In 1987 Fran Rowe became the first woman whose achievements were recognised by the Ronald Anderson award, proudly inscribed 'Man of the Year in Agriculture'. 'A significant moment for women in agriculture,' Fran dryly observed to hoots of laughter at the first NSW Women of the Land gathering in Orange in 1993.

The Rowes see-sawed through the 'horror years', as Peter calls them, until 1989, when stringent belt-tightening and two dream wheat crops helped wipe out their debt. By 1992, Fran was dashing around New South Wales servicing more than 250 clients. She helped other communities set up counselling services and trained new counsellors. The pace was frenetic. Smoking incessantly, eating and sleeping little, rarely seeing her family, she was forced to take stock. She decided to base herself at home, which reduced the travel and gave her time with the family. She whittled her daily agenda and learned to say 'no', but quickly adds, with a laugh, 'That's not yet perfected.'

In January 1995 an unprecedented 98 per cent of New South Wales was drought-declared. By then the quality of life, health of the land and finances, and maintenance of equipment had deteriorated for many farmers. Governments provided money to meet living needs of families as well as interest rate subsidies, and the public generously supported farmers through appeals such as Farmhand. One of the few growth areas was in rural counselling services, which in New South Wales grew from the original core of six to more than 30 in eight years. As drought abated, government focus shifted to education in financial management.

Fran believes that the crisis years from the mid-1980s to late 1995 made Australian agriculture change forever. The *2000 Year Book Australia* published by the Australian Bureau of Statistics, supports her view: 'By the mid-1990s Australian agriculture contributed only around 3 per cent to Gross Domestic Product (GDP), down from 15 to 20 per cent in the early 1950s. The rural sector's contribution to total exports had dropped from around 75 per cent to 28 per cent.' Agriculture now accounts for 4.4 per cent of Australia's employment, down significantly from 10 per cent in the 1950s. By 1998, 375,000 were employed in the sector, nearly two-thirds as owners/partners and the remainder as employees. Fewer young people are entering agriculture, reflected in a median age of 44 years for farmers compared to 38 years of age for those employed in all industries.

On the positive side, Fran says farmers have become much more financially sophisticated. 'There is no longer the "shoebox mentality". If you travel along our Bobadah Road, you would be hard-pressed to find a family that doesn't maintain computerised records. They have developed their power to negotiate. They understand that the banker is not God behind a desk, and seek independent advice.' The impact of further education on farm productivity has been marked. *Australian Agriculture* sixth edition 1997/98, a National Farmers' Federation publication, states: 'Farm businesses that have management teams who hold agricultural qualifications (estimated at 15 per cent), have a mean average operating surplus of $85 024, compared with $58 768 for farm businesses without these qualifications.' Farm businesses participating in at least one training event yearly also have a higher gross operating surplus ($68 102), compared with those who have not attended any training ($39 788).

Another legacy of the crisis years was that farmers wanted to repair family relationships strained by the past decade of concentrating on repaying the banks. As well as financial stresses, Fran's case notes describe the stark realities of marriage breakdown and attempted suicide. She looks forward to the day when rural adjustment policy-makers take into account the importance of social factors to farm business decisions. 'So often they assume that profit, or the lack of it, is the prime motivation in adjustment,' she says.

The stories Fran hears today are not of drought, interest rates and bank pressure, but farm families who have experienced fair to average years and are still finding the going tough because of 'the cost/price squeeze'. 'Many clients are now considering the future of farming and examining whether the farm can support the future generations,' she says. 'Some perceive farming is losing its attraction as an independent lifestyle and question government's and the broader community's interference in the business of farming. The service based at Bombah still cannot satisfy demand and my working hours are long. I'm always behind.'

In 2000, the Lachlan Advisory Group (LAG) broadened its focus to work with other local groups for community development. Like many rural communities, the Condobolin district is identifying its potential for growth and development in response to challenges such as isolation, population decline, the withdrawal of rural services and drug and alcohol abuse. 'We don't just want to survive, we want to prosper,' says Fran. Supported by the University of Western Sydney's Hawkesbury campus, LAG did a social audit of businesses, townsfolk, Aboriginal people, youth and retirees, as well as the farming community. 'Our district wants employment opportunities. We want to develop tourism. We want our youth to have a future,' says Fran.

Today Fran is well known; she has come a long way from her first public appearance in 1985 when she went to bed for the day in sheer terror. 'The passion remains, the skills have developed. Most farmers look at me in disbelief when I tell them what fun we're going to have analysing their figures! I love problem-solving and helping people to become productive Australians beyond what can seem insurmountable difficulties.' Her well-honed ability to see both sides of a situation makes her not only an outstanding counsellor, but a canny political animal and forceful negotiator for rural Australia through the thorny paths of government and financial institutions.

'I don't like adversarial politics,' she says. 'I would like to see more emphasis on political parties working together to create a better country, instead of maintaining power. Compassion has been taken out of the big picture. I know some people may not overcome the barriers. As a nation, we have a responsibility to support them by having a welfare safety net in place.' Fran herself is fuelled by an over-abundance of compassion. She believes that fate stepped in, moulding her into what she is now—strong despite a painful childhood, armed with a formidable range of skills despite leaving school early, finding happiness despite a harmful first marriage. 'Each experience prepared me to better understand those facing difficult circumstances, and left me with the strong belief that we are in control of our own destiny.

'I'm a workaholic, which is disdained as an inability to balance pleasure and work in your life. But my work is my pleasure,' she laughs in her throaty way. 'I feel privileged to get paid to do something that I absolutely love, and to work with people I really care about.'

Triumph of
the Spirit

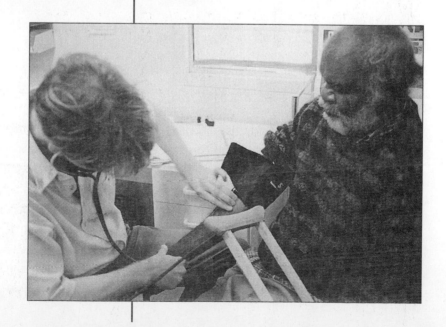

13 | Top End, Top Cattle

Carol and John Armstrong ~
The challenges of isolation

'Carol and I started Gilnockie from scratch in 1985,' says John Armstrong. 'It was 1000 square miles on the Sturt Plateau, totally undeveloped and pristine— no house, no fences and no roads. Carol camped here with the children, without a decent airstrip or road. Her only contact was a radio. Lifting the kids out of a safe environment with their mates at Victoria River Downs to open scrub was probably dangerous. We thought if they wandered off, we'd never find them, but they adapted well.'

Carol spent every second day checking the 200-kilometre boundary fence for stray cattle or feral animals while John was 300 kilometres away at Victoria River Downs managing operations for a company called Heli-Muster in the state-wide Brucellosis and Tuberculosis Eradication Campaign. He would camp with his family when he could. During his flying career John notched up 25 000 hours in helicopters and fixed-wing aircraft, a feat matched by only a handful of pilots in Australia.

Carol and John Armstrong live on a cattle station, Gilnockie, in the Northern Territory, 260 kilometres southwest of the nearest town, Katherine. I first met Carol in 1993 at a national meeting where she represented the Territory Women's Advisory Council and spoke eloquently about a world apart for most Australians—the concerns of outback people, huge distances, poor roads, lack of services, loneliness. Over a meal the vivacious, dark-haired woman told me of her pilot husband, their dream to build Gilnockie station for their three children and the strength of friendships in remote areas.

This is a story of a couple's courage, determination and love, often in isolated circumstances and separated from each other. For these remarkable people, community involvement is in their own vast backyard, the whole state and on the national stage.

o o o

In July 1999 I have a chance to see the Armstrongs and their dream. Our family Patrol grinds over deeply rutted roads, carved up by road trains in the last Wet. The entrance road is 50 kilometres through scrub burnt out in a recent bushfire. A mob of pale grey Brahman cattle loiter under trees. Three bulls lie in a small paddock chewing their cud, ignoring the mob. The long, low homestead on a gentle rise behind them is framed in purple and white bougainvillea. Beside the house, like square, shiny guardians against aerial attack, solar panels that power the house and electric fences turn to face the sun. There is a helicopter parked like a farm ute beside the garage.

Its pilot emerges from a well-equipped office at the back door. John Armstrong is a no-nonsense man, tall, good-looking, used to action. With a firm handshake, straight gaze and gruff 'gidday', he propels us into his ute to inspect Gilnockie, while Carol shows the ropes to house-minders. The Armstrongs are preparing for a week away to co-ordinate 700 competitors at the annual Katherine Campdraft Rodeo, one of their many community involvements.

We head through open bushland along a well-formed road following miles of fences. During his 50 years on the land, John has learned how to deal with wild animals Crocodile Dundee-style, shouldering away docile creatures crowding around as he unloads a protein supplement lick for stock in the dry season. From under a battered old hat he describes his early life, in a matter-of-fact drawl.

A shy, introverted kid wearing 'bloody great glasses all the time' to correct astigmatism and a squint, John grew up on a mixed farm near Toowoomba in Queensland. He absorbed aviation 'every second day' from his World War II fighter pilot father, and kept a scrapbook of aviation events. He has an incredible memory for facts and figures. 'At precisely 7.10pm one Wednesday evening, I remember being out on the lawn searching the sky for Sputnik 1 at the 10.30 o'clock position from a reference mark Dad had. It arrived right to the second.

'I rode a little fat pony to school and had to learn to balance ride standing in the irons. It's one reason I fly the way I do, not getting too excited when I'm half upside down. I daydreamed about being a pilot, but with this eyesight problem I never thought I would. I always felt insecure and used to have nightmares of falling.' John was at boarding school in Brisbane when the first 727 jet arrived. He rode a friend's pushbike 19 kilometres to the airport to watch the landing. 'I noticed the pilot had glasses. I thought, "If he can wear glasses, so can I", and headed resolutely towards aviation. Later, when I applied for a Commonwealth Flying Scholarship, for which I needed a commercial medical, the doctor failed me because of my eyesight. It was devastating at the time, but I finally passed the medical in the United States in 1979. That was a greater achievement than actually flying.' John and Carol had risked all their cash on John's commercial licence.

On a central Queensland property when he was 20, John learned about mind control of animals. 'Cattle have always fascinated me. It's being aware of their moods, already looking at and mentally dominating the flighty ones before they look at you, just before they want to run. They look at the strongest personality in the stock camp first, usually the head stockman. It's a mental challenge like when you feel someone looking at you. They check, and if you're not watching, they charge off. They always go past the most useless idiot in the camp,' John says. Excitable people or flighty horses cause the whole mob to become restless. 'Nine times out of ten, you can mentally block them without actually moving, but with some old bullocks you could fry your brains and get nowhere.'

Their daughter, Melanie, is home briefly, having finished her BA with a distinction in Pacific and European Studies, 'a product of School of the Air', her mother, who was formerly her teacher proudly claims. Over lunch, I ask Carol where she met John. She says they were born in the same Toowoomba hospital, 'but we didn't meet then, thankfully'. Her rich laugh sets off a chorus of barks from Scrambles and Charlie, the family dogs. 'Dad was an ambulance driver and moved the family to Cloncurry, where we met.' When John went to the Territory as head stockman, and then manager of Willeroo, a 3520 square-kilometre station with 20 000 cattle, she followed, and became the first full-time woman teller in Darwin's National Bank. 'I planned to go overseas, but never got there because John asked me to marry him. He was always special, but it was difficult seeing each other because of distances. We married in 1973 and lived on Willeroo for seven years. I knew where I was going in the bank, but I didn't know about station life. I would drive 120 kilometres to Katherine once a month with five dollars and spend it on sewing material.' The Willeroo period forged a loving relationship and deep commitment between Carol and John.

Bryce Killen, Willeroo's owner in the late 1960s and 1970s, also owned Air-Fast Helicopters, which then had 104 helicopters and 30 fixed-wing aircraft. John says Killen first had the idea of large-scale mustering by helicopter and processing the bull beef locally through Katherine meatworks. Prior to that, Territory stations had to walk cattle hundreds of kilometres to meatworks in Queensland or Western Australia, needing a skilful drover to deliver stock in good condition and hopefully break even financially. Tough bull beef was exported to the USA, where it was blended with trim from their high-grade feedlot cattle. John ate hamburger while he was there in 1979: 'a sweet succulent taste, but five minutes later I was still chewing'.

Mr Killen, as John referred to his former rather imperious boss, agreed to put him through his helicopter licence. He trained in Adelaide under legendary British Army instructor Buck Ryan, who 'hammered basic skills into us, so emergency reaction became automatic and always correct. When you erred, he would belt you on the head or shoulder and shout, "Don't stop flying now, moron, or we'll all bloody crash!" We worshipped the ground he marched on.'

A new American owner came to Willeroo promising change. Now having a growing family to support, John had managed on $69 a week for four tough years of low cattle prices, and he asked the owner for a raise. 'He didn't encourage my line of thinking,' John says dryly, 'and gave me 24 hours' notice, although later he had to ask me to come back and muster.' So within the day, the family moved to Victoria River Downs and what became John's job with Heli-Muster. Carol recalls arriving to a dark house. 'I switched on the light and you couldn't see the kitchen bench for cockroaches. It didn't endear the place to me.' Her friends were a long way away, John took off at daylight and was home after dark or was away for days at a time living in stock camps.

For the next 12 years John headed helicopter operations for the Brucellosis and Tuberculosis Eradication Campaign, known as BTEC, which mustered and tested all cloven-hoofed animals in the Territory, slaughtering diseased ones. The job proved particularly difficult because of rough terrain, vast distances and wild cattle. Each state was part of a mammoth national program to protect consumers' health and market 'clean' Australian beef. 'When BTEC started in 1978 I became more laidback because we were daily exposed to hair-raising incidents,' reflects John. 'The Queen Mary could roll over in port tomorrow and it really wouldn't startle me.'

Carol was fully occupied with three children by then—Louise, Melanie and John. 'I asked to enrol our eldest, Louise, in primary school at Victoria River Downs, only to be told they were no longer accepting non-Aboriginal children,' she says, 'so I enrolled her on School of the Air. When you're young, untrained, and two smaller children are running around getting into mischief, it's hard work teaching your own children. There are no yardsticks on what was expected. When the kids met up with School of the Air friends, they never said "hello" but, "What set are you up to?" Now when I talk to young mothers, I tell them to relax and enjoy it more than I did.' She became involved in the fledgling Territory Isolated Children's Parents Association and chaired every school committee there was. A highlight of her life was playing to three nights of packed houses as the bride in a local production of *Dimboola*, a Jack Hibbard play, in Katherine in 1982. Under the direction of bestselling author Terry Underwood of Riveren station, the cast travelled an incredible 14 000 kilometres to rehearsals and formed a close-knit group.

Meanwhile, in any one day John was flying immense areas over mostly unfenced country. Very few owners had any idea of their cattle numbers. Big bulls accounted for up to 40 per cent of musters because there were no fences, numbers bred up and young females were often ridden to death during mating.

That night, over tender home-grown steaks lubricated with gutsy red wine, John describes how Territory herds improved dramatically during the 1980s. His eloquence is light years away from the shy, introverted child he had considered himself. 'I once did a treble muster at a station called Killarney with two other pilots. The owners thought we might get 1500 head of cattle; we ended up in a holding paddock with 6500. Only 700 of these were branded. We had covered 300 square miles of country, not seen each other all day and finished after dark. The ringers or stockmen called cattle younger than three years calves or 'mickeys', but they were twice the size and age of most southern calves, and ferocious.' They tailed, quietened and walked those cattle to the station yard 37 kilometres distant.

'I will carry with me forever the sight of the massive pall of dust going straight up from the heat of the cattle, and then flattening out in a temperature inversion like an atomic bomb cloud,' he says. 'We were flying into the sun setting beyond the dust, a magnificent scene on a brilliant clear horizon. Afterwards we flew home in numbed silence and blackness, relieved only by the flickering strobes on the rotor blades. It was a surreal and motionless passage of time, broken by the feel of a cold beer from the engineers as we landed and they dragged out arc lights to prepare the machines for yet another day.'

In a replay of his boyhood nightmare of falling, he once had control failure at altitude. 'I was a long way off the ground and had to get down and land among all these great big rocks. I did it, but after landing, I remember repeating "Good boy, John, good boy" in relief. Another time, we had a stockhand on a motorbike who was pushing a beast back so I could wheel it into the mob. He got in the wrong place and I misjudged the distance from the ground by about six inches. The two blades hit the earth and we flew into the ground without any control, like running a truck downhill with the steering wheel disconnected. I had accepted that it was going to happen eventually, but it makes you think afterwards. It was a turning point for Heli-Muster, because nobody believed I could ever crash. It shocked them into acknowledging anyone can prang. We used accidents as training regimes for all the pilots.'

John considers that his biggest contribution to the Top End was cleaning up feral cattle, buffalo, brumbies and donkeys. 'There were so many donkeys that some of them were starving to death. The ground underneath them was also starving to death. Nowadays you can see the waterways and biodiversity. Some herds were so badly infected with tuberculosis that shooting them was the only option. When flying a chopper that shoots 1400 animals on some days, you had to look to the future benefits of animal health and export markets. These were rugged areas you couldn't muster except by air. It was very professional. We never left any wounded animals.' But he says the experience turned him off shooting.

Once feral buffaloes and cattle had to be eradicated at Wagait station on the Finnis River; rough estimates were between 1000 and 4000 head. In mercenary-style operations, four helicopters flew line abreast from one end to the other of the long, narrow station. In four and a half days under John's co-ordination they shot 17 500 head, and nine months later another 3000. The flying was extremely demanding in hot, humid weather, at treetop height and down to ground level in the small gaps as the stock inspectors shot out the right door. 'They had to be excellent shots,' says John. 'Working in relays of three hours each, we would do three missions a day. Springfield rifles were more reliable than self-loading rifles (SLRs), the standard issue for the Australian infantry. We reckoned if Australia ever got into a large-scale war with SLRs, we would be doomed. When you needed them most, you could bet your left testicle they would fail.

'It would have been good to get more animals out to markets,' he says, 'but look at our healthy cattle industry today and how well positioned it is in world markets. Where before we had three helicopters flying all day pushing cattle into yards, now one machine in a few hours can push a couple of thousand head into a bore and six horsemen can walk them home.'

John says, 'BTEC would have failed miserably without the helicopters, skilled pilots and stock inspectors. We built up from four to 23 choppers. We cut corners and flew a lot more hours than we were supposed to, because there weren't enough experienced pilots. One day I remember flying 13 hours.'

By 1992, the goal of 'clean' cattle was achieved in the Territory. BTEC had cost government and industry more than $100 million, and banished the open-range system of management forever. 'We contributed to the changing face of Territory herds,' says John. 'With the eradication of bush bulls and the injection of Brahman cattle, stations changed from harvesting low percentages to professional operations. Many stations now brand over 75 per cent.' He represented the Territory on the National Cattle Council from 1995–98, applying the same principles as he has to flying: 'Tread carefully, listen and learn, and keep out of trouble.'

Carol and John had long dreamed of buying their own station, and starting Gilnockie was exciting. 'It was a big deal to count our cattle off the road train,' Carol remembers. The children helped in the stock camp, mustering on horseback or truck as their father hunted cattle to them with the helicopter. She and the children lived in a pop-up caravan, used a tent for a schoolroom and cooked over an open fire. The sink was a wheelbarrow. 'I missed the women and Saturday night parties at Victoria River Downs. It became a quiet life, but that's when you talk.' She recalls having to fix a broken belt on a bore with instructions over the two-way radio from John, who kept saying, 'Make sure it's going the right way or you'll unwind the shaft and all hell will break loose.' 'I was terrified, kept checking and eventually got the belt on. When I told John, there was a big cheer. Half the Territory was listening over the radio!' laughs Carol.

When the last child finished School of the Air, the school radio and its daily contact ended, and even police and church people visited rarely. Carol tells me about meeting a friend in the supermarket one day in Katherine. 'We each asked how the other was. We both said, "Good", and went on our way. Years later, she told me she would go home and think, "How come everyone else is coping and I'm not?" I used to think exactly the same thing, but we never let on. We were in such a hurry, we never sat and discussed real matters.

'Just about every visitor, you could see what they were going to say— "Don't you get lonely here?"—and I used to say, "No, I don't", ' says Carol. 'It wasn't until our last child went to boarding school in 1992 that I thought, "Yes, I know what loneliness is." Our son, young John, could change tyres, fix motors, do anything. The last year he was home, it was just the two of us, a horrendous year of fires and pulling cattle out of bogs. He said to a visiting School of the Air teacher, "What happens when I go to school and want to play football and cricket and don't know the rules?" He never complained and got into everything, even representing the school in cricket in South Africa, but that first year was hard for him. I know now he was too mature,' she says, '13 going on 60 because of the work he had done. We were great mates, and then he was in Brisbane. I was close to going into a big black hole then, but was frightened that if I went down I wouldn't get up again. It's not that I was here on my own, it was that the people I wanted weren't here.

'Now I am part of a group, and when we talk, we do talk, but one woman told me she contemplated suicide after her children finished school. I never got that low. If I was down about something, I would go to the sewing room.' After a Territory Craft Council workshop with renowned quilter Allison Schwarby, Carol took up quilting, 'My sanity outlet!' She shows me some of the 15 quilts she has made in the last 18 months, stitched with care and affection. 'I give them away to friends and family. I love the peaceful colours.'

The Chief Minister invited her onto the Territory Women's Advisory Council, but she declined until her youngest child went away. 'I didn't say much for the first few months, just listened,' she recalls. 'I was amazed at what the other women spoke about—sex and women's problems, subjects I *might* discuss with a close friend. I wanted to do something for bush women, particularly when their children finished School of the Air.' Carol instigated forums in outback areas, so women could be informed and voice their concerns. These still continue. 'We made remote women visible.' She also discovered the joys of bushwalking with a group of friends through wilderness areas like the MacDonnell Ranges and Katherine Gorge.

The Armstrongs are known as people who give a hand, even though their community of Katherine is hundreds of kilometres away. Carol had three terms as secretary of the Northern Territory Cattlemen's Association, and they became involved in a Cattle Stations Issues Group that deals with the loss of health services. They have re-established the service of 'mobile' nurses, who used to give hands-on health care and were like counsellors to women on remote stations (see chapter 4, 'Hey Sister!').

Exporting live cattle to South-East Asia is the Armstrongs' main market. It was badly affected by the 1998 currency collapse, but signs are positive for the future, John thinks. 'We need to build stronger relationships with the importers over there.' Carol chairs the go-ahead Sturt Plateau Beef-Net Group, which is planning a brand name, and group selling and buying of clean beef from 40 000 cattle in the region.

The Armstrongs have two great concerns. One is the effect of native title claims on pastoral land. Five years after they applied to subdivide Gilnockic in order to clear debt they wait, their application now caught up in claims. 'We are not against Aboriginal people having land,' says Carol, 'but we shouldn't be penalised when we have put our heart and soul into land we have bought. Some people think we are the baddies. We feel we are in the wrong place at the wrong time.'

The other concern is cancer. In December 1999, Carol had one kidney removed, and since then has had secondaries in the lung and brain. 'When the doctor first told me, it didn't sink in. He kept saying, "Have you got any questions?" But neither John nor I had any questions. I had more tests in a few days, but all I wanted was to go home. It seems crazy now, but we drove home, 600 kilometres. I went to bed and cried, then John came in and cried with me. The next morning I decided it couldn't be this bad, and I had to get on with life. Some of my bushwalking group came to visit me in hospital, drank the ward out of coffee and ate the nurses' biscuits. They were so positive.'

It is the depth of Territory friendships that has again sustained the Armstrongs during a tough time. Carol needed an extra truck to take home the 40 bouquets of flowers she was sent in hospital. 'I think there must be a reason I'm going through this,' she says. 'I hope it makes me a more understanding and caring person.' John has become an internet sleuth on cancer treatment. After 27 years of living together and apart, Carol says they are best friends as well as husband and wife. 'He's been with me through thick and thin. I'd hate to be without him.'

Carol and I met again when she journeyed to Canberra in March 2000. She was appointed to a Federal government board for Rural Transactions Centres, responsible for funding one-stop centres for small towns which are losing banks and post offices. The journey entailed John flying her in the helicopter to their car parked beyond the floodwaters around their house, then flying back to leave the helicopter out of reach of the cows that are inclined to chew off parts, and swimming and wading through the mud back to his wife. They made it through a boghole, and drove the 600 kilometres to Darwin for Carol's flight to Canberra via Adelaide. She has a quiet chuckle when she hears city colleagues complain of traffic problems.

o o o

Postscript: On 28 October 2000, Carol Armstrong passed away in Katherine Hospital from a virulent cancer. She was a compassionate woman who always put others first. A natural leader and effective advocate for people in remote Australia, Carol brought about change on many fronts—in agriculture, health, children's education and the rights of women. She had the extraordinary courage to have a church service the week before she died to celebrate her life and say goodbye to her beloved family and friends.

As John walked out of Carol's funeral service, he was told that the magistrate had ruled in their favour for their subdivision application over native title claims. 'What a tremendous pity this news could not have arrived just a few days earlier for Carol to hear' he wrote in his Christmas 2000 letter. As John Armstrong continues to run Gilnockie, he concluded his letter with a request for a little prayer for Carol and the family, and a poem:

When the golden sun is sinking
And your mind from troubles free
When of others you are thinking
Will you sometimes think of me?

(Anon.)

14 | Flying Doctor

Dr Rod Mitchell ~

Chipping away at remote area health problems

It is Dr Rod Mitchell's last monthly clinic at Titjikala, a remote Aboriginal community on arid plains excised from Maryvale station, 80 kilometres south of the Royal Flying Doctor Service (RFDS) base in Alice Springs. I am privileged that the RFDS has allowed me a precious passenger seat to fly with Rod to one of his 20 outback clinics. This is a routine flight in one of Australia's most unpredictable jobs. There are no heroes here, but smooth teamwork between the pilot, the fly-in staff, Rod and the senior nurse, health workers on the ground and administrative staff back at the base.

The red and mauve spine of the West MacDonnell Ranges curves beneath the plane and sweeps away from the central Australian town like a crocodile. The striking colours and harsh beauty of the country combine with the excitement of anticipation as we fly away. All this has captured the heart and imagination of Rod, a city-born and bred man in his mid-thirties. He always sets a punishing pace for himself, and today is no exception. He has an open face you can trust, youthful and fringed with laughter lines and bushy whiskers, until weariness settles around his eyes.

Our reception committee at the dirt airstrip consists of two burly young Maoris. The Pilatus aircraft takes off for its next stop trailing the familiar banner of the Royal Flying Doctor Service, a huge plume of red dust. The sight of that dust, signalling help at hand, must have relieved many an isolated outback person struggling with health problems. We receive a warm welcome from Aboriginal health worker Janie Wells, the daily face of health care in this community of 200 people. This is her land and her people. She acts as translator for Rod when needed.

At Titjikala clinic I watch Rod deal with the robbers of health, largely introduced lifestyle diseases such as diabetes and high blood pressure, or the kinds of accidents that could perhaps be reduced with health education and stricter legislation. For example, fireworks are still legal in the Northern Territory; into the clinic walks a boy with a running nose whose eyebrow has been blown off by a firecracker that narrowly missed his eye. The Territory has no speed limits on open roads; the next patient is an elderly man badly injured in a car accident that killed two people. He has progressed from hospital to wheelchair to crutches a year later.

However, it's not unrelenting bad news. In walks an old man. 'Can you hear me, Charlie?' asks Rod.

'Eh?' says Charlie.

'Do you remember last year when you got that hearing aid?' Some sign language here from Rod.

'Eh? Oh, I lost it!' Doctor and patient both burst out laughing. Rod has endeared himself to these people. He is respectful, tunes into their situations sensitively and with endless patience explains the links between their lifestyle and the disease, or whatever treatment might help.

'Some come here to "do good",' says Rod during a break in his busy clinic, 'but as a rule, they don't survive for long. You owe it to yourself to enjoy what you do.

'One of the biggest frustrations is an inadequate basic health infrastructure because of chronic underfunding for Aboriginal health, given the dramatic level of need,' he adds. 'I now have a patient with diabetes who embodies the tragedy of Aboriginal health. A quiet, taciturn man, he never really understood what the diabetes was going to do to his body. First he lost some toes, then a foot, then the other foot. Then he lost a leg, then the other leg. He's now bound to a wheelchair. Chronic abdominal pain led to morphine dependence. He was given large amounts of morphine tablets, which he kept in the house. One night his five-year-old grandson took a few of the tablets, curled up next to his grandfather and never woke up.' The accumulating horror of this story told by Rod in simple facts, with no drama, shocks me. I wonder how the situation could be different.

'Huge losses for this man,' continues Rod. 'His legs, his grandchild, his independence, and his status. It is a recurring story. In the last 12 months in his community there was a car smash with two deaths and another seriously injured, a young man who died of severe lung disease and another young man who died of acute leukaemia. Just one tragic young death after another. With Aboriginal male life expectancy at 48, lots of young people do die.'

o o o

When he was 14 Rod read two books: *Bury My Heart at Wounded Knee* by Dee Brown about the Native American Indians in land wars with the Europeans, and *Killing Me Softly: the destruction of a heritage* by Phyl and Noel Wallace, about how Australian Aborigines in the western desert suffered through contact with white culture. Both told of proud peoples living in harmony with their surroundings as part of the greater world, not as its rulers. 'There's something profoundly sad about those values being smothered by a money-focused Western society, and the loss of that way of life,' Rod comments. 'I began to question things I had taken for granted.'

Instead of launching straight into medicine after finishing school at Scotch College, Adelaide, he wanted a break from study and the chance to earn some money, so he worked for the maintenance section of his old school. Before this, his world had been confined to the social echelons of the offspring of financially successful business and professional people. 'It opened my eyes,' he says. 'I developed a great respect for the tradesmen with whom I worked.'

Rod started studying medicine because he thought it would be interesting and academically challenging. He could work wherever he wanted in such a transportable trade, and it offered interaction with people. Halfway through his degree, after three years study at Flinders University, he wanted to see the world and spent ten months in India and China studying Mandarin at the Beijing Language Institute. Looking for adventure, he travelled in the back of a truck to Lhasa, the holy city of Tibet, and across the Gobi desert of Mongolia. Interacting with these cultures reinforced his belief that the foundations of happiness are family, friends and a job. 'So many things we do in our culture, we see as being the right way, but there's no one right way. I found the Chinese blowing their noses into communal pots a bit hard to take, but they thought us blowing our noses into a little cloth and carrying it around in our pockets all day equally hard to understand.'

During his final year of medicine Rod worked in Mexico and Guatemala and found the best-equipped doctors were those who knew the culture and language. The experience inspired him to work in difficult health areas in his own country. In 1990, he met Sue Sharpe and they married. 'My mother-in-law would have killed me if I'd taken her daughter to Guatemala,' he says. 'I decided I would work in the Australian bush. There was no rural general practitioner training program then, so I designed my own.'

He went to the United Kingdom to work in anaesthetics and obstetrics and returned to Adelaide to gain experience in the Alcohol Unit and the Sexually Transmitted Diseases Unit. 'You could spend a lifetime training. A huge hurdle is the fear of what's going to walk in the door next. You just have to go out there and sink or swim. Common sense and a telephone help; I would often ring from the desert seeking advice from doctors in Adelaide or Sydney.'

In 1993 he was aiming to go to a general practice in Toowoomba, but the Royal Flying Doctor Service (RFDS) was too enticing. He decided to do that. So began his love affair with central Australia. 'What I most enjoyed was being out bush in that magnificent country. I was continually invigorated working with Aboriginal people. I found them fundamentally honest, down-to-earth people, and shared their humour. Alice Springs did not have a conservative country town mentality and many people had similar interests in Aboriginal and environmental issues. We felt at home.'

'The extraordinary becomes the ordinary,' says a radio operator in an RFDS video *Wireless, Wings and Stethoscopes*, 'because every day something totally different happens.' Rod agrees. 'I enjoy practising a wide spectrum of medicine. As I am more commonly seeing people who are acutely unwell, medical intervention often makes more of a difference. It is a professionally rewarding area in which to work. Having travelled in Third World countries, I wasn't appalled by the standard of living in Aboriginal communities. I try to see past the material poverty to what people do have—family and friends. But they don't have jobs and that's a big problem. Women still have a role raising families, but the men are robbed of many of their traditional roles and seem more at a loss for ways of occupying their time.'

The story of the RFDS is full of romance and heroism. It is an inspiring part of our rural history. It provides a mantle of safety over the inland and outback emergencies are its daily work. In 1928 its founder, the Rev John Flynn, aimed to eliminate Australia's geographical loneliness and isolation, not just when it came to physical injury and illness, but also through understanding spiritual unease. Rod has seen the isolation 'come down on people' when someone is sick or there is an accident. 'A radio call is even more isolating when it is drowned out by static,' he says. RFDS staff confront the isolation by providing a voice link with patients and swift access to health care.

'A bloke rang at three in the morning from an isolated station. His wife had gone into labour early and torrential rain had isolated the homestead. We had to get the husband to row her across the water and organise a truck to meet and drive them to the nearest airstrip for the RFDS flight to hospital. For me, it was weighing up all the risks. I wanted her to deliver in a hospital, but not to drown or the plane to crash. As doctors, what's challenging and invigorating for us is not always exciting for the patient.

'While I derive great satisfaction from being able to improve someone's lot, the outcomes are sometimes grim. Two tourists rolled their car west of Uluru and the caller's partner was badly injured. She was very calm. People are either completely calm or hysterical in a crisis. I was trying to get the story and explain over the radio that he might be dying and the most important thing she could do was to comfort him, stop any external bleeding, and hold his airway open if he became unconscious. Sadly, he did die.'

A nurse who heard the radio call later rang Rod and said, 'I heard you talking to that lady and thought you were wonderful, so sympathetic and reassuring.'

'When someone is in a terrible situation,' says Rod, 'it's a million times easier being the nice bloke on the end of the radio. The person who really shows the strength is the woman by the side of the road with her dying partner.'

'How do you cope with a regular dose of such stressful situations?' I wonder.

'I enjoy practising medicine in an area of such obvious need, and in the company of other people in this field,' he says. 'The RFDS is a great place to work. I'm with five other doctors who are employed by Territory Health. I love the land, the timelessness in its presence. I enjoy working with Aboriginal people not worried by the trappings of modern life. The older Aboriginal people teach me to be accepting of life, and keep a sense of humour, even in the worst hardships. They are used to "whitefellas" coming and going, so continuity is important in establishing good relationships with patients. It leads to better health because they feel confident of your abilities.'

Rod observes that health professionals often come to tackle the huge health problems of the Centre fired with zeal and ideas, and quickly burn out when they discover that either their ideas are not so good or they cannot make a difference. 'The workforce is not at maximum capacity because of the high turnover and lack of stability, all of which leads to a sense of not getting there. Enormous resources go into providing interventions for end-stage diseases, such as dialysis for kidney disease. Yet resources are lacking to adequately address the *causes* of poor health and unemployment. The dilemma is that it's morally hard to withhold lifesaving dialysis from someone so that an employment program can be funded.'

Rod learned early to have realistic expectations, to be a good general practitioner and provide the patient with choices and practical advice. 'I want not so much to individually implement change, but to contribute to a collective effort. I was prepared to put up with the hardships and frustrations of the job because I wanted to learn more about indigenous people. And I'm stubborn! When you're here longer, you can contribute more, have fingers in more pies. I've enjoyed being on the editorial board for the third edition of the *Standard Treatment Manual*.' This is the bible for 'hands on' treatment in remote areas, particularly invaluable for newcomers.

'It's easy to make assumptions about cultural values. For example, seeing pneumonia, we non-indigenous people think of micro-organisms causing it and so take antibiotics. Aboriginal understanding is very different. Being unwell usually reflects a disharmony between them and their broader world—the physical, the spiritual and the land.

'When I started working in central Australia, I was told that Aboriginal people take time to speak, and not to look them in the eye because it's rude. A man came to see me and didn't say anything. So we both stared at the ground for a while. I waited patiently. After a few minutes, I asked him, "Did you want to see me about anything?"

'"No," he said. "I thought you wanted to see me."

'"No, I didn't," I replied. So he got up and walked out without another word, both of us puzzled. I'm still wondering,' Rod laughs.

'The tragedies are poignant. They make an impression on you about the toughness of living in the bush. Sometimes the price you pay for the isolation is the ultimate one, especially in Aboriginal communities. Death is ever-present.

'I had a chap out to the east of Alice, who for some reason lit a match in a long-drop dunny. There was a loud explosion because the methane gas ignited in the bush toilet and he was blown out the door. People exposed to explosions in enclosed spaces can be very badly hurt, or if their airways are burnt, they may be okay for the first hour or two, but as the swelling accumulates and accelerates, it can block off the airway and they can die. So we had to go and get him.

'There was no airstrip out there so we had a four-hour drive,' Rod recalls. 'He started driving and so did we in a 4WD ambulance, but we hit a big kangaroo which smashed the radiator. We lost all our water and oil and were stuck in the middle of the desert. That unpredictability would drive some people bonkers, but for me, stuck under a beautiful desert night sky ... you go crazy or laugh. As it happened, the guy was fine.

'The job has its bizarre side. Once at three o'clock in the morning, I was woken by a woman who told me she couldn't sleep! I was struggling to stay awake and counsel her on sleeping!'

Despite the widespread health concerns, Rod remains optimistic about the future of health in central Australia. 'I believe we need to better understand the forces that motivate people to change. I suspect that further advances in education, employment opportunities, and responsibility for local self-government will be accompanied by increases in self-esteem. It is this factor, and being more in control of their own destiny, that will drive people to undertake the changes needed to improve their health. Without people being motivated to change, much of what we do as health practitioners has little impact.

'For example, recently we looked at our diabetes management,' says Rod. 'We found that we have made progress in detecting and reviewing patients with this disease, prescribing the right medications and carrying out the correct investigations. However, we are not actually improving their diabetes. It's technologically correct, but we need to focus on the other end of the disease process to promote good health.'

Rod says that the solutions are long and slow, requiring forward planning and patience. 'Advances have occurred. For instance in the 1960s and 1970s there were big advances in Aboriginal perinatal health. Infant deaths used to be ten times higher than the general population. Now it's much improved, but it is still three times higher.'

At Nyrripi, north-west of Alice, the Grandmothers' Program has involved older Pintubi and Walpiri women in teaching women's health and tribal culture to the younger women. I visit the Titjikala Women's Centre, where boredom is replaced by women painting their land and animals on silk batik squares in all colours of a rainbow and selling them at Alice Springs markets. At the basketball courts men are playing sport. Rod says these simple activities have brought a positive change in community mood.

The Pilatus touches down on Titjikala airstrip at dusk, fully loaded. A motor vehicle accident at King's Canyon has a woman on a stretcher immobilised in case of spinal injuries. Next to her sits her shaken partner and an Aboriginal mother nursing her little child who has a broken collarbone. We fly back in silence, each wrapped in our own thoughts. A magnificent crimson sunset bathes the ridges of the MacDonnell Ranges as we reach Alice Springs.

Rod struggles to find ways of combining all his loves—his family, medicine and the vast arid lands of central Australia and its people. His superhuman schedule of long days and nights flying, followed by clinics and unpredictable emergency flights, exacts its toll on him and his family.

o o o

After six years of working with the Royal Flying Doctor Service, Rod, his wife Dee and their four children, Lucy, William, Jessica and Samuel left central Australia for the culture shock of city living. When I meet him again, six months after my day at Titjikala, Rod is studying anaesthetics in Adelaide. 'We will best remember our family time in central Australia, the walks, camping and barbecues,' Rod says. 'At dawn on the day of our departure, I climbed Spencer Hill behind our house for one last time. Our family had clambered up its rocks and crevices on countless occasions. Watching the sun rise over the East MacDonnells, I reflected on how attached I had become to the central Australian landscape in six short years, and how sad I was to leave it. It is land you can really come to love. I had an inkling of the despair those indigenous people who were forcibly taken away must have felt, people whose families had been here for generations, people who must have felt an infinitely stronger sense of belonging.'

A paradox exists in that he loves central Australia and the arid landscape, yet is living in a modern city. He is laidback yet ambitious, he ruefully admits. Anaesthetics postgraduate students usually allow at least 12 months to prepare for exams. Even then, the pass rate is only 40 per cent. Rod has set himself a pressure-cooker nine months of preparation to minimise the time locked in his study away from his family.

'How are you finding city life?' I ask.

'We loved our time in Alice, but in the end the long hours and being away from our extended family wore us down,' he says. He firmly believes that it's important to recognise when the time has come to move on. 'I'm enjoying the challenge of studying for a higher degree, and eventually see myself using the anaesthetics training for retrieval and emergency work. It takes time to re-adjust to the pace of city life, but we are all savouring what it has to offer, especially the beaches!

'Ultimately, I'd love to return to central Australia with my family, because part of my heart is there.'

o o o

Postscript: In August 2000, an exultant Rod Mitchell rang me, 'I passed the exams!' he said. At last, more time home with the family. He was minding three of the children, who were down with a gastro bug! By November, the Centre had captured the Mitchells again and Rod was working in anaesthetics at the Alice Springs Hospital for three months. After that they returned to Adelaide as Rod continues further study in anaesthetics to expand opportunities for the future and maintain links with the bush and the Royal Flying Doctor Service when the children finish school.

15 | The Sea Gives, the Sea Takes Away

Sylvia Holder ~

From Finsbury migrant hostel to prawning pioneer

Thevenard, port for the South Australian fishing town of Ceduna, is home for Sylvia Holder, pioneer of the prawning industry on the west coast of the Eyre Peninsula. She is recognised as a fighter for her industry and for safety, a powerful voice on the South Australia Fishing Industry Council board and the South Australia Women's Industrial Network for fishing. When I meet her, she is not the weathered, dungaree-clad woman, smelling of fish, I have imagined. Instead, a silver-haired, perfumed woman smartly dressed in a blue linen suit with gold chains at her neck and wrists opens the door of the 1970 customs house building she has renovated.

Never still, it seems, Sylvia also runs an embroidery business and sells craft items and coffee at the customs house. She gives me a quick smile and asks 'What will you have?' Coffee sounds good. I tell her that so, too, does a Holder-netted prawn on a sunny morning scented by the sea. Amused and surprised, she raises her eyebrows but is soon showing me how to expertly shell the sweet-tasting Southern Ocean morsels. The smell of freshly brewed coffee and prawns mingle. As I sample them, the light streams in, gilding the richly coloured ribbons, tapestry cards and plaited embroidery threads.

Ceduna is South Australia's gateway to the Nullarbor, a massive curve of limestone hugging the Great Australian Bight.

Journeying east from Western Australia, my husband and I marvelled at the chalky Bunda Cliffs falling into the pounding waves of the Bight a mere stone's throw from the Nullarbor Highway; a powerful meeting place of sea and desert plain. At home in the swell, two gigantic black and white Southern Right whales cruised east, surfacing now and again to send up a fine spout of spray. Further on we found their destination, the calm turquoise waters of the Head of Bight, winter playground for whales and their calves before they return south to an Antarctic summer. At the entrance was a daily count—69 whales on 24 August 1999. The mighty creatures lolled, floated, flapped massive dorsal fins and tails, and called to mates or calves.

Each year Ceduna receives 400 000 travellers across the Nullarbor. Despite this, Sylvia tells me the fishing, oyster-growing and farming settlement of 3500 people is now in decline, needing a viable new industry. 'The council is, naturally, pushing tourism. We own the only big boat here. Others travel 400 kilometres up from our nearest centre, Port Lincoln,' she tells me. Her accent betrays an English background. She has come a long way from Norwich, the famous seafaring town on the east coast of England.

After the World War II, Sylvia's family applied to emigrate for a new start in Australia. They were turned down for seven years because of her father's lack of skills, but eventually her mother's expertise as a highly qualified nurse was recognised during a polio epidemic. Her mother inspired an independent spirit in Sylvia. 'We were £10 migrants: £20 for my parents, free for we kids. There were five in our family, but only three came out here—me aged 15, and my younger sister and brother,' she says. The two older children stayed to work in England.

'We were told on 3 August 1958 that we were sailing on 16 August. It was a great adventure—30 days on the *Orontes* through the Mediterranean Sea and the Suez Canal. We arrived in South Australia on 18 September. It was pouring with rain. My Dad said, "What's happened to the sunshine?" That's how Australia was promoted in England—sunshine and beach scenes. We were sent to the Finsbury migrant hostel in Adelaide.'

Twelve hundred migrants, mostly from the United Kingdom and northern Europe, were housed in long corrugated-iron sheds separated by large open drains, which were flooding when Sylvia's family arrived. Very hot weather followed, fuelling the already dry Adelaide air. The hostel had bitumen floors and tar-paper walls. 'Mum mopped the floor with kerosene and it went soft and sticky. Circular skirts were in, with hooped petticoats. They would stand out from your body and swirl when you danced rock'n'roll. I can still see mine hanging starched into a half-circle on the clothesline, drying so stiff I couldn't get it off the line without wetting it again.'

As there was no high school near the hostel, Sylvia left school. 'I lived at home for nine months, earning four pound ten and sixpence a week at Woolies in the city, and paid four pound twelve and sixpence a week for the hostel and bus fares. Mum and Dad subsidised me the extra two and sixpence weekly. Because of the polio epidemic, my mum went to the hospital all week and stayed there. We had no car and Dad didn't drive. He was allocated to Kelvinator when we arrived, making coils for the back of freezers. He hated it.'

Sylvia saw a poster advertising for nurses, so she instantly applied. 'They gave me a psychological quiz and asked was I interested in going to country hospitals. I said, "Yes, which is hardest to get to?" I wanted to be away from my parents!' She nursed at Port Lincoln for a year, training on the job.

Dances were the highlight of night life in Port Lincoln. At one she met Thomas Holder, a local grain and cattle farmer. 'He was six feet tall with deep brown eyes that talked to you, soft like a puppy, but dangerous if he was angry,' says Sylvia. She married him in a no frills registry office ceremony when she was 18. Her parents didn't approve so her mother went to work that day instead of coming to the wedding. 'A lot of people said we would be divorced in three months, but we weren't. I wouldn't take "no" for an answer, whereas he was quieter. I'm a fighter, but he was slow to anger,' she said. The farm struggled, so Thomas worked off the farm with the

South Australian Railways. When she was 19, Sylvia had their first son, Tony, and at 20, the second, Dennis.

Thomas was a practical, adaptable man who turned his hand to farming the sea in 1965 when his father sold most of the farm and bought a fishing boat. 'Later he found Jack Holberton, old and ready to retire, and bought his crayfishing boat. The boat, *Diane,* and 30 pots cost us 4000 pounds, no interest. A good price. Without him, we wouldn't be where we are today. He wanted to help a young family with drive.'

So began a series of make or break experiences for the Holders. They paid good wages to 'pick the brains' of expert fishermen, and Thomas learned fast and did well. 'He loved being his own boss and was very motivated,' says Sylvia. Her husband would be away for a week at a time netting sharks, or pulling in cray pots. She and the boys would listen to the fishing fleet radio each morning for his boat to report in. During Christmas holidays Sylvia and the children would go fishing with Thomas. 'Through the year I would crew for him when someone decided not to turn up, but mainly I was the shore manager, at home with kids making shark or whiting nets, preparing cray pots, doing the books, and cooking cakes and casseroles for Tom to take to sea. I was a jack-of-all-trades, master of none.'

Prawning started in South Australia in 1972. Three years later the Holders applied for an exploratory prawning licence and were allotted unexplored territory, the west coast of Eyre Peninsula. 'We didn't know whether we could survive, but we had to try. We explored for six months with few results, then on the way home one night Tom decided to trawl off Goat Island near Ceduna. He made a huge haul, netting two thousand pounds of king prawns.'

For two years Sylvia, Thomas and their four boys, aged from 15 to three, squeezed into an eight-metre-long caravan in Ceduna. 'That makes or breaks a marriage,' she says. 'I had to keep the kids quiet during the day when Tom wanted to sleep. We had taken the children from good schools in Port Lincoln to school in Ceduna, where a teacher told me, "Fishermen don't need to be educated." How little he knew.'

It was full-time fishing 300 days a year. 'We had to be persistent. Prawns were a lousy price, $4.50 a kilo, but fuel was cheap.' Times have changed! They decided to stay, bought land, transported a house, but had no power and no water for six months.

In 1981 Sylvia found a lump in one breast and their lives took a dramatic turn. More than being shocked or worried, she was annoyed at cancer interrupting her busy life. 'I went to Adelaide and had the breast off. Thomas had just bought a new boat, the *Peter Crombie*, so we were $180 000 in debt, I was wondering how long I was going to live, and one of the boys was in trouble at school for fighting and smoking. We sent the youngest to Scotch College in Adelaide, in case I died,' Sylvia says in a matter-of-fact tone. 'Six months later I had another lump removed from under my right arm.'

She said to Thomas, 'It's not the end of the world,' and they set out to see the world together over the next six years. Prawning was again prospering so they entrusted the business to their eldest son, Tony, a qualified skipper at 19. 'We decided to make the best of life. It brought us very close,' Sylvia remembers. 'We went to America, Japan, Indonesia, the South Sea islands, being tourists and looking at how these countries fished.'

In 1985 Sylvia was again diagnosed with cancer, and had an ovary removed. 'I've had no cancer since then. I didn't dwell on it, ate well, exercised, relaxed and spent time with my family.' Since then, she has devoted herself to helping others with cancer through the Anti-Cancer Foundation. 'What gives me the most satisfaction is if in some small way I can support someone. Often it's a matter of tuning into that person and finding out what's needed. Often isolated people need transport to Adelaide or Port Lincoln and I organise it.' She urges them to be positive, for which she is the perfect example.

By 1991 fishing regulations restricted the Holders to prawning 200 days a year. They built a boat, outlaying $500 000 and borrowing another $500 000 from the State Bank of South Australia. Drought had struck the land, and six months later the sea. 'El Niño changed weather patterns, which affected the moon and tides, and brought dry times,' says Sylvia. 'The bottom dropped out of fishing and the government allowed none.' The bank foreclosed on them. They had to sell their new boat for half its value. Fortunately we still had the *Peter Crombie* in Western Australia, worked by a skipper we employed. We decided to bring it home to do the occasional night's fishing.' The boys had that income, but Sylvia and Thomas also had to live.

Together they decided Thomas would have to work in the deep-sea fishing industry. He entered a different world of bigger boats, heavier nets, trawling to 50 fathoms, and working for others as an engineer. Thomas Holder went to sea on 30 June 1994. He called his wife from the middle of the Bight, just before the satellite phone dropped out, adamant that 'this is my last trip'.

'That was the last time I spoke to him.' Sylvia's face crumples. Her voice is caught in her throat, weighed by sorrow. At 10.30pm on 2 July, she was outside in the dark catching moths for tree frogs when the police pulled up. A feeling of dread closed in. 'It has to be Thomas, it can't be the boys,' she thought. They informed her that Thomas had been knocked overboard by the fishing net sometime between 4.30 and 6.30 that evening. 'A wire rope had pulled apart at a splice. It was very rough, 30-foot waves and blowing a 15-knot gale. Thomas went on deck to rescue the gear because he was more experienced. The other two seamen were in their twenties. He was gradually hauling the net in when the skipper decided to bring the boat around,' she says. 'It is a quarter of a mile turn for a boat that size. Thomas went overboard. No-one really knows what happened, but to this day I have not had a suitable explanation as to why the skipper didn't stop the boat when he saw Thomas struggling in the water. My husband was lost in the Head of Bight 100 nautical miles south of Eucla at bearings S3320.282 E12902.755.'

Five years later it is still a battle for Sylvia to describe the events surrounding her husband's disappearance. The memories are fresh. We sip our coffee in silence. Now she is angry. 'It was a Saturday night in midwinter. The police plane was called in, but they didn't leave Adelaide until the next morning. They are only allowed a certain number of hours' flying time before a break is required. They had to fuel up at Port Lincoln, then Ceduna, then Eucla, by which time they had used up about six hours' flying time, and almost run out of time to search 180 miles out to sea, let alone to continue looking.

'The only life jackets on board this boat were the USL [universal safety] standard, which are too bulky to work in, so no-one wore them. Thomas had on normal wet weather gear, heavy TAFT waterproofs and rubber boots. The crew stayed to search for three days. The police told us that the *Orion* was looking. We presumed this was the RAAF plane, but on contacting the RAAF base in Adelaide, they were never called in. The *Orion* they meant was another trawler working on the WA border.

'The boat should have hove to, ridden out the storm and pulled the nets up when the weather turned bad, not continued running into a heavy sea. They lost eight tonnes of fish on board, because only Thomas knew how to operate the refrigeration plant. My husband was never found.'

Sylvia reaches for her handkerchief and weeps. Somehow she is compelled to tell me this harrowing experience. The depth of her sorrow touches me as the story unfolds. 'I was unable to ask questions at the coroner's court,' she continues at last. 'Only my lawyer could, so I furiously passed notes to him. He asked why the skipper did not stop the boat when he could see Thomas trying to swim to safety. The skipper replied that he was afraid the net would foul the propeller. The skipper said he threw Thomas a lifebuoy, but with the boat being over 100 feet long and the lifebuoys at the bow of the boat, it did not have much hope of reaching Thomas, who was at the stern.' The coroner's finding on Thomas Holder's disappearance at sea was 'death by misadventure'.

Sylvia is left with many unanswered questions. She expresses great hurt, anger and frustration about massive, expensive rescue operations that can be mobilised for international yachtsmen and women, but not for her home-grown fisherman. Her ongoing quest is for safety at sea. She is currently campaigning for safe havens, coastal refuges where boats can shelter from storms. On their own boat the Holders wear Tasmanian-made 'Stormy Seas' waterproof waistcoats that self-inflate if a person is knocked overboard. Sylvia spreads the safety word through her various committees.

'Two days after Thomas was lost at sea, some heartless person rang and offered me $2.5 million for our boat and licence,' fumes Sylvia. 'They saw me as vulnerable.' On Monday, two days after his disappearance, she went to their Ceduna bank to let them know what had happened. The relieving manager saw her in the front office. 'He wouldn't take me into his office, and closed all accounts, saying I could no longer operate. We never carried cash and I was unable to draw a cheque.

'I also went to Social Security,' she continues, 'but they were no help either.' She fortunately had some money at the bank across the road and explained her desperate situation to them. They arranged a loan so she had some cash until the papers and finances could be transferred from the other bank. The same relieving manager told her it would take an hour to get them from the safe. She said she would wait. That bank later tried to woo her back.

I ask Sylvia if the grief you feel is different when there is no body. 'Yes,' she says. 'It is a constant searching. You can't put it to rest. It keeps breaking your heart. You can't have a grave because you don't have a body. Where do you go to sit and talk to your loved one, not just on the anniversary of his death, but when you need to talk something through? Where do you put the first flower from the garden which he loved? Where do you go? A grave is a very personal place for your loved ones.'

Sylvia had Thomas' memorial service down at Thevenard, and at Port Lincoln at the marina memorial for fishermen lost at sea. 'It is a beautiful spot on the edge of the water. Many fishermen are remembered there. Hundreds came to pay their respects. He was well known in the industry. In place of a grave, the Spencer Gulf and West Coast Prawn Association and I donated a marine research laboratory in his name to the Flinders University Marine Biology Units in Port Lincoln. This is our memorial to Thomas.'

Locals thought Sylvia would leave Thevenard and live in Adelaide. She decided to stay. 'This was our home and my family and friends were there. He was a loving, caring husband. The loss of Thomas made me determined to continue with our fishing business and prove to others that a woman can do it. It made people realise how much Thomas and I had done together,' she says. 'Thomas inspired me. He always went forward. I thought, "I can do it too."'

The four boys started fishing six days after their father was drowned. They took the *Peter Crombie* to Venus Bay and caught 545 kilograms of prawns. 'It was as if Thomas was watching over us, God bless him,' says Sylvia. She managed the boat for the first year. 'We managed on love. We muddled through with lots of tears, laughter and help from so many friends. That year was very hard on the boys, going out to sea on the boat that their father and I owned. Thomas was always there for his family. I can only imagine what they went through on rough nights at sea. Even now I still wake if the wind is strong and ring them at sea if I can reach them by phone. We often talk about him. My son Tony asked me about something the other day: "What would Dad have done?"'

The family saved so they could build a new boat, named *Bosanquet Bay* after one of the bays near their home, and launched it in October 1998. In seamen's tradition, on its arrival in port the Rev. Tom Beever blessed it with water he had brought back from the Red Sea. 'Thomas would have agreed it's a lovely boat,' says Sylvia. It is the first fibreglass trawler purpose-built in South Australia for prawning. It can venture 30 miles into the chilly, unpredictable southern seas. Sylvia's eldest son Tony manages the crew of three. They can sort and grade, cook and snap-freeze prawns on the boat, fishing 14 days at a time. 'The limit is 120 days a year, and we catch the same amount of prawns as we previously did in 300 days a year. From research we know the peak periods now. We make more money by processing on board and selling locally to a supplier for the big Sydney and Melbourne markets. We have an export licence and could direct market.' Sylvia describes a heavily regulated industry, where they co-operate with two other boats. If stocks are insufficient and two make a decision to stop fishing, the third also stops. 'We need to leave something for the future.'

The migrant girl who started on four pounds ten and sixpence a week has built a highly profitable business in a remote area with her 'boys'. She has weathered storms and developed strength and purpose. 'When Thomas and I started fishing we did it for our family. The fishing industry has been good to us. I love the sea. She rules our lives. She is a wonderful provider but she can turn so quickly.'

o o o

The sea turned on Thomas Holder, but Sylvia is proud that he never compromised his principles. 'He lost his own life because he wouldn't allow the younger guys to go up on deck.'

16 | Men of Peace

Abbot Placid Spearitt and Dom Chris Power ~
The Benedictine monks of New Norcia

'All guests who present themselves are to be welcomed as Christ, for He himself will say: I was a stranger and you welcomed me' (*The Rule of St Benedict*, Chapter 35, Matthew 25:35). This is not the token Bible in the top drawer of a motel room, but a truly warm welcome in framed calligraphy at the glass-panelled door to the monastery guesthouse at New Norcia, which is Australia's only monastic town. Two hours' drive north of Perth, the community of 17 monks follows a Benedictine tradition of 1500 years in offering hospitality to pilgrims.

I walk down the cool, darkened guesthouse corridor to a sunny courtyard. Pausing to admire red flowering gums against the stark white walls of the chapel, I hear the chant of male voices. Peace steals over me.

People are drawn to this place and its feeling of tranquillity. The guesthouse visitors' book hints at the impact on some of New Norcia's 50 000 visitors each year—'a feast of music, peace, fellowship, good food', 'a place to heal the spirit'.

A similar life-giving spirit welcomed the founder of New Norcia, the Spanish monk Rosendo Salvado, in February 1846. Trudging through the alien countryside in scorching heat, seeking a site to rest, his small party could find neither food nor water. An Aboriginal man of these Victoria Plains guided the strangers to a spring near where the settlement was established. The present abbot of New Norcia, aptly named Father Placid Spearritt (pronounced 'spirit') notes the irony for the nineteenth century missionaries. 'Coming from Europe to teach the Aborigines, they quickly realised they also had to learn from them, and if they didn't, they would die,' he says.

It is a shock to come upon this unusual town. Around a corner on the Great Northern Highway, Salvado's legacy almost seems like a mirage in the February heat haze as a group of Spanish buildings rises through the blue–green gums of the Australian bush. New Norcia is named after the village of Norcia in Perugia, Italy, the birthplace of St Benedict in 480 AD. This 154-year-old Benedictine community has had three eras; Salvado's pioneering mission in the nineteenth century, the educational focus of subsequent abbots in the twentieth century, and the third stage since 1991 under Abbot Placid, as New Norcia opens its doors to the world. Central to each era is prayer. The abbot says, 'The first thing Salvado and his fellow monk, Serra, did when they arrived here, was to offer Mass on the back of a dray for their small party. That hasn't changed. We pray six times a day. We've been doing that from the start and we will do it until the end of time. We want God at the centre of our lives, and we encourage others to pray and see things in that perspective, to walk in the bush and to be at one with the universe. We think that can be our main contribution to contemporary Australian culture.'

Abbot Placid, a slight man in his sixties with a direct gaze and warm smile, says God wanted him to be a monk. He grew up in Brisbane and chose Catholicism at 22 after being raised an Anglican. He lives the Benedictine ethos of respect for others, not in a pious way but with great tolerance and good humour. Graceful in his hooded white summer robe with a carved wooden cross hanging on his chest, the silver-haired abbot has an air of gentle authority. Living in England for many years has done his Australian accent irreparable damage, he says in a cultured voice. His right hand man is Dom Chris Power. (The Latin title is shortened from *Dominus*, meaning 'Lord', used for monks and novices.) They combine vision and action for the town's survival.

Flying around the town like a jet-propelled angel in his flowing robes, Dom Chris is the procurator or business manager, not unlike a town clerk. He is youthful and sprightly with a whimsical wit and firm grasp of all facets of New Norcia, from its art treasures to the latest cropping program. In 1980, as a 28-year-old layman uncertain about his future, he came from Melbourne to a retreat at New Norcia monastery and was put to work removing cobwebs from the many verandahs. Two weeks later he had a crick in the neck and a realisation that it was the right place for him. What drew him was the monastic life.

Unlike other Catholic orders, Benedictine monks make a commitment to a specific community, not to an occupation such as teaching. 'In the sixth century, St Benedict wrote the famous Rule that has established him as the father of Western monasticism,' says the abbot. 'It is about living in communities and praying together, doing whatever work is necessary for the maintenance of the community and for the good of the local people.'

'Benedictines don't go out and do "good works",' Dom Chris tells me. 'We have a place for everyone—they don't have to be card-carrying Catholics. We like it that way.' Salvado set the ecumenical tone. When trying to establish his mission and denied money by the bishop, he gave a fundraising concert. In *Lord Abbot of the Wilderness, The Life and Times of Bishop Salvado*, George Russo describes how Anglicans carpeted the Perth courthouse hall for the occasion, a Jewish man provided lighting, decorations and printing of tickets, and the Sisters of Mercy lent a piano. Salvado was in a sorry state, his tunic in rags and his shoes having parted company with their soles somewhere in the Australian bush.

At dawn in the fresh, crisp air I walk through a collection of grand buildings of mainly ochre and white laid out in the form of a cross, in styles ranging from classical Georgian to Gothic and Byzantine. Twenty-seven out of 65 buildings are listed on the National Estate Register, a body maintained by the Australian Heritage Commission. The ornate hostel was built in 1927, originally for travellers, as in the Benedictine monasteries of Europe in the Middle Ages.

All around are the means for self-sufficiency: an orchard, olive groves and two old mills for crushing wheat into flour. The cemetery tells the tale of generations of Spanish and Australian monks and nuns, Aboriginal people and settlers of Irish descent. At the town's centre is the abbey church and monastery, their privacy protected by tall wrought-iron gates. White-robed monks move in meditative procession out through the gates and into church for morning mass. A younger man escorts an older one bent over a walking frame.

Throughout the nineteenth century lay brothers, artisans skilled in all trades, built the town. Queen Isabella II of Spain became a benefactor to the mission, financing the second wave of recruits in the 1850s. She also sent a gold cutlery set 'that must have been a source of wonder to the monks and Aborigines when they sat down to a meal of kangaroo and lizard', commented Dom Chris in a Friends of New Norcia newsletter. New Norcia became a 'a little piece of old Spain', with more than 160 Spanish men and 40 women coming to live and work there from 1850 to 1950. Conditions were tough in Spain with World War I and the Spanish Civil War. Boys who volunteered to come out to New Norcia as monks or missionaries were sent to monastery boarding schools in Spain or Italy to do their novitiate, and came to Australia aged 16. Some never saw Europe again.

'Salvado was a genius at making friends and he showed that ability with the Aborigines,' says Abbot Placid as we settle in a quiet, cool room in the guesthouse away from the midday heat. 'He won their respect because he was interested in them and their language and culture. In 1847, an Aboriginal woman was given sanctuary in the monastery from her husband who was chasing her with a spear. The following day a raging bushfire threatened the settlement. Nobody accused the husband, but complete destruction of the new settlement looked certain. Salvado took a painting of Our Lady of Good Counsel, placed it against a corn crop that was about to catch fire and prayed. No sooner was the sacred image of Mary in place than the wind reversed direction, the fire turned back and the fledgling community was saved. Today the revered painting hangs in the church.

'Salvado learned that the mission had to be self-sufficient in such isolation,' continues the abbot. 'He built up an empire, at one stage owning or leasing a million acres for wool growing, which earned him criticism from some settlers. He used his power and wealth for the benefit of the Aborigines in housing, food, clothing, schools, training for jobs, employment, music and advocacy with government. On the whole his mission was regarded as an example of respect between races.'

In 1900, Salvado died of fever. He was 86. The next abbot, Torres, saw an urgent need for education. He improved the boarding schools for Aboriginal children and built two more boarding schools, St Gertrude's for white girls and St Ildephonsus' for white boys, the latter named after Father Ildephonsus Bertran, Prior of New Norcia when Torres arrived. 'So New Norcia became an educational settlement alongside the original agricultural establishment and Aboriginal mission,' says the abbot. In 1908 Torres asked Mother Mary McKillop for Josephite nuns to run the girls' school. Dom Chris estimates that 6000 students came to New Norcia throughout the twentieth century, about half Aboriginal and, half white children from further north, the wheat belt and Perth.

The past was not perfect. 'The treatment of women between the 1930s and 1980s was a blot on our history,' says Abbot Placid. 'One old boy of the school said there was a definite pecking order—white men, white boys, white women, white girls, Aboriginal men, Aboriginal women, Aboriginal boys and Aboriginal girls. The Spanish sisters, along with the Aboriginal girls, cooked, sewed, washed and ironed for all that mob, a large community of monks and all the schoolboys, both Aboriginal and white. There were not particularly good wages, holidays or living conditions.'

After World War II few boys wanted to be monks. In the mid-1950s, a changeover of cultures from Spanish language to English within the monastery caused upheaval, compounded by a gradual loss of school students with the increased mechanisation of agriculture, fewer farm workers and smaller families. 'Country boarding schools were no longer needed in the 1960s and 1970s,' says Abbot Placid. 'Aboriginal culture was also changing within the wider society, and eventually the government refused to fund institutions for Aborigines. We had to close the Aboriginal schools in 1974 and move those children to the other schools. Meanwhile we had Vatican II in the 1960s and the culture of the church had also changed. The Abbot explains, 'This council of all the Catholic bishops set in train many reforms to adapt the church's structures and procedures to the needs of people of the twentieth century. The bishops wanted the church to serve the world rather than claiming to tell the world what to do. Catholicism started to take more notice of other faiths. Modern languages replaced Latin in much of the liturgy and life in monasteries became less institutional. There was a wider range of training, more respect for the individual, and men joined religious orders later.'

Dom Chris says it was difficult to see the big picture emerging from these events. 'It was only as the school ran down and operating costs rose that the community realised we had to do something, or we would all go down the gurgler.' Abbot Placid was brought in as an 'outsider' from the well-run monastery of Ampleforth in England. He appraised the situation and reported back to the community. 'The monks were faced with a difficult decision about the remaining school because it had been there for as long as they could remember,' continues Dom Chris. 'It was the central business of the town. The Archbishop of Perth said he would lease and run it. The monks were relieved, but the archbishop soon encountered the same problems we had—an increasing deficit and declining student numbers. In 1991, the Catholic Education Commission of Western Australia recommended to the Archbishop that the school be closed.

'We were in shock. The community was informed with three months' notice,' he says. 'There were about 180 students. The Commission found other schools for them. Local people lost their jobs. They were worried and angry. The parents challenged the decision, but without success. The monks didn't know what to do. We are only a small group with few resources. We could have easily sold up and gone to a brick veneer monastery in the suburbs, but we wanted to stay in New Norcia. It's our home.'

For a town that had operated as an educational settlement from the turn of the century, this was a crisis. Overnight it lost 200 of its 250-strong population. The hotel, roadhouse and general store lost most of their customers and formerly bustling buildings attracted only white ants. In an experience many country towns have shared, New Norcia's reason for being disappeared.

'We had a meeting to brainstorm possibilities,' says Dom Chris, 'but none of them "had legs". We gave up trying to work it out and decided to wait and see what opportunities would present themselves.'

He believes the hand of Providence is always powerfully at work. After the school closed, Marge Tanner, a music teacher from Penrhos College for Girls in Perth, suggested marketing New Norcia as a venue for school music camps, beginning with her own students. 'She saw the dormitories and classrooms as an asset, whereas we saw them as a liability,' he says.

'We worked hard to clean up and make it look as good as possible. Where there were cracks in the walls, we bought flowers to hide them. It looked like a florist's! When 130 girls and Marge arrived, we greeted her with, "Welcome, Marge." She burst into tears.' They found ten more schools that wanted the same arrangement and the old school buildings came to life, staff were employed, and customers returned to town businesses.

Dom Chris says the town can be many things. 'We thought—of all the things that it can be, what is sustainable and suits us? If we are to be true to ourselves, we need to be good stewards of our whole heritage. A man came in a white Rolls-Royce wanting to invest in the olive industry, but he had no comprehension of the rest of the place.' The offer was rejected.

An ethos of self-sufficiency, building an ecumenical community on peace and culture, and nurturing connections with Aboriginal people dates back to Salvado's era and his dream of a self-supporting mission village. Until the 1980s the town milled its own flour from its own wheat to make its own bread. In 1991 the bakery closed. Dom Paulino was the baker. It is hard to believe that this vigorous Spaniard with the ruddy complexion of an outdoor worker is 90 years old. He came to New Norcia in 1928 aged 18, recruited in his village by a priest looking for children for the monastery. 'I didn't know what Australia was like. In Spain people live in small villages. Here it was bush,' he rumbles in strongly accented English. 'We spoke Spanish and four monks and four nuns came from my village. I went home twice, in 1953 and 1963.'

Men like him were the community's backbone. He replaced a monk in the bakery, who said, 'You won't be strong enough to do this job.' 'I did do it, for 50 years!' he chuckles. With only one helper he used to start at 4am every day baking 180 loaves, each a hefty four-pounder (1.8 kilograms). 'Special bread,' he says with pride. 'Very tasty because the flour was ground with stones. Each year I used to crush 1000 bags of wheat into flour.' They fed the large community of monks and nuns, the Aboriginal community, hungry schoolchildren and surrounding farmers. He even grew the hard durum wheat much loved by Europeans for macaroni and porridge. 'I had a small packet of wheat, like tomato seeds you buy.' His capable hands sketch a tiny square. 'I grew it in the vegetable garden, then a bigger patch, until it filled a paddock.'

In 1993, New Zealand breadmaker Kingsley Sullivan reopened the bakery to make boutique bread. He understood the allure of bread baked in a woodfired oven at the 100-year-old monastery bakehouse. Before dawn, it is steaming hot inside the bakehouse as the oven heats for New Norcia's specialties of delectable nutcake, biscotti and breads. Demand has rapidly grown in Perth, Adelaide, New Norcia Museum and other outlets in town, and has even spread as far afield as Selfridge's of London.

It's seven in the morning and the delicious smells in the bakery make me think of breakfast—a thick, crunchy slice of bread fresh from the oven with a handful of delicious New Norcia olives. The olives were in decline by the 1990s, having relied on the schoolchildren to help with the harvest. Dom Paulino tends the 140-year-old grove, Western Australia's oldest. It is a long way to walk on his crutches, so he rides in style on a motorbike. Last year he pressed 700 litres of oil from 400 trees. I ask his secret for long life.

'Work hard and eat more oil.'

'And the future?'

'To the graveyard!' he laughs.

Completing a trinity with New Norcia olives and bread, the Benedictine Abbey wine label was reintroduced in May 2000 after a lapse of 25 years. The community's history of vineyards started with Salvado, expanded to 32 hectares under Torres, and reached its heyday in the 1950s and 1960s. By 1973 rising salinity and the winemaker's advancing age forced its closure. Providence was again at work when nearby Bindoon Estate recently suggested a joint venture.

Next stop is the abbey church. The exact moment I step inside, a glorious swell of organ music fills the long, narrow building. Did I tread on a button? Dom Eric Raymond is the organist, a courteous, fresh-faced 32-year-old monk with a shaved head, also being trained by Dom Paulino in olive production. He plays Bach's 'Jesu, Joy of Man's Desiring' like a man inspired. It is sublime, ideally suited to the magnificent pipe organ built by German Albert Moser and imported in 1923. When it arrived at the docks, the Fremantle Port Authority impounded the gun-like pipes until convinced they were harmless.

'It's great being a junior monk in what may seem a small, obscure town in music circles,' he says, 'and having famous musicians like Philip Glass, the American composer, come to us. He gave a concert and workshop last week.' The long musical tradition is being revived through the children's camps, and with increasing attention to Father Stephen Moreno, one of

Australia's most prolific but unrecognised composers and a monk at New Norcia for 45 years.

The community is also home to major collections of European and Australian religious art, including the recent discovery of a masterpiece from the workshop of the great Italian Renaissance painter Raphael. Its treasures also lie in collections of Aboriginal artefacts and rare books and manuscripts. To deepen insight into a unique heritage, the community has opened its doors to guided tours and in 1996 launched an education centre.

The abbot expresses delight at how the centre brings to life Aboriginal culture and the history of monastic life. The education centre's dynamic co-ordinator, Robyn Watson, tells me that children are wary at first, but after meeting Aboriginal people like former New Norcia student Lester Jacobs they don't want to leave. Jacobs talks of his life at New Norcia, teaching them some Yuat words, and gives them hands-on experience of gathering and cooking bush tucker and throwing a boomerang. 'Australia is on about reconciliation,' says Robyn. 'My biggest thrill is to do that on the ground.' A magnificent set of panels forms an amphitheatre for the centre's activities. Painted by a former student, it depicts the Aboriginal seasons and six eras of abbots.

Children also learn about the lives of monks. They make their own frescoes, dress up as monks and create their own plays. 'When I was a religious education teacher,' recalls Dom Chris, 'it was a battle to get students interested. Now the children are agape in the "monk talks" about our life here. They always ask: "Why are you a monk?" "What do you wear under your habit?" and "Do you have any money?" To that, I say, "No, we have to go to Father David for money, then record all we spend and hand in the change." The talks fascinate them.'

The local community wanted to see the town revive. A potent symbol of renewed life in 1999 is the 54 000 trees propagated by Moora High School students from seeds collected on New Norcia's farm and planted around the farm by local groups. Recently retired farm manager Keith Hunt, who has been closely involved in landcare, combats problems such as creeping salinity with extensive tree planting. Today more than half of the 8000-hectare property is devoted to conservation areas.

In 1992 Dom Chris suggested to the abbot that they start a Friends of New Norcia group. In 1999 the Friends donated $65 000 to restore the dilapidated veranda of St Ildephonsus' College to its former glory. St

Ildephonsus was a Benedictine monk and Archbishop of Toledo. The college was named after Father Ildephonsus Bertran, Prior of New Norcia when Abbot Torres arrived. Opened in 1913 and designed by Torres, it was the boys' school and housed 250 students at any one time. There are 18 other restoration projects, funded by the National Council for the Centenary of Federation to spruce up the heritage town. News of New Norcia spreads through its Abbey Press newsletters, prepared by one-man-band Dom Benedict, an austere chap who has adapted from naval to monastery life, from an old-fashioned printing press to 'computerese' and desktop publishing.

Recovery has led to research, initiated by Abbot Placid, into the mission's guardianship of Aboriginal children in earlier days. 'Most students here were the children of former students,' he says. 'We found the monks were not involved in taking children away from their families, although New Norcia did accept children sent by the courts. I understand the regime here was reasonably benign, but there were some severe monks who used corporal punishment. That is also true of schools elsewhere.' In the August 2000 Friends of New Norcia newsletter, he writes, 'I am very willing to say "Sorry", and to apologise to anybody who has ever felt hurt for any reason at New Norcia.'

Appointing a female liturgist is part of the abbot's vision to bring a healthy breadth to the community. The only nun in this community of monks, Sister Elizabeth Murray, answered the abbot's call to help with liturgy, the public worship of the church, the mass and celebration of the sacraments. 'The monastery would fall apart without the 20 or so women in trusted positions in the education centre, the kitchen, the art gallery and museum, and the office,' she says. 'We women really have a big role to play here. Sometimes very troubled people come to the monastery as guests and talk to me in the dining room. So many are touched by being here. It helps them go back and face their lives. It's the peace. One woman whose experience of men was not good found that being at prayer and listening to the gentle way the monks sang touched her. For her, there was a lot of healing in seeing the compassionate side of men.'

o o o

Dom Eric, the organist and trainee olive-grower, is the newest member. He describes his experience of the community. 'People notice that we get on well. It is remarkable because we are not blood relations—we come from different backgrounds, cultures, and generations. We want to live together and adapt to each other. We try to outdo each other in respect for others.'

I ask Abbot Placid if he has a vision for the future of New Norcia. 'I like to leave the universe in God's hands rather than trying to fix it myself,' he responds quickly. With an infectious laugh he adds, 'I keep trying to tell the monks what to do and they never do it right! Eventually I realise that it's not my job to tell them what to do. It's the Holy Spirit of God that will tell the brethren what to do. So I adopt that attitude to the world at large. I don't know the solutions to the world's problems, how to bring about universal peace and eradicate starvation and disease. We ought to be men of peace who respond to demands as they arise. So I don't like having blueprints for the future.'

New Norcia is a beacon of hope for other small country towns to find and build on what's special. Opportunities for revival of the community were all around, in the people and the unique place, but lay hidden until the monks agreed to share its heritage. In its heyday during the 1940s, the town population was 650. Now 50 people live here and the place is thriving. It is a national treasure for more than its National Estate listing. A place dedicated to peace is a rare find anywhere in this troubled world. Even rarer are people like Abbot Placid Spearritt and his Benedictine community who have the wisdom to open the doors to the past and the courage to weave a future from its strengths and its sorrows. What better goal could we have than to 'outdo each other in respect for others'?

'What does New Norcia mean to you?' I ask Dom Chris.

'Being here makes sense of my life and gives it meaning,' he responds. 'I'm a happy, useful person with no desire to do anything else. Some of the younger monks have travelled the world. I have come from Melbourne to here!'

'And what would Salvado think of New Norcia now?'

'He would be scratching his head because it has gone in a different direction from the model mission he envisaged,' Dom Chris answers. 'I think he would be really pleased it is still surviving after more than a century and a half, and that it is a place for everybody.'

17 | Never, Ever Give Up

Marlene Farrell ~
Transforming community service

Nine elderly men and women sit down to lunch together in their comfortable apricot and blue dining room. Beaming, 85-year-old Alf, the tenth Abbeyfield House resident, presents the housekeeper with a bunch of crinkly green spinach from his vegetable garden. Several blocks away, a young out-of-town mother on her way to the doctor hurries in to leave her child at the occasional childcare centre. Across town, a single mother puts a protective arm around two children and settles down to discuss her options with the emergency accommodation co-ordinator. Marlene Farrell is taking me on a Cook's tour of community services for the very young, the old, the disabled and the homeless, which she helped establish in the city of Orange, firstly as a volunteer then as an alderman.

A tall, poised and vibrant woman in her sixties, Marlene has an unassuming humanity that reaches out to the invisible people of society. She is also able to inspire dedicated teamwork in the service of the community.

In March 2000 I am at her home on what was the Farrell family orchard, Emmaville, north of Orange in central west New South Wales. The apple trees have all been pulled out and the large packing sheds behind the house now store other growers' fruit. Brilliant autumn reds and yellows colour the garden. Marlene moves calmly around the sunny kitchen making afternoon tea and Bob, her husband of 45 years, sits waiting in his favourite chair, head propped on his hand. He smiles in anticipation as his wife pours tea from the teapot in its familiar blue and green knitted cosy and passes him a hot apple muffin.

These two have the distinction of being the only husband and wife to both serve as deputy mayors of Orange City Council.

'Bob used to delight in telling people he was sleeping with the deputy mayor when I was elected in 1986,' says Marlene with a laugh. Between them they had 13 years in local government: Bob from 1974, followed by Marlene nine years later.

The afternoon tea scene is the same as always at Emmaville, except for one difference. Bob used to lift a conversation with his dry wit, great knowledge of history and his liberal and inquiring mind. Today he eats and drinks quietly, deep in his thoughts. At times, he looks for something in a distracted way. 'What is it, darling?' Marlene asks, as if he were a lost child. They have now entered the toughest stage of their life together. Dementia is advancing on Bob.

Marlene tunes into his needs, not leaving him by himself for too long, trying to simplify his life yet not making him too dependent. 'At times he's aware of what's happening and apprehensive of what lies ahead, but we can still talk about it. We want to stay in our own home,' she says. She concentrates on the present. 'We would have liked to do things together, like travel overseas, but I can't see that happening now. We are going to a course for dementia sufferers and their carers to learn what to expect and how to support each other.'

A 1996 Federal government report stated: 'By the year 2006 in Australia, it is estimated there will be nearly 195000 people over 65 years of age with moderate to severe dementia.' One in five over the age of 80 might have dementia at present. The longer people live, the more they are likely to suffer from it.

'We are an ageing population,' says Marlene. 'Dementia can affect anyone. We have a crisis in Orange now where funding for counsellors of dementia carers is in jeopardy. When these things directly affect you, you sit up and take notice. We're relatively lucky in this city. It's much worse in smaller communities, which need outreach services. In the country, funding to support people in their own homes will save money in the long run.' Already Marlene is following her pattern of becoming aware of community needs as she solves her own needs for counselling, assistance for carers and accommodation.

By September Marlene has followed a roller-coaster of Bob's ups and downs of ten weeks in hospital. 'Life is "on hold",' she says. 'I feel like I'm losing him. It's not the Bob I have had four and a half decades with. We can't sit and have a conversation or an argument because he loses his train of thought.' For her, it is sad and emotionally draining as she faces the reality that he is changing and she may not be able to look after him at home.

When Marlene can manage time to talk, I learn that she grew up in Orange with four brothers. Caring for others started young: as a little girl she helped her mother with her older brother, Brian, who had cerebral palsy.

'He never walked,' she recalls, 'and had to be lifted and bathed. As a child, I always hoped he would be able to walk, but gradually I accepted he never would. I didn't realise how much he must have wanted to join us at school and play. He never complained. Dad was away a lot working shifts as a psychiatric nurse at Bloomfield hospital on the outskirts of Orange.'

When she was nine Marlene would push her brother in a cane stroller several blocks up a hill to primary school so he could make friends and learn to read and write. She looked after him in playtime, but without school amenities or special teachers for disabled children, not to mention her brother being incessantly tormented by neighbourhood children, the experiment didn't last. His transistor radio was his friend. 'I remember when he was 12, Brian got his first self-propelling wheelchair,' she says. 'He was so excited. He said it was like "having legs".' His acceptance of everything and the love he gave freely had a profound effect on the whole family. When she was building her own house later, Marlene made sure it had no steps. It was the only house to which he had unlimited access and he loved to visit her.

As a child, Marlene spent a lot of time with her grandparents, aunts and uncles in the nearby village of Carcoar, and loved the sense of belonging to a community. This extended family encouraged the young girl to excel. 'At Santa Maria College I wanted to do well and come first in class, and if I didn't, then second was nearly good enough.' She was good at sport and liked to win.

'Sport develops character,' she contends. 'It's a bit like meditation when you are absorbed in hitting a good tennis shot. Sport is still one of my best remedies when things get tough.'

Marlene won a Commonwealth Scholarship to Sydney University after completing the Leaving Certificate, for which only four students at her school sat. She set her heart on going to university to study botany. It wasn't to be; the living expenses were too steep for her parents and she was bitterly disappointed. 'I was left in a void,' she says. In the 1960s nursing, teaching and secretarial work were the main careers open to women. She stayed in her home town and put herself through secretarial training at TAFE, working as a part-time theatre usherette at night and doing full-time office work. She met Bob Farrell on the tennis court.

They married in 1955, when she was 19, and moved to his family orchard. 'I was naïve about relationships and ignorant about life on the land,' she says. As in many farm families, the newlyweds lived with Bob's mother, who babysat when her daughter-in-law helped in the orchard. Marlene missed her privacy and the freedom to express herself. It bred restraint in showing affection to her husband in front of her mother-in-law. 'It could not have been easy for her to have a teenager come into her home, but she welcomed and quietly initiated me into the clan.' Bob's brother Jim and his wife Alma lived within 40 metres. 'We only went to town on Wednesdays to shop, and on Sundays to mass and tennis. I didn't have a driver's licence so I relied on Bob for transport.' Both couples shared the only car, which required constant co-ordination and sometimes caused friction. They also shared a kerosene fridge and a side of lamb each week.

Over the next ten years she experienced a succession of disasters. 'When I gave birth to our first child, Mark, I had a severe haemorrhage. I could see a white light at the end of a long tunnel and someone calling me. I was saying, "No, I'm not ready yet." I was near death then. I could feel myself drawing back. It made me stop and think about how quickly life can change. Youth is no protection against death.'

At the same time, the vagaries of agriculture struck. The cherry crop failed, money was short and the young mother went to work in the office of a nearby abattoir. Bob's mother cared for baby Mark. This became the pattern whenever hailstorms or drought wiped them out. The Farrell clan expanded. Marlene and Bob had four children, Jim and Alma had seven. 'I felt like Mother Hubbard when all the cousins played and fought together at our place.'

The only personal money she had was from government child endowment payments. 'I made the children's clothes. Dad's discarded hospital trousers made excellent kids' overalls!' The two families lacked privacy and independence in financial affairs which sometimes caused tension, but also built close family ties that helped them through the difficult times.

'After my fourth child, Bill, was born in 1963, I was diagnosed with a malignant melanoma on one leg. I will never forget the feeling of dread when the doctor told me,' says Marlene in a low voice. 'All of a sudden, I was again looking death in the face. I was 27, separated from my three-month-old baby and with three other children under seven. I was frightened for my children if I died. I prayed I would live to see them grow up.' The children were farmed out to relatives and friends for three months, as surgery removed the cancer and Marlene slowly recovered. 'I could hardly recognise my baby, by then six months old. From that point, I decided to make the most of every day because you never know what's going to happen next.'

Soon after, Bob's mother died. 'Now Bob and I were on our own for the first time since our marriage. We had shared our home and lives with her for a decade and she had often cared for our children. She even shared her room with our second child Karen, with whom she had a special bond. I still have to have everything in the house right, as if she's there, and I seldom sit and relax during the day.' Marlene laughs at her own compulsive habits.

She began to be involved in the community in 1973 when her fourth child was nine. Marlene decided to go back to work and then discovered she was pregnant at the age of 37. 'I groaned inwardly at the thought of more dirty nappies and sleepless nights. My mum half-joked that she was moving to New Zealand, but the children were so excited and couldn't do enough to help when Melinda was born. Often I have observed that an unplanned late child is a blessing. We have always been close. I tell her she has kept me young at heart, if not in body.'

Melinda's birth changed Marlene's direction. 'If I wasn't to be paid for community work, then I'd do it voluntarily. It was Prime Minister Gough Whitlam's era with its exciting changes, a time of women's liberation and recognition of women's contribution to society.' Whitlam, with his program of great social change, influenced both Bob and Marlene to leave the Country Party and join the Labor Party. 'Our relatives couldn't believe it, but for us here was somebody who was going to change society for the better. Bob said if you believe in something, you should be prepared to work for it, not just talk about it.'

When Marlene's elder daughter Karen turned 16 in 1975, her behaviour and personality changed dramatically. Marlene and Bob suspected she was taking drugs and sought medical help, to no avail. She left school in Year 11 and late one night rang her mother to say she was hitchhiking north. They heard no more for months, until one night she rang from Lismore where she was minding children and had tried to cook eggs in a microwave oven. The eggs exploded. 'I almost laughed in relief,' says her mother. 'It took a small accident for her to let us know she was all right.'

A year later, Karen returned to Orange. 'We soon discovered the frustration of searching for appropriate treatment for mental disorders,' says Marlene, 'as we took her to different doctors and clinics for 18 months. I promised her if we could get her on her feet, I would take her overseas. We went to New Zealand. I had been terrified of flying until then. My dad came too and we three had a ball.'

Recovery didn't last, though, and for Karen's parents a three-year nightmare of sorrow and powerlessness followed. Suffering from a personality disorder, Karen tried to commit suicide 27 times, and had to have microsurgery on her wrists. She became anorexic and spent years in Bloomfield psychiatric hospital near Orange, where her grandfather used to work. She refused to see her parents, although they went to the hospital every week. 'We had to let her know we cared. I can deal with any situation if I know what the problem is,' says Marlene, 'but we could never get a proper diagnosis. I had to accept it and put myself into neutral gear. I used to cry to myself as Bob never liked to see me upset.' Her daughter finally recovered, studied communications and is a successful journalist. In 1980, she gave birth to a daughter, Aimee, whom Marlene and Bob helped raise while she studied.

Karen changed both her given name and surname. She became Keiren. Now a vibrant and articulate woman with a strong interest in human behaviour, she reflects on the past and how the name change was a turning point in her life. She believes it was hard for her because her parents excelled. 'When they are so respected, everyone sees you through the prism of them.' Recently she looked at her hospital files, which were like reading someone else's diary,' she says. She has no memory of those traumatic years.

'It just proves you never give up on people you love,' says Marlene. 'I dealt with this harrowing experience by putting energy into keeping the other children together and working hard in the community.'

Australian society was changing in the 1970s, although more reluctantly in rural areas. Traditionally, women had left work when they married and stayed home nurturing husband and children. Marlene joined a dynamic group of women, some newcomers to Orange and part of a population moving for job opportunities. They needed childcare so they could work because they didn't have extended families. Before that, Marlene had not been aware of women's special needs because she had had her parents' help, but with Melinda she had no childcare.

'I was working in the packing shed for about six months packing fruit for the apple and cherry seasons, and like most farmers' wives, I kept the books. We had half-tonne wooden fruit bins. I would put in a mattress and toys, and Melinda would play and sleep in there. She remembers what fun it was to peer through the holes in the bin at what was happening.'

Bob had been elected to Orange City Council in 1974. 'He was in his forties and needed a challenge,' says Marlene, who encouraged and shared his interest, avidly reading council papers and discussing issues with him. She saw how Bob's confidence and skill rose after doing a public speaking course, so she too did a course and found her voice on social justice issues. Before that she would attend meetings without speaking, lacking the confidence to say anything. 'When you feel strongly about something, it's great to be able to get up and put your point of view. I get passionate about causes.' From the women around her Marlene learned to identify needs, enlist support and apply for grant funding. The timing was opportune, with the Federal government funding innovative community service projects.

As Bob moved into public life his wife became packing shed manager, employer and financial manager on the orchard. Bob and fellow Labor councillors were valuable allies on women's initiatives. Community services in Orange expanded quickly as the City Council became a leader on social justice issues. Not all embraced change, however. Until 1971, there had never been any women on Council.

'Town clerks, brought up in the roads, rates and rubbish era, had real influence,' says Marlene. 'The heads of departments were all male, and many were dragged kicking and screaming into the new era.

'In 1975 we jumped on the coat tails of the International Year of Women to lobby for occasional childcare in Orange. We then found there was nowhere to leave children if you were working full-time, either. This was my introduction to public life and the beginning of a new role for me.' The International Women's Year group continued as another group, chaired by Marlene. They lobbied for a new concept in childcare, and family day care was established in the city in 1976, licensing women to care for children in their own homes. So it created work for young women and provided a home environment for childcare. Next came an occasional childcare centre in 1977, providing short-term care for parents going to appointments, studying or shopping.

'Melinda attended so many meetings during her first four years, she would have known meeting procedure backwards!' Marlene's deep laugh fills the kitchen.

In 1979 the International Year of the Child dawned, with Marlene elected committee chair. The group planned a year of children's activities. Some were held in the ballroom of a well-managed local hotel, but letter writers to the local *Central Western Daily* described it as: 'exposing children to an undesirable environment' and 'placing them in danger'. It was her first exposure to public criticism

'It's hard not to take criticism personally,' Marlene says. 'Men don't seem to. They'll make scathing remarks to each other, but forget it and go to the pub afterwards! I soon learned it is the first shot that counts, and not to answer criticism over and over. It only fuels the fire.'

The International Year of the Disabled in 1981 was an opportunity for Marlene to join that committee and lobby for a bus for people with disabilities. She had seen the lack of independence and physical exhaustion experienced by her brother Brian who had to rely on his wheelchair. 'People like him could now have transport. He could visit us at the orchard, or attend functions without asking someone to lift him in and out of a car.'

When Bob decided not to stand for council re-election in 1984, he encouraged Marlene to stand. She was elected as an independent, and found it exhilarating—a new world of being involved, making decisions, speaking publicly, meeting interesting people and representing her city. This is how I met her. I remember starting a new job as a community housing officer and entering what seemed the hallowed halls of Orange City Council, clutching my first report to present to the community services sub-committee. The chairman who greeted me, Alderman Marlene Farrell, was not the 'roads, rates and rubbish' enthusiast I expected from my previous work as a council town planner, but a youthful woman with smooth blond hair, dressed in white, undaunted at finding herself in a largely male domain.

Intensely dedicated to social justice, Marlene chaired this sub-committee for four years. In the Council chambers she mounted skilful and well-researched arguments for expanding existing services and setting up new services. Orange led the way with new programs such as Operation Oldies, matching high school children with lonely older people, Telecare, with daily phone calls to isolated people from volunteers, and the Community Tenancy Scheme, housing low-income earners.

'I progressed from childcare to aged care as my children grew up and I aged!' says Marlene. When her older brother Brian reached his forties, he needed additional care and was housed in Wontama Home for the Aged because there was nowhere else for younger disabled people. Marlene noticed that older people needed their own space as well as good care and support. The result was the first family-style Abbeyfield housing development in New South Wales, opened in Orange in 1991. A new concept from the United Kingdom, it gave older people independence yet allowed them to continue living in the community. We worked together on this project, Marlene always steering the project and airing astute advice about how to achieve results politically. It took years of lobbying to obtain funding from the NSW Department of Housing and land from the Council before the spacious brick Federation-style house was built. It was a great success, housing ten older people who thrive on having the privacy of their own rooms, companionship in the shared common facilities and the support of a housekeeper. 'We didn't give up,' says Marlene.

She and Bob worked as a team over the 1970s and 1980s. 'We had lots of other councils coming to see how the city provided childcare, Abbeyfield housing, emergency accommodation for women and children, and the community bus for older and disabled people,' she says. 'We just accept these services now, forgetting the hard work and fights we had to get them established.'

One of the hardest battles was establishing emergency accommodation for homeless women and children. Many people opposed it, saying Orange didn't have domestic violence or drug problems. At the time, only homeless and sometimes drunken men had accommodation provided. 'I was taken aback by the depth of antagonism,' says Marlene, shuddering at the memory. 'It was my worst experience of a public meeting. I thought we were doing something good for the city, but neighbours around the proposed facility were so agitated and forceful, I felt attacked. There were phone calls from people who were "anti", not wanting such accommodation in their neighbourhood. We had to tackle it a different way.'

Marlene's sense of justice for those less fortunate was affronted, but she was prepared to listen to arguments for and against. Eventually homeless men were accommodated separately, and appropriate housing was purchased for women and children.

'You need to toughen up or you won't survive,' she says. 'We often had issues we had to fight for, but I learned that you can't win everything. It taught me not to be dogmatic. When you know in your own heart what's right, you just have to keep going, otherwise they win, don't they? In local government, I found it's better to try and delay a vote if you don't have the numbers. You have to do your homework and talk to other aldermen about issues. And the media can make or break a project.

'Now twenty-five years later there are few needs, from the cradle to the grave, not being met in our city and jobs have been created for a small army of community workers. But there seems to be a blind spot still about special needs such as disabled access.' She praises volunteers and their role in saving governments hundreds of millions of dollars across the country. 'But what will happen in future as families get smaller, and both parents work so they don't have time for volunteer work?' she wonders.

Looking at the bigger picture, she is concerned about the loss of services in smaller country towns, the heart of Australia. 'Everyone has been talking decentralisation for so long. Towns like Orange and Bathurst will survive and there is spirit to fight back in some towns, but they need more support from State and Federal governments. Service provision is the key. Rural people are resilient enough to substitute bank closures with credit unions, for instance, and communication networks like the Internet will play a big role. We have to be less insular. I believe we are over-governed and too parochial. More local governments could be amalgamated into decentralised, larger regional centres, which could share resources more effectively.'

Marlene thinks her Catholic school training and basic tenets of caring for your fellows, fairness and justice, have influenced her attitudes and work. 'Deep down I always wanted to be a social worker, to be more than a housewife and an orchardist, and to make a difference for others,' she says. 'I'm prepared to speak out on things I care about, and I don't take on any cause unless I really believe in it. Bob has encouraged me. My involvement in politics, social justice issues and community services is Christianity in action. And I'm proud to be Australian. If you can make your country just a little bit better, then that's a buzz.'

After leaving Council in 1988, she worked for the Commonwealth Employment Service (CES) in Orange. 'Women would come to see me. They were in their forties, often their husbands had left, and they were trying to make a new life. I would say, "I was over 50 when I went back to work as a typist, and within 10 years I was manager of the CES. If I can do it, anyone can. Give it your best, find the opportunities and be prepared to work hard."' She thinks all that is just being an ordinary person.

Orcharding was profitable for the Farrells in the 1970s. In the 1980s hailstorms wiped out the crop three years in a row, and in the 1990s drought struck and fruit prices deteriorated. 'I came to dread November to February, because so often a good crop was devastated by hail. Finally in 1990 our son Terry, who had managed the orchard with Bob, told us we should sell or end up with nothing. This was a blow to Bob. He felt he had failed. The final sale was completed in January 2000—a new millennium and no Farrells on the land,' Marlene reflects sadly. They kept a small house-block on their former orchard, which had been subdivided and sold to hobby farmers.

Her 45-year marriage to Bob and their five children have given her more satisfaction than any achievement in public life. 'If our house is empty of children and grandchildren for a few days, we wonder what has happened!' Over the last three years, she and Bob have been on their own for less than three months. When she took redundancy from the CES in 1996, her daughter Melinda wanted to backpack overseas for three months before taking up a working visa in London for two years. 'She asked me to go with her,' says Marlene. 'I was over the moon. How many 23-year-old daughters want to travel with their 60-year-old mothers?"

Marlene's elder daughter, Keiren, thinks her mother is set apart by her capacity to overcome life's challenges—not only for herself, but also for the wider community. 'No matter how many champions like Cathy Freeman there are in the bigger pond, the ripples of change will spread no further unless there are people like Mum in the smaller ponds,' says Keiren.

18 | Hearing the Cry

Margaret Appleby ~
Preventing suicide

A priest from a country town has phoned Margaret Appleby to ask advice about a funeral service he is about to conduct. A month earlier, he had buried a young man who had died by suicide. Now the boy's younger sister has killed herself. 'It's never black and white,' says Margaret. 'It wasn't only sadness at her brother's death that led to the second suicide, but a web of contributing factors. The priest agonised about what he should have done in the previous service, and what he would do for this one. No-one can bring these teenagers back to life. The priest can only walk with the family in their grief. Sometimes it's simply a case of, "I don't know what to say, but I'm here for you." It is situations like this that motivate me to try and prevent more suicides. At these times it feels like my body has been hit all over by huge waves of pain,' Margaret says. In complete contrast, a few days later *Better Homes and Gardens* came to photograph her roses and plant a herb garden. She says how bright they were, bubbling with life.

Margaret has a life-affirming aura, an open face and a ready smile. Her eyes are thoughtful and compassionate. She is one of those rare people who may not agree with what a person does, but will not judge them. She works with total commitment in a field most find frightening. Her own respite and therapy is growing roses. Her astounding garden, 70 kilometres south of Sydney, is a veritable explosion of colour and perfume established in 18 months on solid clay soil and a haven from demands that are beyond the imagination of most people. The organisation she created for donations to suicide awareness is called the Rose Foundation.

Margaret's energy is prodigious. Her work with the Rose Foundation takes her all over Australia and New Zealand and she heads Lifeline Macarthur, a crisis telephone counselling service for Sydney's most heavily populated fringe and pockets of people scattered through the Great Dividing Range. At Lifeline on any one day she might work with a bereaved by suicide group as well as attend to administrative tasks, deal with the board, raise funds and support staff and any of the 200 volunteers.

There are more suicides in rural Australia than road accident deaths. At 2700 per annum, it is the equivalent of losing the entire population of a country town each year. It is a feared problem touching many people, but is only slowly emerging from the closet. As New South Wales Rural Women's Network co-ordinator, I trained at one of Margaret Appleby's Rose Foundation workshops and put together a file of suicide prevention contacts and strategies. I frequently referred people to Margaret and she was my own adviser in a tough family time, always empathetic and helpful.

Brewarrina, in outback New South Wales, was Margaret Appleby's childhood home. There, mustering on horseback on the 6000 hectares of Killarney station easily overtook the doubtful joys of studying. Her schooling was by correspondence, helped by her father, a former teacher. Highly organised even then, Margaret would churn through the bulging envelope of a whole week's schoolwork in one day. Then she was free to ride.

An only child, her friends were mainly four-legged: lambs, dogs and always horses. She yearned to be a vet, and still loves animals. Growing up in adult company, she became independent and resourceful. When

Margaret was eight, a tractor crashed through the bridge at Brewarrina and the family was marooned for six months. They ate from her mother's flourishing vegetable garden and were airdropped essential items like flour and yeast for their daily bread. She learned to value simple things. Aged 12, her idyllic life was shattered by boarding school at Armidale Presbyterian Ladies' College. Margaret missed her animals and, unused to other girls, thought them rather childish.

After high school and Sydney Teachers' College, she veered off the normal teaching path of schools to take on angry, alcoholic, often neglected teenage girls in the care of the courts. 'I was never happy just to go with the tide,' she says. The juvenile detention centre of Reiby in Campbelltown held young women who had committed serious crimes, such as attempted murder, along with others charged with neglect who were themselves neglected. Margaret recognised something worthwhile in each girl. She began to realise that circumstances had caused their downfall. She saw it as an opportunity to develop their potential and taught them how to type and do shorthand, practical skills for life 'outside'. She introduced a game where they could take their three most important items down into a bomb shelter. She set the real challenge in the whole group having to agree on which three and why. For the first time in their lives, these disturbed girls started to believe in themselves. Margaret was showing them how to communicate and sort out what they valued in life.

One of these former students, Karen, who had been on drugs and had her three children taken away, later visited her former teacher with a toddler in tow. Shown a business opportunity by an Amway distributor and using the entrepreneurial skills learned from Margaret, she had her children back and was planning her first family holiday.

Between shifts, Margaret wanted to do something different, and volunteered for Lifeline Macarthur. Dr Gloster Udy, director of Lifeline Parramatta, saw her abilities, asked what income she needed to live on and offered her the directorship of Lifeline Macarthur. It was half the salary of her Reiby job, but she accepted. That was 16 years ago.

Back then, suicide was a whispered word. Far from choosing her vocation, Margaret says, 'It grew like Topsy. I hopefully grew with it, trying to keep one step ahead, responding to needs as I saw them.' The new Lifeline director found she needed to train telephone counsellors not just in listening and communication skills, but in dealing with an increasing number of suicidal callers. There were no 'how to' books for such a taboo subject. Margaret started going to conferences and meeting experts in the field in the US. She returned concerned about the lack of helpful, practical information in Australia. In 1990, she wrote her first book, *Hearing the Cry,* with a colleague, Margaret Condonis. It was groundbreaking, soundly researched and written from the heart. Publishers weren't interested, so the two women published it themselves. 'People, especially professional workers, were hungry for basic information, often buying the book in lots of 40. It was overwhelming,' Margaret said. They sold 5000 copies in three months. Ten years later, its sales have topped 25 000. When I commented that it was a bestseller, Margaret seemed surprised. She was so focused on educating the vulnerable and the bereaved that she hadn't ever considered herself a bestselling author.

The ABC-TV presenter Peter Couchman was one of the first courageous enough to air the subject of suicide on his popular television program, against the advice of leading mental health and medical people. Margaret encouraged to him to 'do it, but do it well', a dictum she lives by. She spoke on the program with two psychiatrists researching suicide, Professor Brent Waters and Dr Michael Dudley. For the first time, people watching at home heard suicide talked about: vital messages including 'it can happen to anyone, these are the warning signs, these are the myths', and the widespread misconception that anyone who talks or hints about suicide is not serious. They told viewers where they could go for help. The response was immediate; hundreds of phone calls. She is convinced that that program saved lives.

The program also opened the floodgates for workshops and conferences from one end of Australia to the other. Margaret's way of keeping up with escalating demands was to write a practical training manual with fellow pioneers Dr Ray King and Barry Johnson. At the same time, people bereaved by suicide were crying out for help. Together with ten people who had lost a loved one through suicide, Margaret wrote *Surviving the Pain* in 1992. The mother of one of the contributors had killed herself more than 20 years before. The family never mentioned her; it was as if she had never existed. When the daughter was asked to contribute to the book it caused a family feud, but as the siblings began to talk and question their father, they found preparing the story a healing process.

'Being with families left behind is working with the "whys" and the "if onlys",' says Margaret. 'It's listening to the pain of people needing to tell their story over and over until they don't need to tell it any more. It's helping them understand that the person chose the way to their death themselves, and others will never fully know why. Then it is helping them start along the path of acceptance, and not blame themselves.'

Margaret discovered she didn't need to be frightened, but to listen, support and help them to see options. Professor Edwin Shneidman, pioneer of suicide prevention and founder of the American Association of Suicidology, was her prime motivator. He likened the tunnel vision of the suicidal person to a screen of black. He told Margaret that her task was to help the person see one spot of grey and steadily enlarge it. He encouraged her to go forth and educate.

She took up his challenge, educating anyone and everyone—communities, the media, funeral directors, health professionals, school children and teachers. One of the hardest areas was children. Margaret was seeing children as young as five with suicidal tendencies. 'Could a small child feel so bad? A mother and her son aged seven came to me. He was to be expelled from school. Twice the boy had tried to hang himself. Three professionals, including a general practitioner had described him as "attention seeking".' Her response, faced with such lack of knowledge and understanding, was another book, called *Understanding and Helping Suicidal Children*. Her books are all self-published.

During the 1990s governments were forced to face the glaring fact that suicide rates in rural areas dwarfed those in metropolitan areas. Government dollars funded innovative programs, 'but even with all the education, it is still the ambulance at the bottom of the cliff, instead of the fence at the top,' Margaret says. 'We need to build the confidence of health professionals to ask the hard question—"are you feeling suicidal?"—and provide resources to help.' In 1997, within a five-week period, a small New South Wales community was devastated by five people killing themselves. All were men, several were good friends. At the last funeral, the minister holding the service broached the unspoken subject and invited the community to a public meeting. Two hundred people arrived to support each other and find a way forward. The inevitable questions were asked. 'Why? Who next? What's wrong with our town? What can we do?'

Margaret was invited to work in this community with the minister and a high school counsellor. They wanted to give people back confidence that they could do something. They helped people to stop blaming and encouraged them to come up with simple ideas to care for each other such as a picnic invitation or a spontaneous phone call. People began to look out for their neighbours. 'This community came to understand that the five individuals chose their own exit through their own overwhelming pain, and that the cycle could stop.' Men preferred the pub to the counselling room, so the minister and school counsellor rubbed shoulders with them there. 'They were real. They listened and they cared. There is a higher rate of suicide amongst men and they often use deadlier weapons. The true blue Aussie male masks his feelings. If he shares them over a beer with a pub mate who does not understand, he may be told "she'll be right, mate" because the other man can't handle it well. Women make more suicide attempts, but tend to use fewer lethal means.'

Many people who die by suicide have not previously seen a health professional or counsellor. Margaret believes ordinary Australians need to know simple self-help strategies, and how to reach out to others. 'Take time to smell the roses! I can never forget the woman who told me when her daughter killed herself, "None of my friends brought me a casserole." Others have told me that people they knew crossed the street to avoid talking to them,' she says.

Research printed in the *Kids' Helpline Newsletter* (1999) predicts that by 2004 depression will be one of the major issues for adolescents. 'What is the point in identifying depression as a major issue and not trying to address it?' Margaret asks. 'We need to give young people skills to help themselves.' She sees huge pressures on them, especially where many factors collide. The straw that breaks the camel's back may seem to be a small thing, but it may come on top of exams, a broken relationship, and perhaps parents in the throes of separation. 'We can build self-worth. Praise, don't criticise. Learn how to deal with stress by meditating and relaxing, and develop these sustaining skills early in life. Then a person can say, "Yes, when I feel down, I do this. It works,"' Suicide is the result of something tragically wrong, not the cause itself. Just as people go to a gym to strengthen muscles, Margaret wants to help people strengthen their emotions: 'emotional immunisation'. Her next book will show how.

'I have met the nicest people in the saddest circumstances. They have made me a far richer person.' Margaret does not believe she has to experience the same pain as another to understand. 'I try to use empathy, not sympathy, which might drown me in someone else's grief and sorrow.' Cultivating roses has enabled her to switch off from the tragedies of others, and her own enormous pain of marriage breakdown.

'After my first marriage ended, I cried for years. I remember the day he married a friend of ours, I felt like I could die. I thought, "If I just slip down into the bath and drown, I will not feel the pain." After my second marriage, I was left in enormous financial difficulty, but emotionally stronger. At 55, I had no home and little money left.' She acknowledges that growing another rose garden has helped her own grief. What strengthened this woman who had dedicated her life to supporting others was the belief in her held by family and friends, and her own faith. Margaret's two sons, David and Peter, organised a roof over her head, which she now shares with one of them. She treasures time spent with young William, her grandson.

When I visit her home, the wealth and perfume of roses is overwhelming. 'It's over the top, isn't it!' she laughs, taking me along rows of bushes crowded with blooms, through arches already covered by riotous climbers. I think about my own garden and wonder if I maybe bought pygmy varieties.

'How do you do it?' I wonder out loud.

'Fertilise every month except when they are dormant,' Margaret says. She shows me the Lifeline Rose, a magenta beauty donated to Lifeline for its constant fundraising by her friend Richard Walsh, a leading amateur rose breeder.

I ask Margaret about the importance of role models. She speaks of her friend Pat Farmer, famous for his incredible physical and mental tenacity as an ultra-marathon runner. In 2000, Pat completed a 14 500-kilometre circuit of Australia, supported by the National Council for Centenary of Federation. 'Pat and I were asked to speak to a group called "Spirituality in the Pub" at Campbelltown. One month before, Pat had lost his beloved wife Lisa to heart failure. With great courage he decided to speak. He rose and said he felt he was meant to be there that night and spoke of his grief, adding "how easy it would have been to run in front of a car when on the road." It was the thought of his children that stopped him.'

Many have recognised Margaret Appleby's special gifts. In 1997, Narellan Rotary awarded her an honour rarely given outside Rotary, a Paul Harris fellowship, for her suicide prevention and community work. She constantly treads new paths. Early in 2000 she launched Mission Australia's Youth Suicide Prevention Appeal, followed by a hectic round of media interviews. In April 2000 she gave the Australian perspective on suicide in schools at an international conference in the USA. 'We need to get back to basics. Do more of what keeps people alive.'

'If I died tomorrow, I would feel I've had the privilege of helping a lot of people. I've taken opportunities, not spent my life dreaming, but doing. Being a Christian is my motivation to help people. It's like being God's hands and feet. He can't walk beside a person who has just lost a loved one to suicide, but I can in my body. It's tough work and I'm required to go the second mile. Sometimes I'm tired out and would like to take time out and relax in my garden. I'm sustained by the old prayer of "serenity to accept the things you cannot change, courage to change the things you can, and wisdom to know the difference".

'In the future, I would like to breed a new rose, something unique. And have more fun!' Margaret Appleby continues to walk the second mile to prevent more suicides in Australia, is chief executive of Lifeline Macarthur, and grows stupendous roses. After our third interview she hands me a basket crowded with fragrant roses from her garden. They are her favourites, Joyfulness and Spirit of Peace. 'These are for your mum.' She didn't know my mother, but she knew she was unwell. These bright blooms from a complete stranger lit up my mother's withdrawn face.

'My recipe for rose growing—plenty of water, plenty of fertiliser and give them away to bring happiness to others,' says Margaret.

Photographic credits and captions

Page 17: TOP: 'Hearing the beat'. Aboriginal children at a school health screening, Borroloola NT, 1977 (chapter 4, Hey, Sister!). (Reproduced with the kind permission of Margaret Carnegie-Smith.) MIDDLE: The Littles' (chapter 5, Jack's Dream) marriage by Pastor Stan Eldridge at the Aborigines Inland Mission church at East Arm leprosarium, Darwin NT, 1971. (Reproduced with the kind permission of Mrs Connie Eldridge.) BOTTOM: John Thompson (chapter 1, The Man Who Loves Trees) says goodbye to an old friend, his 1956 Polish Wilga, Pinnaroo, SA 1999.

Page 19: John Thompson—innovative farmer, adventurer and inventor brings forth plenty from the desert. Pinnaroo SA, 1999.

Page 28: Jill Jordan, leader in community development, outside her converted milking shed home. Maleny QLD, 2000.

Page 41: Pat and Peter Lacy of Mt Elizabeth station, pioneer new paths in the rugged north Kimberley WA, 1999.

Page 51: A mobile baby clinic at Mudginberri Station, NT 1968. Sister Margaret Carnegie-Smith weighs and checks a child from top to toe. (Reproduced with the kind permission of Ann Trinder.)

Page 59: Jack Little—'ringer', first Aboriginal Health Worker in the Northern Territory, recipient of the World Health Organisation Award for 'health services to Aboriginal people', and founder of Bulla community— is looking for self management for his people. Bulla NT, 1999.

Page 68: LEFT: Michael Eppler, German immigrant farmer of Packsaddle Plains in the Ord River Scheme, is phasing out the use of chemical sprays and fighting pest insects with beneficial insects. Kununurra WA, 1999. RIGHT: Steffi Eppler, Ceres Farm marketer, tractor driver, financial planner and melon and pumpkin grader. Kununurra WA, 1999.

Page 77: TOP: Cullen Winery, in the Margaret River region of WA (chapter 9, First Vines to First Wines). MIDDLE: Hugh Lovesy presents an early version of the Money $tory™ at Mimili community store, central Australia, 1994 (chapter 11, One Land). (Reproduced with the kind permission of Hugh Lovesy.) BOTTOM: Fran Rowe (centre) advises clients Roz and

Owen Weber at her farmstead office, 50 km west of Tottenham NSW, 2000 (chapter 12, Fighting Broken-down Cocky Syndrome).

Page 78: Cathy McGowan, farmer, rural consultant, President of Australian Women in Agriculture (AWiA) and chair of the Federal Government Regional Women's Advisory Council. Indigo Valley, Wodonga VIC, 2000.

Page 90: TOP LEFT: Stanley Mirindo, cross-cultural worker, dancer and actor, on location with his mobile phone for the film *Stranded in Wasteland* where he plays Mudo Mudo, the tracker who found two German aviators dying of starvation in the land of abundance. Broome, WA 1998. (Reproduced with the kind permission of Peter Bibby.) TOP RIGHT: Rose Hillman, Pitjantjatjara woman, poet, community worker and Australia Day Citizen Award winner for Whyalla in 1994. Bayulu Community Fitzroy Crossing, WA, 2000. BOTTOM: Joe Ross of the Bunuba people, up to his neck in the fight to save the pristine Dimond Gorge on the Fitzroy River from being dammed for cotton development, 1997. (Reproduced with the kind permission of WA Newspapers/Mohens Johansens.)

Page 104: Di Cullen (OA)—Margaret River wine industry pioneer, winner of the region's first national trophy in 1977, and joint founder of the Vasse Conservation Council which succeeeded in halting sandmining along the Margaret River coastline. Margaret River WA, 2000.

Page 116: Ian Dickenson, peacemaker, with one of his 40 000 streaky-barked gums. Blessington TAS, 2000.

Page 125: Hugh Lovesy, cross-cultural worker and brilliant creative mind, developed the Money $tory™ to shine light on incomprehensible accounting figures and empower Aboriginal communities. Alice Springs NT, 1999.

Page 135: St Francis of 'Bombah'. Fran Rowe, rural financial counsellor. Tottenham NSW, 2000.

TRIUMPH OF THE SPIRIT

Page 145: TOP LEFT: Thomas Holder testing gear while unloading fish into the hold of the *Peter Crombie*, off Port Lincoln SA, 1987 (chapter 15, The Sea Gives, the Sea Takes Away). (Reproduced with the kind permission of David Holder.) TOP RIGHT: Margaret Appleby in her magic garden. Catherine Fields NSW, 2000 (chapter 18, Hearing the Cry). CENTRE: Heli-muster Captain John Armstrong's eye on the world from his helicopter at Pigeon Hole station NT, 1985 (chapter 13, Top End, Top Cattle). (Reproduced with kind permission of John Osborne, Telecom.)

BOTTOM: Dr Rod Mitchell takes the blood pressure and pulse of Paulus Wilyuka, recovering from an accident. Titjikala Aboriginal community NT, 1999 (chapter 14, Flying Doctor).

Page 146: Carol and John Armstrong, best friends and husband/wife team from remote Gilnockie station in the Top End, 2000. (Reproduced with the kind permission of Louise Armstrong.)

Page 157: Through his work with the Royal Flying Doctor Service, Dr Rod Mitchell contributes to a collective effort tackling the huge health problems of the Centre. Alice Springs 1999.

Page 166: Sylvia Holder, tireless cancer support volunteer and pioneer of prawning on the west coast of the Eyre Peninsula. Ceduna SA, 1999.

Page 175: Dom Paulino Gutierrez, a 90-year-old Benedictine monk. Since immigrating from Spain at the age of 18 he has baked bread, made and mended shoes and grown olives at the monastery. New Norcia WA, 2000.

Page 186: Marlene Farrell, orchardist and former deputy mayor of Orange City Council. 'Emmaville', the family apple orchard near Orange NSW, 2000.

Page 198: Margaret Appleby, CEO of Lifeline Macarthur and executive director of The Rose Foundation, searches for what keeps people alive. Molong NSW, 1999.

PUBLISHER'S NOTE:

According to traditional Aboriginal customs and beliefs, seeing a photograph or mentioning the name of a deceased relative can cause distress. All reference to the names of deceased Aboriginal persons have been removed from the stories in this collection. The photographs in this book have been reproduced with full permission of the subjects, and each subject has read and approved the contents of their story. It is the Publisher's sincere hope that this does not cause any pain or distress to any Aboriginal person in the future.